OPEN MIC FOR ANIMALS
EVIDENTIAL FAIRY TAILS

Praise for Open Mic for Animals Book

"Shannon is a natural-born storyteller and truth warrior. Open Mic For Animals is a powerful, magical, and funny book. By bravely unlocking her caged spirit, Shannon continues to free countless animals who need a friend with a fearless voice. You'll love this book that will heal your heart and open your mind's eye."

-Deborah King, spiritual leader, New York Times bestselling author of Be Your Own Shaman and Heal Yourself—Heal The World.

"I've known Shannon Spring for many years through our common bond of animal advocacy. Shannon does everything with passion and a very big heart. She is one of the most singularly unique people I've ever met and I know Open Mic For Animals will amuse and delight animal lovers across the globe. She leads people into an unseen world, giving hope and a connection to love and life that is so different than everyday existence."

-Amy Luwis, author of For Dog's Sake! and creator of the viral cartoon, RedandHowling.com

Praise for Open Mic for Animals Presentations

"Shannon's fun-filled animal communication presentation for the Leukemia Lymphoma Society fundraiser had people mesmerized. Book her for your event now!"

-Maureen Famiano, former Executive Producer WTSP and WFLA-TV

OPEN MIC FOR ANIMALS
EVIDENTIAL FAIRY TAILS

SHANNON SPRING

SPP

All attempts have been made to preserve the stories of the events, locales, and conversations contained in this collection as the author remembers them. The author reserves the right to have changed the names of individuals and places if necessary and may have changed some identifying characteristics and details such as physical properties, occupations and places of residence in orden to maintain their anonymity.

Published by St. Petersburg Press St. Petersburg, FL

www.stpetersburgpress.com

Copyright ©2024

All rights reserved. No part of this publication may be reproduced, distributed, or transmitted in any form or by any means, including photocopying, recording or other electronic or mechanical methods, without the prior written permission of the publisher, except in the case of brief quotations embodied in critical reviews and certain other noncommercial uses permitted by copyright law. For permission requests contact St. Petersburg Press at www.stpetersburgpress.com.

Design and composition by St. Petersburg Press

Cover design by St. Petersburg Press and Isa Crosta

Print ISBN: 978-1-940300-86-3

eBook ISBN: 978-1-940300-87-0

First Edition

❀ Created with Vellum

Mayor Puppypants, Jack, Grover, and Kermit

INTRODUCTION

"And those who were seen dancing were thought to be insane by those who could not hear the music."– Friedrich Nietzsche

"Why don't you stop talking about it, and just do it already?" – Tinkerbell the Cat (upon my telling her dad I'm going to write a book...here it is!)

Who is this book for? Animal lovers, pet parents, skeptics, believers in magic, people who've walked easier with an animal by their side, and those who fear they'll never see their animals again. It's for the child within who knows this book holds truths you knew long ago, and for adults whose hearts feel broken beyond repair. It's for your playful inner puppy and kitten, and the senior within questioning your value. It's for those indoctrinated to believe God is a bearded, old, white man in the sky, and those who know God has paws.

Welcome to the true story of how I remembered I'm an Animal Communicator. I've helped thousands of animals and their people live happier and healthier lives through intuitive conversations addressing behavioral, emotional, and medical challenges. To be the animals' voices, I had to clean up my life's litter box and unleash myself. Animals of all species around the world take the microphone to share their stories and communicate messages they most want their people and you to know.

My daily visits to the Rainbow Bridge bring comfort and closure to grieving pet parents when animals in the afterlife share their unlimited wisdom and wit and signs they're still with us. Discover how to communicate with your own furry, feathered, finned, scaled, or hoofed friends by learning how they talk with me. We don't need to guess what they're thinking and feeling. We can communicate right now telepathically with all creatures, wherever they are, to better understand and care for them. Compassion and connection transcend cultures, species, and worlds.

Whether two or four-footed, open hearts open doors. Step outside your comfort zone and into what many of us have been told is the Land of Make-Believe. What's make-believe is the human misperception that there's just this one world, and only we communicate intelligently. When you stop caring who thinks you're crazy, you'll start having more fun in life, and new worlds will open up.

Before I remembered I could talk with animals, *and* hear them back, life was flat. It's weird how we can know we're missing something, but not quite know what it is- a restless emptiness- a missing piece. I didn't realize how shallow the waters I'd been swimming in until life led me into the mystical deep end where I met my soul and my purpose.

While I knew my pets' lives continued after death, I couldn't always *feel* their presence, and that's not because they were absent. It's because grief sucks, messes with our minds, and sometimes our ability to receive signs. Animal communication saved my life and is my life's mission. The good news is we don't have to wait until The Big Paw in the Sky calls us *Home* to reconnect with our furry loved ones. We can do it now.

Animal communication is something everyone can do, although at different skill levels. Everyone's born with the ability to sing, dance, and play sports, but we're not all going to be rock stars and

Olympians. Certainly not me, unless competitive cupcake-eating becomes a sport!

I understand the viewpoints of skeptics and atheists. So often the worst of things happen to the best of people, leaving us confused, shattered, or wondering what kind of God could allow animals to suffer. Whether you pray to a specific God or no god at all, this book cannot answer all of your questions. I do hope it answers many about the inner lives of animals and opens your mind to animal communication, and an afterlife that awaits all species.

I have many questions myself, including, "Will I ever get to pee alone in my own home?" Four bathroom attendants seem excessive, and their barking is more rude than helpful. Maybe I should just start peeing outside, and bark at myself instead.

I don't know why life has to be so hard. I do know animals make it easier...and funnier to be human. I'm dedicated to making life easier, and more fun for them, by holding myself and my species accountable to be more animal-like.

I hope the true stories here challenge beliefs that this life is all there is. It's not...not by a long shot. People will always have their own mental filters, fears, and opinions, but they can't take away our experiences. While many of my stories may *sound* fictional, this book is filled with my real-life adventures and those of my human clients and animal friends. We've lived these events the same way you've lived the best and worst days of your lives.

Scientists can keep doubting whether or not there's a party going on they can't see, hear, or feel. The animals and I are going to just keep enjoying the party. My invitation has been with me since birth; I just needed to show up. You're invited to the party too... and it's a wild one! This is an interspecies invitation to play between worlds, transform, and put pain in perspective.

As I tell my worldwide clients, your pets don't need to be present "in person" for our sessions. They can be eating, sleeping, in the bathtub, or at a nightclub—the process is the same. It's a telepathic, heart-centered conversation that transcends human barriers, including culture, language, religion, time, and space. I can speak with animals that are on my sofa, your lap, in the ocean, jungle, or afterlife, as well as people—living or deceased.

Animals speak TRUTH—straightforward, common sense, unfiltered truth. You can learn to speak "Animal" too. They send images, words, sounds, songs, feelings, and even jokes to communicate with me about their needs, wants, and ways to help themselves and their people. I use the names God and Spirit interchangeably, as well as Heaven and the afterlife for what happens after we die. I respect there are many more terms to describe these concepts.

I sure hope you treated animals kindly on your journey, as this book will be a hard lesson for those who haven't and a welcome reward for those who have. Thank you for RSVP-ing, "Yes," to this unusual party, where shirts, shoes, and pants aren't required, as most of our guests never wear them. It's Open Mic For Animals, and time to welcome our first star to the stage ... Teddy!

1
FOR THE LOVE OF TEDDY

Happiness is a warm puppy.
Charles Schulz

When it comes to choosing one's battles, this one chose me ... and I was ready. Grief fueled my adrenaline to challenge a priest who dared lie to me about my dog's soul.

"No, Shannon. I'm sorry, Teddy won't go to Heaven. Heaven is for people only. Dogs don't have souls," claimed the priest at my Catholic elementary school when Teddy died. I'm pretty sure I heard Jesus say, "OMG!" as the chapel's stained-glass windows cracked, along with the innocence of childhood. Teddy was my first dog, the center of my world, now shattered.

Dressed in my blue polyester uniform and freshly polished saddle shoes, I'd somehow trained for this moment since birth. Hold my lollipop...this holy man was about to get schooled by a ten-year-old girl whose dog had her back. Father John forgot The 11th Commandment—the most important one: "Dog is God spelled backward," and that's no coincidence.

While Sister Julie was fine with teaching kids about a man with a crown of thorns being nailed to a cross, comforting an inconsolable child whose dog died was outside her comfort zone. So, she sent me to Father John, whose job was to provide timeless wisdom. "Time heals all wounds" may be timeless, but isn't wise. Ironically, Father John didn't do what Jesus would when he preached to me "Dogs don't go to Heaven."

Father John's claim made no sense. If we're all "God's creatures," then aren't we all loved the same, whatever our skin color, gender, age, or species? Why do only people get to live forever in a magical kingdom that sounds a lot like Disney World, without the lines? Despite girls not being allowed to be priests, I knew something apparently "Father" didn't. And so, I preached, "YOU ARE WRONG! Dogs do go to Heaven, and you should never tell a kid her dog doesn't go there." I stormed out and earned myself a demerit for talking back.

Demerits were given to shame us, but, I was shameless. Besides, I knew it wouldn't hold up in real court. After all, I watched a lot of *People's Court*, (the original Judge Judy) and never saw a kid arrested for defending her dog. It wasn't even in my awareness that someone could believe pets simply die…THE END. I was born talking with animals, and Teddy told me he'd be back, and I believed him. Dogs don't lie. Adults do.

After all, adults told me a fat man slides down our chimney once a year to deliver gifts on the backs of reindeer, and a giant bunny lays chocolate eggs in spring. Now they want me to believe dogs DON'T go to Heaven? I don't think so. My faith was in my furry brother, not any human authority.

When someone utters words that are so opposite to the truth we hold so dearly, we can either double down on our convictions or we can break down, thinking this presumed wiser person in a white robe or funny hat knows better than us. They don't, but animals do. When Father John told me I'd never see Teddy again, I knew better. #BeastsBeforePriests would've gone viral, but this was way before Twitter.

If I could go back in time, I'd award my younger self a pink Pope mobile with a megaphone to blast throughout the land: "DO YOU HEAR ME? ALL DOGS, CATS, AND CREATURES GO TO HEAVEN!" Then, when not struck down by lightning, I'd take a bow and sign "Shannon the Great" autographs before being hung by my rosary beads. I'd once given myself this title on a name tag for my school desk. A not-so-humble title for a not-so-humble kid.

In fairness, Father John was sharing what he believed to be true. Something misguided authority figures taught him. He didn't have the answers but did his best to provide them. As passionate of a debater as I am now, I'd be more terrified to debate my fifth-grade self than adult me, because *that* girl just knew stuff, and had NO FEAR WHATSOEVER.

My courage during that epic battle of faith vs. fiction practically baptized me into my career of talking with animals, including those in the afterlife. Someone who knows the truth of what happens when pets die...they live on.

I know because I've talked with thousands, and not just dogs and cats.

I don't remember much about my childhood, but I do recall begging for a dog for years. Finally, on Christmas morning 1980, I unwrapped a dog ornament. It was then my parents told us the life-changing news: "WE ARE GETTING A DOG!" Our family briefly became the one in *It's a Wonderful Life*. That's the magic a pet creates.

Even my mom, who didn't want a dog initially, (thinking she'd be doing all the work) ended up dearly loving Teddy and regularly cooked him scrambled eggs. Loving a pet is winning life's lottery. They're often the only beings who truly both know *and* love us.

Teddy was my first dog, a black and white mutt—the only family member with whom everyone was always on speaking terms. Pets are the missing piece—the donut hole they're responsible for unapologetically eating. Teddy would forever change my life in ways I couldn't imagine, and he'd also change Father John Joseph's life many years later. I was eight years old when my family got Teddy, my baby brother.

Technically, I have a human sister. I think her name is Kelly. I'm joking... my sister has never been proven to be human. Kelly was the Cruella De Ville of sisters, and we haven't spoken in 112 dog years. She never wanted a sister much like how some pets don't want a puppy or kitten brought in to steal their thunder. Fur is thicker than blood in my world.

We had no idea what we were doing when Teddy arrived. We bought him from a pet store before those became the worst places on earth—puppy mills and income for animal pimps. Insincere apologies to the countless breeders I've now offended, but I think you owe many cats and dogs apologies before accepting mine.

We're all mutts, making it comical that so many people are obsessed with pedigree. Perhaps dogs and cats should ask to see our "people papers" before they choose us. I'm just grateful we didn't have to show ours because we weren't the most stable family.

Puppy Teddy joined our family and changed all of us in different ways, but it was me he changed the most profoundly. When he was "put down" just two years later, I experienced the greatest grief I'd ever known. It was a grief that screamed childhood isn't supposed to hurt and an unwelcome preview of how much more grief awaited. But, it also spoke a higher truth- of course, all dogs go to Heaven. It wouldn't be Heaven without them.

Teddy was the world's fiercest rabbit chaser. His stealthy cheetah technique when stalking his prey decades ago on Canterbury Lane was a lesson in persistence. He never caught one, but he never stopped trying. Persistence is one of the most important things animals count on me to be when their messages are urgent, especially when their life is on the line. I was eager to celebrate Teddy at school for "Show and Tell." Strangely, I don't remember much about that day. Perhaps I was in an altered state of sheer bliss—showing off my baby brother. Maybe a traumatic math test (a subject that still haunts me) subtracted my brain's memories. I do remember how proud I was of Teddy, and what it felt like to have a true friend. Something I still only ever feel when I look into an animal's eyes.

"Show and Tell" the prior year was thankfully before the internet. I brought in my first Valentine's Day card from a boy, John Tucker. He wrote in pencil, "I like you very much." Being the theatrical kid I was, I decided to erase "like" and change it to "love". When my mom saw the *improvements* I'd made to John's like-letter, she asked if I'd changed his words. I confidently replied, "It's what the people want, Mom. No one wants to hear about a boy *liking* me." A reality show producer was born!

The next day, I proudly presented the revised *love* letter to my class audience with great applause. It was the pilot episode of *Elementary School Bachelorette*, before reality shows were a thing, and before I knew more boys than just Father John and John Tucker. I hadn't even met my first love, Teddy, who'd *be* a LOVE letter forever etched on my heart.

Please be assured I've since matured, and no longer forge love letters nor exaggerate truth for dramatic effect. My life is a daily wild adventure with animals so weird and wonderful, that any embellishments would be excessive. Also, telepathic communication happens lightning fast, leaving my inner child no time to use her eraser.

I say this because the stories in this book are far down the *rabbit hole,* and will require some to suspend disbelief. Of course, others already know the *rabbit hole* is real. As for John Tucker, I imagine he learned to stop using pencils and started notarizing romantic notes.

Teddy was my best friend and hero who lost his life too soon for "being aggressive." Thousands of animals of all species are unfairly labeled aggressive and lose their lives or quality of life for it. In Teddy's case, like in many, it's human mistakes that cost an animal his dignity or life.

There's not enough space for the labels that'd be placed on my shelter chart if I were a dog. And the only accurate one would be: "Plays well with others if you treat her right." My bite history would be longer than a CVS receipt.

It was a lively Saturday afternoon playing PacMan in our basement when my sister's friend Kathy let out an excited scream, startling Teddy who'd been resting on her lap. Frightened, he bit her on the lips. I don't remember much after that, only that Teddy would soon lose his life for it.

For something a child did wrong, he would die. Adults must teach kids to respect the sensitivity of animals and their boundaries. While Kathy wasn't being a bad kid, Teddy wasn't a bad dog. It was Teddy's instinct to protect himself from perceived threats. Only one of them bears ultimate responsibility for his death (or blame both sets of parents), just don't blame Teddy. Tragically, it's always the animals who get blamed and punished. Kids are then left with scars on their hearts, like mine, or lips in Kathy's case.

I'm sorry, Teddy, I couldn't save you. I tried, but I was just a kid. My voice didn't count, but it does now and so does yours. After the bite incident, Teddy was sent to stay with a trainer. It was more of a holding cell until my parents decided what to do. I can only recall my fear and sadness, powerless to help my brother and hero.

Childhood is both magical in its innocence, and hell in its captivity. Kids know the right answers but aren't the decision-makers. The day Teddy was scheduled to be euthanized, I was sent to New York City to spend the day with my father—a man I adored and feared. An abusive man I don't speak with anymore who lost his title of Dad. Dad is a term of endearment, but Paul is just a man.

I begged Dad to call Mom and cancel the appointment. I believed Teddy could be fixed, that he wasn't bad. Teddy did die that day, and when I came home, I saw Teddy's lifeless body on a sofa wrapped in blankets. Our family had lost its MVP. The fragile joy he brought to our dysfunctional family was gone. We dug his grave in the backyard. I know I cried, but I'm not sure if Kelly did. She learned pretty early on to shut off her feelings and use mine against me.

Even as a kid, I desperately tried to take action in overwhelmingly tragic situations. I wrote Teddy a card to take to Heaven with him, that would be "delivered" via U.S. ground mail, via his tear-soaked grave. I chose poems from Shel Silverstein's book, *Where The Sidewalk Ends* (which seems like a fitting title about death), to read aloud. In the letter, I told Teddy to "be good for Jesus," and then I watched my hero's precious body laid to rest. I saw his Spirit rise and never told a soul.

Despite my consuming pain, I trusted I would see Teddy again. He told me I would. My trust was well placed. Teddy has found many ways to show me that no matter how many tears fell, and how many years passed, he was right by my side. Always.

Against my will, I returned to school after Teddy died. Despite being in the fifth grade, I think I should've been allowed to graduate, as I'd just learned way more about life and love than I ever would sitting behind a desk.

An unexpected plus side to staying in school included receiving the best dating advice from Sister Catherine, a nun who was constantly asking us kids to pray for her. I don't know what she did, but it must've been good!

I do know while teaching us how to sit like ladies, she cautioned us, "When the bridge is open, the boys will look." Wow... thanks for the tip, sister! She also asked us to "Consider marrying Jesus." I was far too boy-crazy for that, and I think even Jesus found that a little inappropriate.

Father John, like these nuns, was simply doing his best at the time and didn't intend to hurt me. I'm grateful to my younger self though, for standing my ground. And most importantly, for knowing, not "believing," but wholeheartedly knowing Teddy was still with me. I know he got that letter I wrote him, and sees how truly brave a friend to animals I grew up to be. Of course he does; he helped raise me.

Teddy visited me many times throughout adulthood. He's the hero who sent me the telepathic White Rabbit (you'll meet later), who guided me from my mental war zone of depression back to beautiful butterflies and talking animals. I'm not sure if Teddy visits Kelly, but I wouldn't begrudge him if he did. After all, she could use some lessons about how siblings should treat each other.

I felt Teddy sleep next to me the night after he passed, even though he'd never been allowed in my bedroom. I used to sneak him up there sometimes. Spirits, of course, aren't limited by human rules, stairs, walls, or really anything. I imagine many dogs return to wherever they'd been banned and tear down those absurd "NO DOGS ALLOWED" signs. Perhaps I'll do this too, and with Father John's help, as anti-dog signs no longer define his beliefs.

Many years later, about 38 to be specific, Father John Joseph searched me out to speak more of his truths. Well, to apologize. It was now his spirit, not his human robe talking. Mediums often meet in mediumship circles where we continue to hone our skills with each other. While taking turns reading for each other, a medium whom I'd never met said, "Shannon, there's umm...a priest here...with an apology? Does this make sense to you?"

My heart opened wide, as of course I knew who it was, so many years, so many dogs and heartbreaks later. It was Father John, and he had a much different message for me than he did back in 1982. The medium continued, "Shannon, Father John wants you to know he's sorry, he was wrong, you were right...heaven is full of dogs. Teddy is here, as well as so many other animals."

I could see Father John smiling, and feel what was in his

heart—sorrow for what he'd told me at such a tender age. It was all he knew at the time until a young girl challenged him. I felt deep love and gratitude. Thank you, Brother Teddy and Father John. Perhaps one day, Father John will officiate at my dog's wedding. And by that, I mean when I finally do marry my dogs!

The Spirit world, where Teddy resides, is all around us, and there's not so much a *here* and *there*, as an everywhere. Imaginary friends abound, except we know some of them, and they're not imaginary. I don't need to fully understand the afterlife to accept that life and love continue, whether I can GPS the route or not. The animals show me the way.

Animals were my first career counselors. When my 2nd-grade teacher asked me what I wanted to be when I grew up, I answered unequivocally, "A veterinarian and a comedian." Both of these dreams came true in a way I couldn't have imagined.

Teddy's tragic death helped guide me to become a Humane Educator, someone who teaches respect for animals. And many years later, an Animal Communicator-—a professional who understands, and intuitively hears, talks, and laughs with animals (and gets paid to do all that). I have the greatest clients/employers in the world: the straight-shooting, snack-stealing, underwear-chewing, face-licking ANIMAL KINGDOM!

As a professional Animal Communicator, I use my extraordinary intuition, a subject not taught in school. Luckily, I can still suck at science because I don't need to read labs to read Labradors. To satisfy my inner class-clown, I lead *JustHumorMe*™ inspirational and comedic keynotes, retreats, and online fun and games. I bring recess back to adults!

I've created and taught kindness to animals programs, along with my furry *pawfessors*, so kids learn to advocate for all voiceless creatures. That *shameful* childhood demerit would make a great business card today. Proof of my dedication to animals, whatever the cost. It's only a shame I didn't use it back then, as it's never too early to build a client base...of all species!

Teddy's message of education lives on through me, and now our many students too. It's human aggression in large or consistent micro-doses that ends up having red flags stamped on the permanent records of innocent animals. There are many animals of all species whose reputations I've helped restore and protect by being their voice—challenging the "human as victim" story.

My skills in animal communication provide the animals' perspectives and facilitate understanding and compassion from their people. Animals know when they're amongst unstable people and situations, which is often the cause of their behavioral, emotional, and even medical challenges. They need to trust their leader's character to feel safe.

For the love of Teddy, may all kids grow up to be trustworthy friends and voices for the animal kingdom. May they use their hearts and minds to challenge those who don't value animals, and project untruths about their souls onto them. May everyone love and respect all the Teddys across all species. Speak up for them, you might be the only one who does.

Trust that even when the outcome isn't favorable, they know at least one person cared enough to show them the only love they've ever known. Trust they'll remember you when you join the Spirit world too.

Teddy has appeared to me many times over the years, including 39 years after his death in a lucid dream. He showed himself as I knew him, and I was able to pet him as my child and adult selves *together*. He and I were smiling, and I didn't want the experience to end. It was a portal in time—the past and present simultaneously, and pain wasn't possible. He was sitting next to Teddy #2 (whom you'll meet soon).

Teddy #1 has been "good for Jesus," and makes sure kids' letters and prayers of all kinds are delivered and answered (including mine as a big kid now). He runs, plays, and knows how many days are left until I join him in Spirit. What feels like an eternity to me here on

Earth is just a moment in divine time. While I miss him in the physical form, our energy is never apart.

Teddy tells me it's a lot like the cartoons I watched with him as a kid. One second we're young and playing ball, and the next he's back in Heaven chewing bones with Teddy #2 who's not born for decades later...and I haven't yet met. One moment I'm a middle-aged woman writing a book missing them, and the next I'm a Spirit on the beach petting both Teddys...and my future cats I've not yet met... and I'm back to being a kid!

If this were a cartoon, it would all "make sense," but when trying to process the limitlessness of our souls, it scrambles our brains. To unscramble them, let's just start with the concept of time and impossibilities being only human constructs and constraints. If I could, I'd blow up Jesus's phone asking, "Am I there yet? Am I done being human? I'd like to be together with all my animals from all lifetimes now... and just eat cake." Jesus is busy though, and has me on hold with music. "Halfway to Heaven" is playing. Always with the jokes, that one.

Many times we feel alone, and that our sorrows go unheard and our prayers go unanswered. I once felt so alone, I drove to a secluded parking lot where I screamed at God for allowing so much trauma in my life. Angels heard and surrounded me, as I begged for mercy which was soon shown in a way I couldn't have conceived would unfold.

Once in a while, I have to concede and say, "Well played, God" when a prayer is epically answered. Other times, I give Spirit the silent treatment because being a human is insane. It's a job I never applied for that I can't quit. In theory, my soul signed up for this, and she might've been drinking at the time.

I prayed as a child that Teddy wouldn't die that day and yet, he did. I don't know why my prayer wasn't answered. Perhaps because if he'd lived, I wouldn't have had that experience with Father John, who ironically solidified my faith with his woefully bad guidance.

Perhaps because then, maybe I wouldn't have grown up to do this work, connecting so many people with their own beloved Teddys.

While my childhood prayer wasn't answered how I wished, it was answered in the way that matters most: Teddy's life continues. There's no reason to worry about not being reunited with our pets because the reunions are already in progress.

Death be not proud, I hear them all, barking...LOUD.
Our pets do not sit and wait, lost and alone.
They play, they laugh, and guide us Home.
One day, when my life's over and done-
  there shall be my animals, each one.
Smiling, woofing, "Run, Shannon, run!"
They'll gather me in a furry embrace
  in this special time and space.
Call it Heaven, my happy place.
Recess is calling...an eternal game of chase.
Indeed, I'd won my first divine court case.

Teddy can hear and feel my heart's wishes and love for him, just simply by my thinking of him. It's the same for you and your furry and human loved ones. My thoughts and feelings of him are an instant energy transfer where he receives my love. He's watching over the child in me, and the grieving adult who alternates thanking Spirit, and being angry at It.

Our pets are strong enough to survive death. And whatever God you believe in is strong enough to handle any feedback you have on unanswered prayers. So...be thankful, be angry, be unapologetically you. Your pets and people are waiting to be reunited with you, whichever way your prayers are answered and by whom.

2

BEST IN SHOW

When I went to school, they asked me what I wanted to be when I grew up, so I wrote down 'happy.' They told me I didn't understand the assignment, and I told them they didn't understand life.
John Lennon

I don't know if I would've been more or less scared as a kid, knowing adults know even less about life than kids. My imaginary reality show, where I was the producer, director, and star, wasn't so imaginary after all. Turns out, my life's path was mostly up to me. Welcome to ADULTHOOD!

My story isn't about religion. I'm spiritual, not religious. Still, Jesus of "WWJD?" fame often drops by in dreams, animal communication, mediumship, and meditation. He brings peace and a playful sense of humor that initially surprised me. I've also had spiritual experiences with Buddha, The Cheshire Cat, Maya Angelou, Muhammad Ali, Robin Williams, faeries, and strangers who've miraculously crossed my path.

I once received a letter inviting me to "leave behind your wicked ways and find Jesus." Jesus and I snort-laughed over that one.

There's nothing wicked about my ways, except perhaps when I used a garden hose to spray a neighbor for smoking near my trees. Although, protecting nature is a holy mission. #Wicked for Jesus.

One of my biggest fears as a kid was no one would believe me if I ever saw Jesus. I think I knew there'd be many things which people should believe, but didn't. I'm just glad I believed Teddy and he believed in me. No one person, religion, scientist, or musician has the answers, but the animals do. Animals are the only ones I could ever fully trust to love me, stand by me, and tell the truth. And the truth was that I had to clean up my life's litter box and unleash myself to be the animals' voice. To claim my crown in Narnia, I needed to get sober. Magic and adventure awaited.

For far too long, my social life—okay, all of my life—centered around drinking. At times it was fun, but it was always borrowed fun—unsustainable without alcohol. Finding trouble was my specialty, and entertaining people with my psychic skills was always a fun time. I even kept a shell game, like street hustlers play, in my purse that scored me many free drinks. I wasn't your average barfly. Not your average anything.

One time, in an upscale Atlanta bar while wearing a tight mini-dress showcasing cleavage, and where the song playing, "It's Getting Hot in Here" was an understatement- I seriously pissed off an FBI agent. This was my idea of foreplay. While sipping Pinot Grigio, I approached him and his equally handsome friend. Out of nowhere, I proclaimed I could guess what he does for a living. He took offense, and defensively proclaimed right back I *definitely* could not.

Within about 2 minutes of accurately telling him things about himself, I confidently laughed and said "AHA! This is weird. Here I am profiling you, and yet you, yourself, are AN FBI PROFILER!" The agent turned red, his ego torched and cover blown by a smart-ass in stilettos, nonetheless.

Agent Johnny Law (for anonymity purposes) glared at my friend and demanded to know. "How's she doing this?" My friend shrugged, knowing I was just playing around, flirting in my unusual way. Infuriated, Johnny Law insisted I disclose my "parlor trick." I laughed again, asserting, "I'm right, aren't I?"

He stood and motioned for me to follow him outside. For a normal girl, this would be a bad idea. For me, so much bad stuff had happened, that I statistically hedged my bets I'd be alright. Besides, at least my friend was witnessing this strange mating dance unfolding in case I needed backup.

Agent Johnny showed me his badge and gun in his car. We decided it had gotten hot in here, took off our clothes, and treated each other like Most Wanted Criminals with one last conjugal visit! It was dangerous, delicious, and like any true crime scene, riddled with DNA.

While my drunk days had some happy highlights, most were ultimately just finding friends in equally low places. Partying is a bit of a misnomer when you're no longer present for the party. Parties should be fun and celebratory, but when you're blacking out, and bottoming out you're betraying yourself and missing out. My friend DJ once nicknamed me "The Original Party Girl" before I'd spiraled into the "After School Special Girl."

Drinking dulled my gifts and made magical experiences rare. Life had turned into slow motion, and booming Spirit voices had faded to whispers. Why was I drinking so much? I had to find out. The animals collectively staged interventions in all areas of my life step by step, one by one. They had their work cut out for them because denial is a powerful drug too.

Visualize your addiction on one side, and your pets' faces on the other. One is pure darkness, and one is pure light. It's easy to know wrong from right, but addictions don't go down without a fierce fight.

Once when arguing with my live-in boyfriend, I saw my Golden Retriever Lucy sweetly and sadly looking at me. Her wise face and gentle energy let me know it was time to let go of Jason and unbreak my own heart and hers from seeing me so sad. Instantly, I saw things through her eyes, and how helpless and trapped pets feel when mom and dad are fighting. It's no way for them (or us) to live, and I ended it right then with my MD-PHD boyfriend. A golden ticket, a pedigreed future husband versus a non-pedigreed Golden Retriever. No contest. There is no greater wealth than unconditional love. Lucy rescued her rescuer.

My dogs would come first, and I'd learn how to create a happy home for all of us. Lucy, aka Lucy Goosey, aka Gooseypants, reminded me that being a great dog mom is my number one priority, and no relationship is worth causing my pets pain. We don't get our time with our pets back. The time is NOW to put their needs first, make hard decisions, and move on. (Alcohol would be a much harder breakup—and it was the worst boyfriend of all.)

I'll never forget an ex-boyfriend (don't try to keep up with the boyfriends, just the dogs—keep up with them) who waited to announce a Thanksgiving dinner we were heading to was at a "dry house," a term that meant miserable to me. He told me right before the host opened her door, so I couldn't run. But, it was just me that was miserable. Their family and home were full of love and laughter. They didn't need alcohol to have a good time, and that's when you know you're free. When you don't need someone or something to escape yourself or your life.

I'm not Bible-thumping here. I don't even own one to thump on. Even when I was drinking, I often lamented how as an adult, *everything* revolved around drinking. I missed the simplicity of childhood play—good old-fashioned recess, the kind our pets offer us daily. "Adult beverages" are never more fun than the fun kids and animals have just being themselves.

Animals can reach our souls even when we've lost ourselves by communicating with a look, a meow, or an invitation to play at just the right time with a message, a purpose, or a second chance.

As a kid, my psychic abilities threatened my parents who lied and told me my instincts were wrong when I was frighteningly accurate. I spoke the truth—something they couldn't even tell themselves. Training me out of my instincts removed the very thing that could keep me safe in the world...and from my family. They reframed reality as my imagination and tried to systematically erase me from my own story.

I feared one day no one would believe I existed because my reality was constantly denied. I once asked my mom, "Am I still alive?" She laughed dismissively. Narcissists need control of narratives, and I was asking too many questions challenging her lies. I was so concerned for my safety, that I'd often write the date, exact minute, and weather in my Snoopy diary next to the day's events as evidence I was real.

When I learned fingernails continue to grow after we die, I began storing mine in a jar, physical proof I'd once lived, in case I suddenly disappeared. If you'd like to hug that kid, go ahead, she needs one. I felt I had a target sign on my back for most of my life.

Like how animals smell fear, human predators target wounded people to reduce their own pain. People trophy-hunted me. Especially the unholy trinity of my family. My father was a dangerous narcissist with a score to settle from his childhood. My fear was his glory. He was repeating a cycle, and I was ending it. The battle was epic.

My mom was a codependent who denied the truth of how unhappy she was and the danger we lived in. "Everything's fine," she'd say while my father terrorized us, and she insidiously manipulated us and called it love. Whenever I'd ask, "How do I look?" she'd answer, "Fine," causing me to obsess and wonder why I never looked beautiful. Fine never actually meant fine. It meant something was terribly wrong, and I had to fix it.

Outwitting sociopathic mind games is exhausting for seasoned psychiatrists and detectives, let alone a sensitive child. I had to learn to see myself as separate from their wounds. The cruelty, confusion, and betrayal served as bootcamp—surviving daily psychological warfare. I learned to think like a chess champion, anticipating ten moves ahead of my opponents—special ops trained in the womb on reading energy.

Recognizing deception, and learning to trust the truth of my experiences, versus what I wished were true or lies others told, were key to my survival. I was a sensitive, fire-breathing dragon armed with a teddy bear and truth serum. Adulthood didn't provide much relief, as adults lie to themselves the most. My quest for truth grew stronger.

A shaman once advised, "Shannon, people are going to shred you so much, you'll eventually be much happier because you'll become almost immune to criticism. People are only attacking you because they recognize your power." I knew this was true in my soul. Jealous, false friends were everywhere. I was eager to be done being shredded wheat and wanted to enjoy the flip sugar side of my life's cereal already.

Using the powers of time travel, let's visit me at thirty-eight when I experienced "the dark night of the soul." Unlike Amy Winehouse sang about, I *wanted* to go to Rehab. I needed help, and I knew it. I hit rock bottom when Teddy #2, a beautiful brown Aussie mix with a white heart on his chest, died. The day he died, I was suicidal and unrecognizable to myself—crippled with grief.

If only I'd known that every last traumatic thing I'd survived, and that was still to come, was preparing me to be a voice for animals, I'd have shouted, "Yes, sir! I'll have another trauma. Make it a double, as long as one day, it'll help me best serve the animal kingdom."

When my beloved "Baby Bear," Teddy #2, passed, I couldn't stop crying and wanted to die. I didn't plan on surviving his death and took 60 benzos. I'd been spiraling into addiction for a long time, numbing pain that screamed louder. By suppressing it, I'd multiplied it.

My heart shattered upon each furry child's passing. But, when Teddy #2 died, I had no emotional reserve to pull from to survive the loss. I was in trouble.

I planned to overdose and be in Heaven by the time he arrived. Teddy #2 made it safely into Spirit, but I was stuck here. Spirit deemed I had to remain a human in this lifetime a while longer, and much to my horror, I miraculously survived. I just woke up.

While Baby Bear was gone, there were thousands more animals around the world for me to love and learn from who needed me. My death wish became determination to fight my demons and win. Teddy's life would be honored, mine salvaged. Maybe one day, *happy*.

My self-destruction was an attempt to remove something deep inside that didn't belong to me. Growing up in a house of domestic violence and deception is complicated, and its wounds run deep. I learned that ancestral trauma imprints on our DNA. We can inherit fear, emotional pain, physical characteristics, addictions, and psychic gifts.

It takes a stubborn, brave soul to break the ancestral chain of pain, and I am this soul. I was fighting battles that predated me for centuries. No wonder I needed a drink!

Being exposed to physical and emotional violence over periods, or even one instance in some cases, can lead to PTSD for people and animals. I had to learn how to set myself free from debilitating despair, and in turn, I'd set countless species of souls free too. I'd learn the purpose of my suffering, and everything that happened would make sense, as much as it can while human. My mission was about to be revealed!

I'd discover how my severe depression would one day, among many things, help an abused pig get a new life, and even a girlfriend! You'll meet sweet piggy Benny later. But, before miracles happened, things would suck for a long time. Buckle up, buttercup—more storms are coming, and your umbrella is inside you.

At 39 years old, I collapsed and went blind and paralyzed from suppressed trauma and tolerating the intolerable. My mind said, "No more fucking pain!" and sent the signal to shut down my internal hard drive, which anyone who's watched their computer crash knows is a BFD. A BIG FUCKING DEAL.

I was having seizures and stroking out in front of my mom, who continued to do paperwork. With a rapidly shutting down brain, instincts kicked in to coach her to take me to the hospital and keep talking to me so I wouldn't go unconscious. Denial was Mom's drug of choice, and it nearly killed me. When the hospital intake lady asked me my name, I couldn't answer. (Interestingly, my name was soon to change.)

As I sat paralyzed in a wheelchair, my mother flirted with my doctors, and while this confused them, it was just an ordinary egregious episode of *her* reality show. Granted, the doctors were all exceptionally handsome (unfortunately), and in my most non-sexy, vulnerable moment, they carried my deadweight body behind the curtain.

Doctors confirmed I technically had sight and the ability to walk. But, the signals my brain was sending to my body said otherwise. A traumatized mind was tricking a healthy body into being disabled. I had also abruptly gone off benzodiazepines. Never go cold turkey off of those drugs. My mind felt like a machine gun, a merciless assault weapon on my spirit and body. Welcome to Detox. Except this wasn't a colonic. It was a rickety ass screaming roller coaster with no seatbelt. Pray for your life...beg for death.

Getting high was never my goal. I wanted relief from grief. But grief wasn't going anywhere until I faced it. It was the non-returnable gift that kept on giving. Even though doctors explained to me my paralysis and blindness were real, but only in my mind. I still wanted brain scans. Surprisingly, they humored me.

When Doctors Steamy and McDreamy showed me my brain was "normal," something I wanted notarized, I conceded maybe this was all caused by trauma (as these dudes already knew). That's a lot for a traumatized mind to process. I then joked, given how exceptional my brain looked in the scans, perhaps they'd award it a "Best in Show" ribbon. One out of 5 doctors agreed this was funny. The rest remained deeply concerned for me.

The chuckling doc seemed to sense somehow I'd be okay. Ultimately, he was right. But, until my subconscious negotiated the hostage release of my soul, I was literally scared out of my body and mind. I took scalding hot showers to feel the water but only heard it fall. My limbs had gone numb, particularly my right side—metaphysically connected to moving forward with life.

When I spoke, I wasn't sure if I made a sound. For years, I had dreams where I'd scream, but no sound came out, and no one heard me. Now it was happening in real life.

My body had converted emotional pain into physical disabilities. I'd been a hardcore player in the game of life for too long. I needed my coach to call a Time-Out to devise a new strategy. The problem was I was the coach. And I couldn't drink, drug, or fuck away the pain or responsibility.

I could sit with and listen to it and ask it to heal. I could walk my dog Ducky, and I could dream of feeling the joy that's buried within me despite what's happening.

As I lay in a raw subconscious, fragile state, a trauma nurse whispered to me, "You're probably always going to suffer from depression." I whispered back, "We'll see about that," blocking her attempt to barbwire my mind for life.

For as out of my mind as I was, my soul was wise enough to know she'd just projected her shit onto me. Someone needed to give her a demerit. I read her energy and saw her pain. She was a wounded healer feeding off of her patient's pain. And I wasn't having it.

Never tell a person or animal they can't get well. (Even when we're dying, we're actually "getting well" by transitioning into a new form. Like a butterfly.) Miracles happen, and no one has the right to deny you yours. Never lie to someone in pain either, though. Just remember "The Golden Retriever Rule"—treat people as a loving pet would. (#GoldenSprings...all of my Goldens rule!)

If the nurse had been wise, she'd have "taken advantage" of my subconscious being fully at the wheel. My mind was so powerful it had physically disabled me. Now was the perfect opportunity to plant seeds of wellness in my mind. Not only was that the kinder, ethical thing to do, it also would've worked. Now, please validate my parking and get one of those hot docs to wheel me outta here!

Minds in acute trauma are mental sponges and can absorb positive or negative energy on a deeper level than ordinarily. It's why hypnosis can be so effective—the conscious mind is taking a nap, and the subconscious mind, responsible for most of our behaviors and decisions, can get reprogrammed into a healthier, happier existence.

My mind was wide awake and listening, craving nutrients of compassion and truth, but Nurse Negativity fed it SPAM®. I will not *always* suffer. Don't you dare label me a victim for life. Yet again, someone projected their reality onto me, and I rejected their truth for my own.

When people throw emotional knives at you, RUN, preferably in flats. "Intelligent disobedience" is what a trained service dog knows to do when given a direct command that'll put its person in harm's way. My subconscious had learned to be an intelligent, disobedient service dog. Questioning authority and listening to animals saved my life.

Before diagnosing yourself with depression or low self-esteem, first, make sure you're not surrounded by assholes causing your problems. Being surrounded by assholes can wreck your mind, spirit, and health. Too many people and animals get medicated for conditions that don't originate with them. If you change their circumstances, they'll heal.

Animals bore witness to my pain and didn't judge. They saw and loved the real me and the broken me. They needed me to fight and win. They'd planned a party, and I was the Guest of Honor. I walked out alive. I'm returning their kindness by teaching people to see their souls and change their circumstances. Animals can also lose the will to live. Depression doesn't discriminate. Animal rights should be in the constitution: Freedom from harm, right to bodily liberty, and unconditional love from people.

My beloved friend DJ, now in Spirit, lost his battle with depression at 44 years old. DJ was/is a naturally fun spirit whose laugh I can still hear in my head 20 years since I last heard his joy. I miss him A LOT. We were soulmates, spoken for by other soulmates.

I helped him get his first dog he rescued from a bathroom. Darby Dog is the first who greeted him upon his arrival into Spirit. DJ beamed with joy and love at the sight of his first dog who broke his heart when she passed. I can see him holding her paw now.

My friend, an angelic soul with a beautiful heart, wasn't crazy in the least, just in crazy pain. Most people who attempt suicide aren't crazy, they're grieving. Their sensitive hearts simply can't pump blood fast enough to reach all the wounded places. They're emotionally bleeding out. All broken-hearted souls can't be saved, but all deserve compassion.

If I'd succeeded with the overdose (enough to knock out a blue whale), I'd have been there with Darby to greet DJ. Divine intervention is mysterious. DJ joined the afterlife angels and is on his sacred mission. I was asked to stay behind and do angel work on Earth. Spirit blew up my blowhole and breathed me out a bonus life.

Given blue whales have no predators, I'll likely remain an Honorary Mermaid until my song is sung. Angels and animals blocked my escape route. My work had just begun.

DJ is also *alive*. He visited me in a dream—healthy, happy, healing, smiling at me from a swimming pool. Souls who pass from suicide are welcomed Home with love. I've spoken with many and their grieving families. If you believe in a God that punishes beautiful souls like my friend, I wish you and your God peace.

Many years later, I learned a snake named Molly helped suck the poison out of my body from the overdose. (They never pumped my stomach.) While showering mid-shampoo, I suddenly felt compelled to read a snake—a species I'd despised after a copperhead bit my Lucy, nearly killing her. I'd held a grudge ever since, but spontaneously decided I should make peace.

When I hopped out of the shower, a text message awaited asking, "Shannon, can you read a snake for me? Here's a picture of one that's chosen my front porch to sunbathe on." Had snakes been reading my mind in the shower rattling around ideas in my head? Of course, they had.

At least this time, it was a nonvenomous one. I asked what name she'd like and she answered, "Molly." Sometimes a name has meaning, and sometimes it's just a preference. (Later, I realized she was being clever, as "Molly" is also the name of a non venomous drug.) Molly answered my questions about her impromptu vacation on the porch and shared a heartfelt message. The spirit of the snake species sucked the poison out of me to apologize for the pain one of them caused Lucy. They could withstand the toxins my body could not. Molly said they "owed me one," and showed a group of snakes swimming around inside me like I was a pinball machine. They were the pinballs hitting and healing my various organs neutralizing the poison. I was shocked I had a friend in them, given how my human self had wanted revenge for so long. I'd even told my boyfriend he needed to "find the evil snake who bit Lucy and make boots out of it!" (Not my finest moment.)

Molly gently explained the snake who'd bitten Lucy wasn't being evil, only protecting itself. I knew she was right, and instantly I felt guilty for holding a whole species responsible for the acts of one snake just trying to survive. Molly went on to say that the same things humans dislike about snakes, snakes dislike about humans. The two species aren't so different. Both can be sneaky and dangerous, or innocent and helpful. It's often hard to tell the good and "bad" ones apart. Both species need understanding and respect. Hateful ignorance only hurts both.

Like Molly, people have feared me too, and used to burn my witchy kind at the stake—misunderstanding our powerful healing abilities. I thanked Molly and apologized for maligning her species. While some characteristics remain across a species (humans harm the environment; snakes scare the crap out of people), we're all individual souls, many of whom are decent.

It's been a true gift having experienced how powerful the mind is to shut itself down *and* fix itself. I recall musing aloud, "If my mind is so powerful it can create disability (paralysis and blindness), I wonder what similarly powerful, but positive abilities can it create?"

I discovered the miraculous answer by opening new portals in my mind and traveling between worlds. Being a witchy woman wasn't going to get me burned at the stake again in this lifetime! Besides, I'd just reincarnate anyway.

We all have parts of our minds we aren't using that if accessed can wildly strengthen our talents and abilities, including our intuitive ones. Athletes and patients rely on various forms of visualization, meditation, and brain training to achieve goals and recover from life-threatening illnesses. A metaphysically focused mind can make real what already exists in other realities and dimensions. Communicating with animals here and in the afterlife is real. It's happening right now. Just ask your pets!

Major life changes can take years, or happen lightning-fast once we're ready. A song lyric, book title, photo, animal sighting, or random comment from a stranger can be a total game changer for a happier life. These things assisted me in getting sober, increasing my power, and accelerating my telepathic abilities. There's no way I could be doing this work I love so much at this level if I hadn't gotten sober.

While looking at a photo of my grandmother, "Nanny," and my dogs, Rowdy and Stormy (all in Heaven), I heard Nanny gently say, "You need to stop drinking. It's not good for you. Please stop drinking." Rowdy and Stormy had messages too, and bounced from the photo into a peaceful stream, smiling and serene, side by side. Crystal clear, these Golden Retriever angels were now in front of me in spirit forms.

Stormy's eyes beamed with deep love, compassion, and total acceptance of where I was at in my life. She filled my heart with self-forgiveness and worth. Stormy (whom I didn't name) was always a gentle soul who never asked for anything, but to be loved. Now she was asking me to love myself as she did, unconditionally. Stormy is all of nature's healing elements in one, pure sunshine. Her dark red coat is shiny and soft and her smile is just as bright.

Rowdy, the beach blonde comedian always ready to play ball, was there to give me courage, and a direct order from his soul. He had a handwritten sticky note on his paw. I zoomed in to see its message: "Be in Charge." He wanted me to reclaim my independent spirit—my life force—and stop giving my power away.

Two Golden messengers who know me better than anyone,

together in life and the afterlife, cheering me on. Both dogs' spirits, alive and well, asked me to be the same. Briefly feeling their divine love and grace made it bittersweet to have to stay on Earth.

Nanny was an alcoholic, and it was obvious this was a curse/disease/choice she didn't want me to carry on. No antidepressant or happy hour could make me happy or cure my PTSD. My struggles were spiritual, not medical in origin. I needed to heal the source, not the symptoms. We can heal our wounds, and our ancestors' wounds too, but only if we make the courageous choice to do so. Fear motivated most of my choices, and fear was a shitty team captain.

I Googled "Things to do besides drink" to amuse myself. (My Google searches should be a coffee table book.) I saw what I thought were useless ideas like "take a bubble bath, join a gym, take up knitting…" and recall thinking none of these things would hold my attention or be any fun. I needed Pinot Grigio like I needed air. Besides, "taking yourself out on a date" sounded like it was written for the undateable—the people who really *should* be drinking!

Finally, one random blog stated, "I never woke up one day wishing I'd drank the night before." Wow! Here was logic, something I couldn't debate or make fun of. It was truth and truth heals. Fear lies. FEAR: Face Everything And Rise, aka *Fuck fear and make it your bitch*. And stop saying the F word. Keep it classy!

One way I fucked fear was getting sober. I did it by myself and engaged in high-stakes humor at my one and only AA meeting. I accidentally chose an AA group of scary-looking ex-cons and seemingly aspiring ones.

The mannerly thing to do in these meetings is admit you're a disaster, and adopt your failure as your new tagline: "Hi, I'm Shannon and I'm an alcoholic." This is dutifully celebrated in solemn solidarity by your fellow train-wrecked peers: "Hiii Shannon." It's said with as much enthusiasm as one has for winning $1 on a scratch-off ticket they paid a dollar for.

I preferred the reactions I'd enjoyed for many years when leading my humor workshops: "Hi, I'm Shannon Spring. It's true what's written on the bathroom wall...when you're looking for a good time... I'm who to call!" That landed me many clients (and offended all the right people). This new, non-rhyming AA introduction was a bummer.

When the AA sharing commenced in the saddest circle of adult kindergarten ever, I knew I needed to play by AA rules, and by my own if I was to be authentic and get well too.

When it was my turn, and all mug-shot faces turned to me, I solemnly introduced myself: "Hi, I'm Shannon...and I had a really hard time admitting...I'm an alcoholic...until I realized *(peppy excited tone)* I'M ALSO A DRUG ADDICT *(giddily laughing at the horror of what my life had become)*!

The scary people burst out laughing, feeling much better about themselves now. Despite the success of my joke, I refrained from doing a whole stand-up act, as I think I'd have gotten beat up... deservedly so. This was a place of self-hatred, and I needed to be respectful of that.

It was at that moment that I knew I'd recover. Because as badly as life sucked, I was laughing at myself and loved myself for it. I knew I could choose to get well or spend my precious life in dark, smoky rooms of toxic energy, the kind that ironically feeds addictions. If AA works for you, you do you. But for me, it was going to make me sicker.

Claiming "ALCOHOLIC" as who I am, and being "powerless over my addiction" wasn't too empowering a way back to health. I didn't have a problem with the truth of my drinking problem, but I didn't believe it was wise for me to forever identify myself by something I planned on recovering from permanently. My goal was to be less of an asshole than the day before, and sobriety has a huge success "asshole to good soul" conversion rate.

I was so thin I couldn't hold up a pair of size 0 pants. I was so broke, my debit card was rejected for $2.16 for fries at McDonalds. I was a lifetime short of a Happy Meal. So wherever you're at, just know you, too, can recover if you keep your sense of humor, do it your way or the AA way, and for the love of God, stop eating McDonalds.

My sense of humor saved my butt a few times. Animal and human spirits often use humor to deliver their messages and heal their grieving loved ones too. They know how I work and they'll "hire" me for my style as much as for my skill.

When we're ready to get real with ourselves, life gets real with us. Choice by choice we decide how our story, our show, and our lives will go. While I lost my cocktail-centered social life, I gained back the self-respect I'd lost. "Self-respect" is somehow not the name of a popular shot. I wonder how many people would order it if it were.

Animals needed me to take care of myself so I'd be able to help them. I promised my furry friends I'd get well, and I did. I discovered having fun the way the entire Animal Kingdom does, by simply PLAYING, is why they're always so much fun to be around. Animals don't need a cocktail, cocaine, or coffee to be fun. They use their imaginations and are curious and excited about simple things. I learned how to be like them (but stopped short of playing with cardboard boxes). I learned how to be ME again.

As it turns out, I'm pretty fun, and had a whole business based on being fun that I wanted to get back to running. With renewed life force, my psychic senses were supercharging—clairvoyance (seeing), clairsentience (feeling), clairaudience (hearing), and claircognizance (knowing). Now, a Party Animal in the purest sense, I offer Party Animal Events—group pet readings that are a funny, furry good time. Shannon's Party Animal Ark set sail for a new adventure! I was back at the wheel of my life, steering a steady course.

Sobriety rewarded me with manifesting *and* remembering mystical adventures. Getting sober was the greatest gift I could give my dogs and the animals. I now feel unshakable confidence in my telepathic abilities and know which realm I'm in, who's communicating with me, and the degree of love, honesty, or fear my clients of any species are experiencing.

If I could go back, I wouldn't have drunk so much that my pets needed to be my unofficial sponsors. I truly wish I'd liked myself more back then, the way I so deeply loved them. That's all they want, for us to see ourselves the way they see us...deeply lovable.

As Rowdy and Stormy say, Love yourself, Be in Charge. Even if your pets are in Spirit now, you're still together and they'd love to see you quit smoking, get sober, dump the loser, write a book, or learn to salsa. Make your gift to them a happy, healthy life story. I did this when I moved into a new city and a new me.

I left Charleston, SC, and landed in Saint Petersburg, FL—partly chosen for the word Saint in its name. I asked myself where I could go, "where everyone has to be nice to me," and found my way to First Unity Church—voted friendliest church.

I was going to need all the kindness they had to offer because sobriety isn't just about stopping an addiction. It's about facing what made you self-destruct. Grief is a traitor that tests us every day. Luckily, I was done betraying myself, but I still had to learn to walk again, as grief brought me to my knees. At First Unity, I met a kind soul, a former Navy Commander turned Medium Suzanne Giesemann, who was giving a talk on her book, *Messages of Hope*.

In so much grief I couldn't speak, I wrote her a note asking for a reading someday. Then, I waited in line to thank her for her powerful, healing talk. She kindly looked up at me and I handed her a note. I knew this was strange since I was standing right there. She immediately understood I was one of those people who'd collapse from the pressure of having to answer "How are you?"

Suzanne's eyes grew wide as she sensed my anguish around losing "a male loved one." She didn't yet know he had a tail and four feet (Teddy #2). She gently asked me to follow up later, as there was a line of people waiting. I graciously thanked her and went home. All I had left was prayer, and a desperate e-mail to write.

Today, my grieving clients can hear in my voice when I tell them I understand the type of loss that brings terror on top of tears. The type of pain so many people come to me with after losing their animal and human loved ones. Even if we trust we'll see our loved ones again (as I do), getting through the days until that happens can feel scary, lonely, and merciless.

Suzanne said something was different in my message that got her attention, and I believe that something was the force of the Animal Kingdom trying to save my life. My heart was beating, but I was dead inside. She was a somewhat new medium then, and I got lucky.

In my first ever mediumship reading (as a client), she brought through Teddy #2, my brave-hearted boy. She hadn't connected with a dog this way before, and I was relieved she didn't get upset when my loved one turned out to be "just a dog." Many come to her having lost a human child, but for me, my dogs are my children...my entire family.

Suzanne is an animal lover herself, so she never judges one person's loss as less than another's, but many do. Her focus is being a people medium working with grieving parents. Yet, Teddy sent me her way for which I'm so grateful. Connecting with Teddy #2 (something my grief had blocked on my own), helped relieve relentless, debilitating grief. While I knew my dogs' lives continued, I didn't know how to do life while feeling alone, fighting too many major battles at once. To be honest, I've never really known how to do life. I feel like I'm my own species, and pray I'll wake up a dog/cat hybrid (something in a way I already am).

Teddy #2 showed himself as a hero who fell on his sword for me. His sacrifice set me on the path to awakening to my divine mission. Both Teddys played a pivotal role in shaping my life's work with animals and in my recovery. Suzanne later became my first mediumship mentor. She teaches with love. Teddy #2 knew the plan all along.

Ten years after Suzanne met my broken spirit, I'd triumphed over my past, and become a very gifted professional Animal Communicator and Psychic Medium. This story came full circle when I did a reading for Suzanne's pets. If she liked my work and my talents proved themselves, she'd send me client referrals. I was excited, and in need of pee pads. Her dogs assured me I'd do great, and were excited to be a part of the process.

Among many things her dogs shared, they referenced how Suzanne took great care of her jewelry (she smiled as she'd just returned from having it polished). Her dogs were also obsessed with reviewing boating safety, stating, "Bad things happen on the water." Just a month later, Suzanne, her husband, and the dogs narrowly avoided a life-threatening disaster on their new boat!

These furry-footed captains, like their former Navy-commander mom, were wise to the ways of the sea. They communicated wonderfully with me, and Suzanne was pleased. Victory! Ten years ago, she'd helped get my tail wagging again, and this experience of reading her dogs honored my soul's furry growth. Thank you Teddys, Suzanne, and your canine crew. Ahoy!

Around the time I first met Suzanne, I was lucky enough to meet Master Spiritual Teacher, Energy Healer, and *New York Times* bestselling author, Deborah King. Her triumph over trauma is one of the most extraordinary stories I've read. When Deborah walks by you, an ethereal breeze sweetens the air—the presence of an angel.

She asked what was hurting me. The image of Darth Vader came to mind. "A special kind of dark force," I answered, feeling spooked by its power. Finally, I gave voice to the superhuman force suffocating the bright light within me. Sometimes "HELP" is whispered, and other times screamed. Deborah heard the scream in my whisper.

Her fearless eyes were ablaze with LIGHT over this battle, bold enough to show up on her stage. A fierce lion held captive inside this fair-skinned-looking lamb gasping for air. There'd been so much slaughter inside me and so little love. Deborah held a calvary of compassion while performing shamanic healing on me. "I see great things for your future," she proclaimed, as her eyes flashed purple. Truth in her eyes. The author of *Truth Heals* and *Be Your Own Shaman* was healing me. Deborah also has a little white dog named ...Teddy!

Transforming from anxious addict to sober mystic was one strange trip for sure. For those with chemical imbalances, medicine can save lives. But I had an imbalanced life, a homeless spirit. The "party" was over. Ironically, when I checked *into* reality soberly, rather than out of it with drugs, I experienced incredible adventures with animals and spirits that *sound* drug-induced, but are my natural state.

The elusive storybook character, the Cheshire Cat (a true party animal), has served as a Spirit Guide and muse for me. Just wait for this party animal to take the stage! Am I suggesting the "fictional" Cheshire Cat is real? Oh, I'm not suggesting it...I'm full-blown living it.

My colorfully striped muse materializes a few times throughout this book, regaling the times he infused me with good mischief, prosperity, and an all-access pass to mystical realms. Clearly, I no longer care who thinks I'm crazy. So enjoy my madness and The Cat's, if you're lucky enough to summon him. Animals live in a magical state every day. So can we.

The book *Alice in Wonderland* (the Cheshire Cat's birthplace) was banned for various reasons at times around the world, including the belief the characters do drugs (no), the perception animals were elevated to human status, and religion and government were mocked, which encouraged personal freedom. Many answers to spiritual crises reside in banned books making library cards the real "get out of jail free" cards.

Being comfortable as my naturally weird self (like my feline muse) is where my bliss lies. It's the only way people can know and like the real me…including me. As The Cheshire Cat wisely hisses, "My reality is just different than yours." I'd rather be mischievously smiling like him too.

3
MAYOR PUPPYPANTS

Someday we'll find it, The Rainbow Connection. The lovers, the dreamers, and me.
Kermit the Frog, from *The Muppet Movie* (1979)

"You'll get a little white dog who'll do very important work with you," predicted an angel reader. I laughed. "Little white dogs are for little old ladies," I said. "And besides, I'm a big-dog person." The psychic smiled, not needing my validation of her vision. I tucked away her prophecy until one day I heard a booming man's voice sounding like Morgan Freeman playing God, commanding, "GO TO THE SHELTER NOW!"

Strangely nonplussed, I simply cocked my head to the side like dogs do when trying to comprehend what people are saying. I looked at my rescued black mutt Ducky. "Did you hear that?" Ducky, of course, like all animals, easily hears and sees spirits. What's labeled supernatural by people is just an average Wednesday for animals.

And on that Wednesday afternoon, I hightailed it to the shelter just before closing time.

Instead of thinking I was losing my mind, I wondered aloud, "Which shelter should I go to?" There were many nearby, and it was almost closing time. The Voice quickly answered, "Go to the Hillsborough shelter...GO TO THE SHELTER NOW!" I've always wanted a hotline to God, and now God was calling me!

I got in my Jeep and dutifully sped up to the Tampa County shelter, now known as The Pet Resource Center. Upon entering, my heart filled with unbridled JOY, my soul supercharged. I recalled the psychic's vision: a little white dog who'll change my life and join me in my work. Magic was afoot! All of my senses were heightened. But, like a stubborn cat who won't be told what to do by a human, I purposely inquired about non-little white dogs. Each one was somehow unavailable for adoption, causing me to laugh at my arrogance trying to outsmart God.

I turned the corner in the county shelter, home to hundreds of homeless pets. There he was, the little white dog with a mischievous smile and all-knowing eyes. The loudest, scrappiest trampoline-jumping terrier mix was on a mission to introduce himself by outperforming the entire Dallas Cowboy Cheerleaders' pep. "PICK ME, PICK ME!"...(cartwheels, splits, high kicks)..."PICK ME, PICK ME!"

The Truth of the prophecy was in his eyes. All kinds of truths that would change everything I thought I knew about myself and life. "Sammy" and I were about to fall in LOVE. I noticed the sign on his cage with a red line: "I can go home with you today for $50.00." My destiny was on sale! This indescribable force of nature was marked down for being labeled a handful, something that's kept me on the market for a while too.

I haven't met Cupid personally, but he does excellent work, ensuring I don't miracle-block myself from true love. "Do you want me to be your mommy?" I asked hopefully. ("PICK ME!") The twirling terrier rolled over and flashed his freckled fairy belly at me. I smiled and smooched this *Dog Bachelor* presenting me the final rose. We were off the market. My heart pounded... *"THIS IS MY DOG! He's the little white dog who'll join me in very important work."*

What the psychic didn't tell me, but Mayor Puppypants knew, was that I had a natural gift for talking with and healing animals of all species that I'd long forgotten. Animals around the world were waiting for me to find my voice and hand them the microphone.

I quickly ran to the front of the shelter to adopt the dog that God (or Morgan Freeman) called me about. When I told the shelter staff, "I want to adopt that loud little dude that's on sale," they smiled, but told me I must "Go ask the couple that's already been looking at him if they want to adopt him. If not, he's yours."

Would the couple refuse the winning lifetime lottery ticket, making him MINE? I'd bite them if necessary. I stayed calm though, like The Dog Whisperer Cesar Milan taught me: Be calm and assertive. I quietly walked back down the adoption alley, but my nerves were doing a fierce line dance.

With my head shaking, "Say No," I asked the young couple if they planned on adopting "that loud, scrappy, hyperactive, semi-hairless, little white dog." I scrunched my face like I'd stepped in poop to really sell it. Clearly, they'd met my imaginary husband, as they calmly "Cesar-Milan-d" me back. "We've chosen another dog. Sammy's not the right energy for our family."

Laughing maniacally, I exclaimed, "AWESOME! BECAUSE I'M ADOPTING HIM RIGHT NOW!" (Mental cartwheels and somersaults up to the office...I was the right energy for him!) As I filled out paperwork, I could hear my furry angel celebrating loudly from his cage: "GET ME OUTTA HERE! LET'S GO, MOM! LET'S PARTY!"

He is incredibly impatient, and I sincerely love that about him. As soon as I paid the best money ever spent, they handed me my little party animal. I was now the mom of an angelic superhero—a magic portal with paws.

His mischievous "Catch me if you can!" face matched mine as we broke out of animal "jail," where every resident's only crime was trusting a person. He rode shotgun in my Jeep with the wind in his fur, a free spirit now freed. His swagger begged for a title, so I renamed him Mayor Puppypants. His high energy is a blessing, not a behavior issue. A mutt on a mission.

As we rode home, I noticed my new son never stopped smiling. I initially named him "Guy Smiley," as he resembled that Muppet from Sesame Street—the game show host with a microphone asking silly questions. Mayor Puppypants is a natural-born game show host who sang into his virtual mic to spring free from the shelter.

Some people train the dog out of their dog, but I didn't want to change a thing. I wanted to be more like him. He's a well-behaved wild card. It'd have been a karmic crime if he'd gone home with a magic-less "master" who mistook his playful energy for disobedience. Many of the best pet parents still don't understand AN ANGEL IS LIVING IN YOUR HOUSE. So, yes...share your bed. Puppypants and I unlocked each other's cages that day.

Animals set people free to live a life they never knew was possible, or long ago stopped dreaming about. Mayor Puppypants, aka "the Mayor," and I are one. We finish each other's sentences and he finishes my snacks that he wizards out of my hands and swallows whole before I can yelp, "Why you little @&*#!" He's a freaky little teleporter who appears out of nowhere like a cartoon angel/devil (mission depending).

My magical muse knew I'd desperately sought a one-way ticket to Oz, Narnia, or Wonderland to escape my life, and he guided me to discover all three lands within myself. Puppypants fetched my ruby slippers, opened the magic wardrobe, and pushed me laughing into a *rabbit hole* of no return.

Here we are years later, co-writing a book for animal friends around the world to tell their stories too. And he's smiling every day, strutting his stuff, and wherever we go, he thinks he works there. The Mayor needs a "Members Only" jacket to be a Bouncer at a nightclub, where the only one who gets in is mommy, and those who know the secret password: ADOPT! Mayor Guy Smiley Puppypants needed a platform to unleash his puppy powers. "Puppypants Town" is a mythical place where he's the mayor, and all the unwanted animals are forever safe in loving homes.

A couple of years into his teaching career, I ran a Change.org petition, contacted the City of St. Petersburg's Mayor's office, and let them know of his campaign to be the first "Dog Mayor" of St. Pete. He was the only dog running and...he won! Mayor Puppypants earned his title for his hard work promoting kindness to animals. At his inauguration party, he was presented with "The Bone to the City" by the human mayor.

While his inauguration story took a backseat to Hurricane Irma, there was still a party, a delicious cake with his likeness wearing a crown and cape, music, and animal friends. Puppypants shined, while I ate cake and straightened his bow tie.

He addressed his Hispanic constituents as "Alcalde Perrito Pantalones." He's a natural-born pawlitican, promoting, "Adoptar, no comparar...Adopt don't shop!" Pantalones performs a few tricks in different languages, which always impresses the kids who believe he's multilingual. (Shh...he's secretly following hand signals paired with cultural words.) In fairness, his native language Animal is "mutt-i-lingual."

This superhero-fairy-fido is a Jack-Russell-Terrier/Maltese...a "Jartese." Oh, look...I've created a whole new breed—a "designer" breed, aka MUTT. The breed is always DOG...superhero. God spelled backward. Cats aren't thrilled about this spelling "coincidence" that dogs enjoy.

Cats are just as close to the Creator as dogs. CAT spelled backward is TAC—Telepathic Awesome Creatures. Use that the next time someone insults your cat. Tell them your TAC is reading their mind, then watch them squirm.

You'll never get a better pet because you pay more money, just a more expensive one. And in case you're wondering, I'm a "Norwish-scot." That's my heritage, and I'm up for adoption!

Mayor Puppypants LOVES the spotlight and has been on TV a

few times, always stealing the show. He appeared on the NBC show "DayTime TV" with hosts Cyndi Edwards and Jerry Penacoli. I'd first seen this show while riddled with depression after Teddy #2's passing (also the year Puppypants was born), and it planted a seed to visit St. Pete, a very dog-friendly city.

The Mayor spent his debut on TV staring at himself on camera and Jerry loved it! He laughed about the Mayor's self-approval. I joked that Puppypants needed to go to "low self-esteem camp" to humble himself a notch, but he reminded me when I was his age, I called myself Shannon The Great. Like mother, like son.

Mayor Puppypants is the magic in every fairy tale ever told. My then senior dog, Ducky, who'd lost her best Golden friends, fell in love with him too. Together, we created children's humane education programs, and hit the speaking circuit in elementary schools, The Children's Cancer Center, and various nonprofits. The Mayor demonstrated how special animals are and how to kindly care for them.

We teach that even if we don't like certain animals, they're still worthy of respect and compassion. Of course, all the kids love the mighty mayor. A self-proclaimed celebrity, the Mayor scream-yodels (for himself and the kids) as soon as we arrive on a school campus. He and Taylor Swift need a duet of her hit song, *"You Need to Calm Down."* Telling him to calm down always backfires into even louder, unapologetic performances that would make a lesser stage mom embarrassed, but makes me proud. Pro tip: Always sing louder than the Mayor, or you'll forever be his backup dancer...just ask Taylor.

The Mayor's magical presence creates mutually excited kids and teachers. We've taught pet care classes to hundreds of kids including at Sawgrass Lake Elementary, where the Mayor enjoyed much praise for his many laughter and learning lessons. Sawgrass enthusiastically invited us back for an encore with a fluffy twist of focus—Animal Communication.

Mayor Puppypants shocked the crowd with exactly how magical he is by understanding the energy of his young constituents around him. About 30 second-graders sat in a big circle while the Mayor in the center threw a toy to himself, seeming to be in his own world.

I was teaching the kids that animals understand our thoughts and feelings and have their own too. Animals communicate with us all the time, I explained. Upon hearing this, a shy, soft-spoken little girl who didn't speak much English said very quietly while the Mayor's back was turned to her, "I wish Mayor Puppypants would talk with me because I love him."

At that exact moment, Mayor Puppypants twirled around, and tossed his toy right into this child's lap! Jaws dropped. The little girl's face lit up as classmates cheered. Teachers silently mouthed, "How did he do that?" Applauding his clever perfection, I proudly proclaimed, "Well...that's animal communication!"

I didn't and couldn't train him to respond to a wish a child would unknowingly make. It was a miracle, and just one of many this scruffy "Jartese" mutt does every day of his existence. His innate awareness of what to do and "say," along with his comedic timing, makes him the superstar he is just by being himself. He made this child feel special by honoring the language of her heart. My fluffy-butted pawfessor demonstrated animal communication in its purest form. Exactly how much does the Mayor energetically understand? From what I can tell...everything!

After we finished a kindergarten class there, the teacher excitedly called after us down the hall, "Ms. Spring, the kids have a very important question for you and Mayor Puppypants!" The Mayor and I excitedly pivoted. "Yes, of course, what is it?" In genuine curiosity, she asked, "Where are Mayor Puppypants' pants?"

I looked at my hero, and confidently replied, "He wears invisible, magical pants!" The teacher didn't miss a beat. "Ah! Yes! Of course—invisible, magical pants. He's the coolest. The kids will love that!" Fun-inspired, wise teachers know silly questions are just as important as serious ones. Who knows what will be discovered? Silliness is often the answer, whatever the question. What's the best way to handle adulthood? Magical pants.

I wish adults could teleport back to this sweet innocence, away from the angst of adulthood for just one more happy day of childhood on the playground. Technically, we can, but that's another book. I've experienced some time travel with Teddy #1 and my kindergarten teacher—all of us, holograms smiling together. I didn't want to leave that bliss-breathing portal where the joy of our spirits escapes the density of our human forms.

We can travel through time, and return to the present with lighter hearts and minds outside of dreams. Simultaneous realities exist and animals are willing, time-traveling tour guides. They shape-shift and can travel the multiverse. Worlds like humans love to explore in fantasy books and movies...and then doubt exists until they discover their spiritual passports to access them.

Mayor Puppypants has traveled with me to many alternate realities. In this world, he attended a meeting at The National Speakers Academy. Members sat at long rows of tables listening to the MC drone on about success. The Mayor was asleep at my feet, snoozing away unseen under the banquet cloth. It was lunchtime, and the MC was speaking overtime, a serious faux pas. I wanted to open a trap door below him.

As soon as I had the thought, "OMG, when is this man going to shut the..." Right on cue, Sleeping Beauty himself, Alcalde Perrito Pantalones, sang out, "AWOOO!" Laughter exploded, and the MC nearly fainted, startled by this wacky alarm. The Mayor kicked it up an octave, and when the MC regained his balance, looked at his watch and said, "Oh look...it's lunchtime...and here I am...still talking."

The Mayor and I, being big talkers ourselves, are in no position to judge fellow chatters. But, we were hangry and so was everyone else. The Mayor saved the day again just by being his bossy, silly self. Best Woofin' Speaker of the Year!

The Mayor entered two "Fido Idol" singing contests. Just to be a little stinker, he sang the whole way there, and the entire drive home, but not one woofing-peep during the contests. He loves playing pranks on me and reminding me who wears the magic pants. He "won" 3rd place because only three Fidos were competing. Lacking a competitive streak, but maintaining his showmanship, he likes winning contests where the odds are stacked in his favor.

He sang so loudly at an outdoor concert, held at the restaurant perfectly named, "The Chattaway," that the stunned musician stopped playing to ask, "Is that little dude singing? Bring the cute little fella up here!" A dog-man duo sang their hearts out to thunderous applause proving he does not ever need to calm down!

Puppypants loves to co-emcee "furry fundraisers" with me. At an SPCA event, he dressed as a classy gentleman in a furry-tailed tux with a purple feather in its pocket. Everyone adored his shameless bravado and irresistible smile with an eager underbite. Guests generously donated until, like a pack of wolves, they became distracted by food. Donations dried up like kibble.

I looked at my pimped-out pooch and gave him a wink. He's always got my back, and we got festivities back on track to raise money fast! I coaxed the deejay to dim the lights and "play something swanky and spotlight my furry superstar."

Channeling my inner Magic Mike, I shouted, "Ladies and gentlemen, LET'S GET WILD AND MAKE IT RAIN!" while undressing the Mayor, taking off his tux one piece at a time. Mayor Puppypants became the first mayor to publicly strip for charity. First Place Funny Fido. Laughter and donations flowed—a drooling success! He's especially proud when he makes me laugh. The sound of happy, human laughter is one of the things that makes our pets happiest.

In one of his greatest pranks, and most disturbing moments of my life, I looked up during sex to see Puppypants humping my lover's leg while (let's say, Todd?) was "humping" me. Puppypants locked eyes with me while maniacally grinning and acting out what he learned from watching boyfriends over the years. "STOP!" I yelled, pushing Todd off me and laughing uncontrollably. Puppypants and I knew Todd wasn't bone-worthy, and needed to get dressed and lose our number. We never spoke of this menage-a-paw again...until now.

Puppypants has comedic superpowers, and I don't mind embarrassing myself to entertain him, too...with the exception of humping his friends! Animals of all species find clever ways to invite us to play hoping we'll play-bow back. (Go ahead...stick your butt in the air!) I'd love to see a comedy club where people entertain their pets, or pets perform standup acts about their people. My dogs are surely performing sold-out shows in the afterlife!

It'd been a while since I heard a Spirit voice with an insistent message like "GO TO THE SHELTER NOW." One afternoon while petting Ducky and Puppypants, working on my humor biz, I mused about the Mayor needing a play buddy his age and energy level to goof around with. Right on cue, I heard an Oprah-like voice say, "Go to the dog park now." *(Note: These mysterious voices don't order me to streak around town. They are my spirit team, guardian angels cleverly making sure I don't miss a miracle.)*

It wasn't our usual park time, but Spirit supersedes my schedule when magic's underway. "*Rabbit Hole*" rules apply. It's always "tea time"— tea being whatever magic Spirit is brewing.

Luckily, following the rabbit down the hole never disappoints. We lived near St. Pete's Vinoy Park on the water. Dolphins would often hear the Mayor singing and come right up to the sea wall to perform appreciation for his playful spirit, wisdom, and land dolphin qualities!

Ducky, Puppypants, and I entered the park and began playing ball when a tricolor-coated flash of fur running faster than greyhounds racing for freedom sprinted past in the distance. I was captivated by this wild spirit. I called out across the park, "WOW! COOL DOG!" His foster mom Emily hollered back, "HE'S UP FOR ADOPTION! DO YOU WANT TO MEET HIM?" My inner child (now able to sign legal documents) cheered, ABSOLUTELY!

Emily brought "Banjo" over, and Ducky and Puppypants immediately liked him. Ducky was never impressed by other dogs, except her big sisters in Heaven, and Puppypants. So, when she smiled at this Happy Hound Beagle mix, I knew he was divinely sent. And now I knew why we'd been summoned to hurry to the park. The Puppypants Town family fetched him just in time.

Banjo immediately tackled me with kisses, and I laughed like a puppy. Banjo was Emily's first foster dog. She said he was very sweet, and her dog Charlie loved playing with him. She cleverly left out that Banjo was redecorating her home with his furniture and curtain-chewing hobby. I'm glad she had his back like that though. My dogs didn't rat me out for my worst moments either.

I filled out the adoption forms, and once approved, the Mayor and I went to pick him up. He tackled me with kisses again while the Mayor dug into Charlie's toy box. He smiled the whole way home, licking my face as I told him he'd now be known as Kermit the Dog, named after a heroic friend to all kids and animals, Kermit the Frog.

Kermit lives up to his namesake's character—kind, zany, wise—teaching us to be our best selves. Kermit the Dog chose to teach me a lesson long overdue through his hobby of performing unwanted home makeovers. A test of sanity and priorities. He was also very hard to walk and nearly pulled me into the lake to swim with ducks a few times. I was humbled by a mannerless mutt with movie star good looks. If a boyfriend ever willfully destroyed my things, he'd be listed for sale on Craigslist. But a pet doesn't rent my heart, they own it. Unconditional forgiveness.

It wasn't until I came home one day, and saw he chewed a

designer tote bag and left it shredded on the floor, that his philosophical tough love message got through to me: Let go of my materialistic ways. Be free like he was when I saw him in the park, not worried about getting his fur coat dirty. Kermit was just the life coach to set me straight. After my initial horror, I laughed at the trashed tote bag wondering, "What kind of asshole spends $600 on a tote bag?" The answer was on my next credit card statement. That asshole still had to pay for the bag.

Kermit was surprised by my Zen reaction. He was relieved to see he wasn't in trouble, and I was grateful to be more like him. Free of baggage. Like Marie Condo, the famous organizer who asks if an item sparks joy, and if not, gives it away. Kermit sparked more joy than all the glittered, glamorous swag ever could. And I'd never give Kermit away. I still love nice things, but won't tote around misplaced values again. (I did give away my scale…instant JOY!)

Kermit needed to know after many failed adoption events where he "didn't show well" (people chose puppies over Kermit, who got jealous), he was finally HOME. He was testing me to see how much I loved him, and who came first—him or my stuff? In Pets vs. Prada, he won, and unpacked his fears for good.

"Kissing Kermit" is an expert empath who feels things deeply and has a side gig puckering up for profits in his smooch booth for charity. My bank once hired Kermit to work their lobby, and I pressured people to make out with my dog and pay him for the privilege of spraying dairy-free whipped cream on their faces or hands for Kermit to lick off. I encourage customers to choose faces reasoning: "It's so gross, ya gotta do it!" Kermit wags with pride checking his breath between customers as I count donations.

Kissing Kermit is an exceptional canine shaman. A little pooch-smooching goes a long way toward feeling better. The harder you laugh, the more he'll kiss you, until you fall over laughing like a kid again. "Laughter opens hearts, minds, and wallets" is my slogan for furry fundraising. Doing silly, sober things like animals do is drinking pure laughter from the Cheshire Cat's vial. Hangover-free bliss from a sloppy canine kiss.

Animals remind us to be comfortable in our skin and inspire us to act more like them. Whatever's happening, PLAY. Animal coaches will never bench you. Head for vegan ice cream after your games and alternate licks on the same cone. "Dog germs" and laughter are a cure for whatever ails you. Cats disagree, and remind you their purring sounds are healing powerhouses!

Puppypants is the main pawfessor at pet camps. Kermit usually comes as a guest woofer and was home alone once while Puppypants and I were teaching. When we returned, I saw the seat cushion of my favorite cherry red armchair badly torn, with stuffing strewn on the floor. Kermit sheepishly cowered when he saw my expression. I know that feeling and never want my kids to be afraid in their own homes. I want them to trust it's okay to make mistakes. Let's not repeat them, let's learn.

I knew it was an accident. His face spoke more than sorrow. He'd simply burrowed into the blanket on the chair and dug too deeply. He'd accidentally overachieved! (His other hobby is "landscaping" our yard. I have fallen into many of Kermit's caverns!) Kermit didn't fall off the "Good Boy wagon" and relapse into destruction. He'd gotten lonely and went too far trying to comfort himself. Something I've done, but thankfully stopped short of fracking furniture.

` All of us need a safe space to learn and be forgiven. Come to think of it, the Mayor's never once looked remorseful...that little stinker!

I smooched Kermit, forgave, and reassured him he wasn't getting re-homed (something pet "owners" do), then devised a creative solution to fix the chair. I put photos of Kermit's smiling face in felt flowers and sealed the holes shut with them. What could have looked like a destroyed chair was transformed into Kermit's pawtographed priceless art. Kermit taught me the value of playing with a problem. My shift in attitude is what shifted his behavior, and he's never destroyed anything since (unless you count stolen snacks from counter-surfing).

Puppypants mostly just chewed me out of underwear and pens. At ten years old, he recently chewed/de-crotched another pair of undies. Is the lesson that he's still a puppy inside? Or that going commando is cheekier? When I ask him, he laughs hysterically. "I'm teaching you to be more like me...pantalones optional."

Puppypants still sometimes holds his leash in his mouth, walking himself while I hold the other end. He sing-speaks for minutes at a time in his own language, determined to be acknowledged, loud, and proud. After baths, he play-growls and silly dances on the sofa. He will never grow up, and for that, I'm most grateful. In my eyes, he'll never grow old either—he'll only ascend closer to the rainbow's center, one day helping fly me Home too. As I type this with him on my lap, he says to "pack a jacket, the flight can be a bit breezy."

Animals are natural shamans with a keen sixth sense they don't second guess as people do. In this regard, their intelligence supersedes ours. Ducky once sat by a stranger on the beach glued to his side. I was throwing the ball for Lucy when I noticed Ducky's unusual behavior. I called out to the man and apologized, "I hope she's not bothering you. She's never done that before." The man smiled and said, "I'm happy she's here. My wife just died, and I needed this."

Ducky intuitively knew to use her healing powers to comfort a stranger in need. Animal Communication isn't all about conversations between us and them. It's about being present emotionally with love. The man asked what breed Ducky was and I said, "Maybe a Flat Coat Retriever mix...she's from the Humane Society." And as if Heaven started raining rainbows, he replied, "I'll definitely get my next dog from there too. Ducky's an angel."

Many angels like Ducky and my other pawspring don't make it out of shelters because breeding unconscionably continues. Let's breed unconditional love for furry souls and choose rescue over milling and killing. Ducky cared about the man's pain, not his pedigree. She followed her heart. There's a rescue group for every breed. Rescuers are so passionate because WE'RE SAVING LIVES! Everyone has the arms of an angel when we choose to use them as angels would.

Be like Ducky, and greet a lonely stranger. Exercise shelter dogs, comfort stray cats, or fetch a treat from the fridge for any slobbering soul within snacking distance. What the fluff are you waiting for?

4

THE ANGEL & THE AWAKENING

And the day came when the risk to remain tight in a bud was more painful than the risk it took to bloom.
Anais Nin

I never really believed in past lives, but that changed when I heard author Dr. Brian Weiss, the Father of the Past Life Regression movement, lead the audience in a past life regression. I doubted I'd experience anything in such a crowded room. Eventually, my overactive mind succumbed to his calm guidance and I saw...drumroll, please...A GIANT BRICK WALL!

This wasn't a comforting sight. But, it perfectly represented how I'd experienced life so far—an insurmountable brick wall I was determined to surmount if I could figure out how. An unlikely hero emerged before I could begin telepathically banging my head against it. Cartoon character Wile E. Coyote appeared and blew it down with dynamite!

Both real and imaginary animals can show up to rescue us. Sound crazy? Maybe, but it worked. Our subconscious minds know just which messenger (serious, sensitive, or silly) to send, and sometimes we're the messenger for someone else.

Brick wall demolished, I ended the hide-and-seek game I'd been playing, searching for my soul. "Shannon... McDevitt...Shannon... McDevitt." Only the faintest voice had been replying because that was no longer me. Caterpillar me was dying. Butterfly me was out shopping for paint colors to decorate my new wings.

My last name, like my former religion, no longer suited me and needed to be changed. I easily chose Spring—my favorite season, representing rebirth for my new name. A judge approved my new legal name and I felt more at home in myself.

Shortly after my brick wall collapsed into smithereens, I attended a second past-life regression workshop at the bookstore, Wings. I was curious who I'd been and what advice my past selves would have for me now. Would we all get along? Or would we fight over clothes and men? Did past versions of me also eat chocolate cake for breakfast? I had so many questions.

When the meditation ended, attendees shared their epic, detailed experiences of revisiting their past lives. Some guests experienced their past selves as pharaohs or queens, and some connected with deities I'd never heard of. My entire meditation involved seeing a silent white rabbit sitting by a stream of gently flowing water. That was it. I didn't have any big epiphanies, travel anywhere exotic, or recover past life memories.

Just a rabbit by a stream sitting in silence, not even holding a cue card for me to read. No secrets were revealed, not even a "Psst...Shannon, the secret of life is..." Just a chill, content rabbit...waiting. I initially dismissed him as cute, but insignificant and almost missed the *Alice in Wonderland* symbolism soon to unfold through this magical hare.

In hindsight, I did have an epic experience and just didn't recognize the gift or the guide. This mysterious rabbit was a Spirit Guide preparing to take me on a beautiful adventure. The rabbit knew the way to where I was going and didn't need to speak. I needed to listen, with all of my senses, just as rabbits do.

Trust that when you're ready, your perfect animal guide, silent like the rabbit, or chatty like Puppypants, will appear too. Or maybe a dynamite-carrying coyote to demolish your brick walls. Each animal is a teacher embodying spiritual qualities and messages. A white rabbit symbolizes abundance, creativity, new beginnings, joy, good luck, and more. Their big round eyes see in almost every direction, and this rabbit saw me coming from lifetimes away!

Coyotes are known for being clever and symbolizing revealing truths behind illusion and chaos, resourcefulness, and balancing wisdom with playfulness. The cute rabbit, (now likely deaf from the explosion) had been patiently waiting for me to show up. Was I late to this mystical party? Or right on time? Was the rabbit a friend I hadn't yet met? Or one I'd always known?

It was 2014 when I awoke one night to a wild surprise. Mayor Puppypants and I were both LEVITATING in bed while Ducky slept nearby. I'd heard about levitating, but never gave it thought until I was...LEVITATING! The Mayor and I floated above the bed in a semi-dream-like state where a loving and assertive angel was chasing me.

No matter where I tried to hide, or how fast I ran, she stayed by my side, smiling like an angel. She held in her hands a gift I was destined to receive. I imagine she felt like rescuers do when trying to catch a stray dog. First, gain trust before treating, trapping, and releasing them into a better life. Catching a stray dog or a suspicious Shannon can be tricky, but the angel had the upper halo on me. Patiently insistent, she wasn't giving up.

The angel looked like Glinda, the Good Witch from *The Wizard of Oz,* a favorite childhood movie. Angels and other messengers will often appear to us in forms that make us feel safe, someone we'll recognize and trust. Spirit knew the best way for a Light Being to appear to me was this gentle fairy-angel archetype. Had she been perhaps a scary Giant Squid chasing me instead, I might've telepathically tased my miracle and gotten slimed.

When Glinda the angel finally cornered me (the way I do my dirty dogs for baths), she exposed the gift she'd been holding was her heart, and she had merged it with mine! And just like how I always remind my dogs they love how they feel after a bath, I instantly felt completely transformed, light, unburdened by life. Naked with truth.

After the heart implosion, she led me into an old-fashioned, empty movie theater where I lamented, "Oh no, I'm late." She smiled kindly and said, "No, Shannon. You're right on time."

The curtains pulled back revealing the movie title, *Kierkegaard*, who I only knew was a philosopher. Then I heard, "You're becoming who God intended you to be." When I awoke, I felt an incredible sense of peace, joy, and LOVE. I felt "at one" with everything around me. Everything made sense to me. Situations and people I'd been angry at no longer affected me. When we die (or achieve enlightenment), we're able to see things through every other human being's eyes. I was experiencing this while alive. This kumbaya feeling was Heaven on Earth.

Mayor Puppypants floated around, laughing, wagging, and resisting the urge to bark, "WE'RE NOT IN KANSAS ANYMORE, MOM!" The Mayor was born wearing ruby slippers.

My thoughts were instantly manifesting into reality, and all of my questions felt answered. I started researching what was happening. Some online sources suggested it might be drug-induced euphoria or a mental breakdown. Nope. I wasn't doing drugs and already had a breakdown. Woohoo!

The peace and calm within felt like an endless infusion of chocolate bliss without a diabetic coma. No emotional highs or lows, just a steady state of loving contentment. I simply felt at ONE with everything in both a surreal and grounded way. Clairaudience (psychic hearing) informed me I was having a *kundalini awakening*—a spiritual transformation. Hallelujah!

In the Hindu tradition, kundalini awakenings are considered a type of religious experience. It didn't matter that I'd grown up

Catholic. When it comes to mega spiritual orgasms like this, it doesn't matter which god you pray to because you're too busy saying, "OH MY GOD!" to check identification. OMG expresses gratitude for all gods, covering your bases.

I experienced a gift of transformation that some people spend a lifetime meditating to manifest/achieve. I simply went to sleep one night with my magical, invisible-pants-wearing dog and woke up in spiritual "Oz" where magic lives. Alive with divine love and wisdom, I was eager to learn how to play with my new gifts.

Discovering I was both right on time in my own story and its co-writer, I stepped into my power and tossed aside human measuring sticks of success. Most people are unaware magic is all around and inside us, and misplaced wands, ruby slippers, *rabbit holes*, or psychic gifts appear when we reclaim our power.

It's socially acceptable to be die-hard fans of *Alice in Wonderland*, Harry Potter books, and the Hocus Pocus movies, but people who live "supernaturally" are often viewed as tinfoil-hat-wearing-lunatics trying to cast spells on you and your little dog too.

It was a bummer when the spiritual elevation eventually leveled off. From Nirvana to I-don't-wanna (be human again). While I was a new me, others were still them. UGH! Still, I became permanently more peaceful, confident, and connected to Spirit. I felt like the only kid without a curfew ready to play, but no one to play with. Luckily, animals are always ready to play and don't have a curfew.

I finally realized when people sense my reclaimed power and try to steal my sunshine, it's because they lack similar courage to lose their minds and find their souls. Like Dorothy, I stand my glittered ground. You can never advance as a soul by harming others.

#GetYourOwnDamnRubySlippers!

I'd tried reading *A Course in Miracles*, a book many people study in discussion groups, but I struggled with its Bible-like language and found it too frustrating to be freeing. My reading glasses never quite fit right, and I complained about the book and my glasses in front of

Mayor Puppypants. Whether we speak our thoughts aloud or just feel them in our hearts and minds, our pets know.

Upon returning from errands, the Mayor had chewed the bridge on my glasses and pages in the book. When I put my glasses on, they fit perfectly and stopped slipping off my nose. The pages he chewed were on forgiveness. He's a clever miracle worker, and there was nothing to forgive. I could now see straight, stopped reading the book on miracles, and started having them! I focused on the Mayor's chosen lesson on forgiveness of many people who'd hurt me without remorse.

You don't have to read (or eat) books on miracles to manifest them, but I do think it helps to ask for signs. I regularly talk to angels, and they frequently visit in and out of my dreams. Spiritual enlightenment is possible for everyone to experience in their own invisible magical pants. Reiki is a great way to restore people and pets when feeling energetically off balance. Power up your chakras, it's time to party like an animal!

In my first reiki session, the healer told me while working on my energy, she saw something mind-blowing. She shared, "The room filled up with animal spirits, and not just dogs and cats, but wild animals of every kind to give you their love and support. So much love for you." One of these *invisible* friends, an amphibian of like mind, introduced himself to me just weeks later when I traveled to Costa Rica.

I hadn't vacationed in 10 years and leaped at the chance to join an Animal Communication guru leading a retreat in Costa Rica. When the retreat guests gathered in the hotel lobby, I disappointedly noted they were ALL WOMEN. I asked if there were any men in our group. "IT'S JUST US GODDESSES!" they squealed. I groaned.

The leader Denise was uptight, but desperately wanted to appear easygoing. In every photo, she's wildly laughing like she's just heard the funniest thing, concealing a serious condition known as RBF—RESTING BITCH FACE. If she and I were cast in a production of *The Handmaid's Tale*, she'd be Serena and I'd be June.

When we headed out for an adventure, my seasoned travelmates were well prepared with bug spray, sunscreen, pocket knives, and ponchos. I was the unseasoned asshole in the jungle with a designer turtle backpack carrying only a wallet and lipstick. Was I planning to bribe or seduce predators? No idea. (In fairness, have you seen the muscles on some of these beasts?)

I sensed Denise trying to read me and I secretly, sarcastically wished her luck with that. She asked me to hand her my bracelet. Amused by her thinking she'd out-foxed me, I obliged. She held it in her hand doing psychometry (the psychic art of reading objects, which I happen to excel at). I witnessed her confusion trying and failing to label me. I'm not a one-dimensional character after all. Don't break your label maker trying to categorize me.

Denise led us on a walk where she quickly scolded another guest and me for laughing in the forest. She was like a librarian on steroids fervently shushing us. Meanwhile, none of the animals gave a flying feces if we laughed. I'm sure if animals had been our troop leader, they'd have gleefully insisted we share what's so funny with the rest of the class. Animals love to laugh and find party poopers rather insufferable.

We were gifting nature with joy, and leaving only our footprints. While humans might not like it, we can be great entertainment for the animals too, especially people who take themselves too seriously. Ever heard the Guns 'n Roses song, "Welcome to the Jungle?" It's a party song, not a lullaby. Lighten up, Denise. Laugh on, Shannon.

Denise was regurgitating a lot of nonsense down our beaks about meditation being the only way to connect with the animal kingdom. Meditation is wonderful for healing one's body and mind, but it's not necessary to talk with animals. (#You don't need to be Zen to talk with a hen.) Speaking of hens, Denise led our group of all women (Where's the beef?), in the jungle that I paid over $10,000 to see, and told us to close our eyes.

No way was I closing my eyes and missing a second of the beauty around me that I'd paid to see IN PERSON. Closing our eyes in a picturesque forest to picture something peaceful was ridiculously human. Denise held up a picture of a rare tree frog, and directed, "Close your eyes and visualize seeing this frog that you'll only spot if you're silent, specifically at a level zero."

A group of grown-ass women playing "the quiet game" like I'd done with kindergartners (and sometimes Puppypants). Denise wanted us to be minions. While the others obeyed our laughter-less leader, I quietly wandered ahead in self-respecting rebellion with eyes wide open. I looked back at everyone trying hard to achieve inner peace to align with the elusive frog. Denise was no doubt winning the award for quietist, despite being the only one talking.

Within about 100 feet of thinning myself from the herd, I spotted the rare little Señor Froggy or rather Sapo (Spanish for frog). He cheered for me, rebelling from his own frog commander's orders- AWOL from his frog army nowhere in sight. It was a clever mental high-five, as we smiled at each other, frog to human...neither of us being at a "level zero". We were just being ourselves.

Once Denise finished her frog-finding foreplay, I pointed and triumphantly croaked, "Hey, Denise, do you mean this frog right here?" The group was excited for me, but Denise was not amused. Sapo and I laughed like two schoolgirls skipping school. All I needed to be was myself to locate Señor Sapo or any other creature who vibes with my inner tadpole.

This fun frog empowered me more in five minutes than human therapists ever could in years. Probably because he saw the real me, not some mislabeled person who needed to be fixed. Animals see souls. Señor Sapo instantly knew me and invited me to play. It's an intimacy, unlike any connection with people. Animals enjoy pureness, a Pura Vida that humans are born with, then lose, and then regain through death. Animals remain pure throughout their lives.

Señor Sapo saluted me as a soul on a mission to recover myself and do it my way. Pura Vida, Sapo! Much like when *trying* to have an orgasm, it's likely to elude you; it's the same with animal communication. Don't *try* to orgasm out a frog sighting. Just relax, and let him expose himself to you. It'll be a whole lot more fun that way. "Relax. Ribbit. Repeat."

Speaking of not forcing orgasms, and letting nature simply take its course, my monkey amigos—los monos (known for eating bananas the right way and fierce mating selection), reminded me to give a sexy shout-out to Esteban. He's the Darwinian selected tour guide who led me on one wild *canoe ride*. By the way, sexy in Spanish is also "sexy." Now you're fluent in what happens next. What Happens in the Jungle makes it into my book!

I was dying to go horseback riding, but my legs weirdly swelled up making that impossible. Before I could curse my luck, I felt a sprinkle of laughing fairy dust dance on my mind. "Your injury is good luck." There was another guest, a psychiatrist (the universe has wicked humor) who needed a second person to register for her canoe trip to be able to go herself. So, my leg injury kicked up some fun for both of us, and Esteban. I'd found the beef! (Caution: lusty river rapids ahead.)

Before taking off in our canoes, Esteban looked at me with a prey drive. (I've sent and received these eyes many times, usually after a few shots.) This was now sober mating, a whole new animal for me. He confidently confessed, "I can only take ONE of you in MY boat and I'll do ALL the work for YOU. The other one (glancing at the shrink) can ride separately."

Into our riverboats we went, gliding on hormones until he docked us on a riverbank, showing us Amazonian clay that women pay top dollar for in spas. Shrink didn't speak any Spanish, so Esteban flirted with me in a few dirty palabras while the shrink shrugged.

It was clear we were getting ready to romp when Esteban solved the issue of our third-wheel-cock-blocking-head-shrinker by literally sending her up the river but with a paddle. He assured her to just go with the flow and we'd soon follow. She drifted out of sight, learning third-wheel lingo...probably diagnosing me as a puta. Puta or puma, I pranced like a wildcat.

Listen, go to "level zero." Can you hear the howler monkeys still howling about it? "Welcome to the Jungle!" Ooh, Ooh, Ahh, Ahh! Esteban and I mated in the river as nature intended. He was blessed to be born with a boulder that rocked my world, and my world is a seasoned traveler with a tight grip on innuendo.

Los monos voted "People Mating Rituals" their favorite reality show to judge. Thankfully my womb is only equipped to breed sorceress cats and silly dogs. We got back in our canoes smiling like honeymooners, and located Shrink who'd learned "AYUDA!" So, we helped her by towing her canoe on ours, as Esteban indiscreetly called me Sweetie, mentally stroking his indefatigable oar.

Back ashore, Esteban kissed me goodbye and I joined the group bragging like a horny sailor. I laughed at how my injured leg was a great wingman in getting my *canoe paddled* expertly in this jungle book twist. "Karen" asked, "Did you get his phone number?" I sighed, as there's always someone who misses the point—always a human.

What Esteban, los monos, and I shared was about exchanging international banana, not last names or numbers. First names were even a bit formal, but he was wearing a name tag, so it was only fair he knew mine. Esteban gave me a rock to remember our riverboat romp. La roca rests on my headboard reminding me sometimes that what looks like a setback is an invitation to carpe someone's diem. Pura Vida, Esteban!

My customer satisfaction survey raved: "Dios mio! Esteban gave me a truly personalized tour of his jungle, leaving me both satisfied and wanting more." (No doubt Esteban had los monos sign an NDA, but I'm howling away.)

It's our positive energy and intentions that animals respond to, not our Zen minds or credentials. Frogs, monkeys, (and Esteban) responded to my ability to play in the moment, not tame myself into submission. Laughter is the highest vibration along with love. Whether you meditate, laugh, or howl your way through life's jungles; animals know a good time and an honest soul when they meet one. A lady armed solely with a wallet and lipstick came to play!

Separate yourself from the herd, and maybe a sassy, rogue frog will help you flipper off your fun-impaired commander too. While you don't have to get jiggy in the jungle to have a good time, it helps get your international groove back. Why do you think monkeys are always smiling? Animals don't care what language we speak, or if we wear a tinfoil hat and invisible, magical pants. They just want us to respect their wild hearts and homes.

5
BORN TO BE WILD

At times in my life, the only place I have been happy is when I am on stage.
Bob Dylan

When I ask animals if there's sin, I hear one word: Betrayal. It sums up everyone that's ever hurt them. According to my team of Goldens in Heaven, the *Animal Bible for People* would simply state The Golden Retriever rule: "Do unto animals as you would have done unto you. Treat everyone as a beloved pet." The Animal Kingdom saved my life many times over and made it worth living. In return, I'd lay down my life or lunch for them.

There are only a few people I'd share my lunch with—the ones who keep their paws off my plate. I've never liked sharing my dessert or fries (unless we're sleeping together). If you want dessert or fries, order your own, and let's share conversation instead. Feel free to use that line next time you're around that annoying person who steals food off your plate. What are they...an animal?

While out driving on a hot summer day, I noticed a homeless

woman standing alone. Not begging, just standing and smiling with faint hope. She was so thin her ribs poked out. I waved her over, smiled, and gave her my sandwich, apologizing for not having napkins. She blessed me, thanked me profusely, and left to eat. I quickly waved her back over before the light turned green, and asked, "Would you like some dessert too?" Her eyes widened in disbelief.

I handed her my strawberries. She cried, "I haven't had fresh strawberries in YEARS. I LOVE STRAWBERRIES! But, I couldn't take these from you, then YOU would go hungry." A lump formed in my throat at the pure kindness she'd spoken. I assured her I'd be fine, and she blessed me again in more ways than one.

Angels come in all forms and species, and she was a human angel. She had the heart of an animal showing selflessness even though life had been cruel. While my dogs regularly and unapologetically steal my snacks right out of my hands, they also do what this woman at "the light" did. They remind me who I want to be, and who I am.

I'm someone who shares my heart, my strawberries, and my strength. I'll give you the shirt off my back unless you shame the homeless woman with "Get a job!" How do you know her job isn't to teach you to be a kinder person? Or stop you from stealing my fries?

I don't believe in organized religions that hold good people prisoner to punishment, shame, and judgment like my former Catholic religion and other religions do. Religion feels more about control than love. It seems quite silly to believe someone or something as powerful as "God" worries about whether we pray in a church, a forest, or not at all, or loves conditionally.

Life is a prayer in itself, waking up every day believing there's a purpose, and doing our best to be good people. Many religions teach that men are somehow closer to God, and therefore qualified to control everyone. My t-shirt collection alone challenges patriarchal culture. My favorite has the nativity scene of Mary, Joseph, the Wisemen, and an angel looking at baby Jesus joyfully proclaiming,

"IT'S A GIRL!" Jesus is a confident dude; it's humans who can't take a joke.

Overall, religion teaches that men are somehow closer to God because they have a swinging pendulum between their legs. (Not exactly, but I read between the lines/legs.) For the record, I'm truly grateful men have that swinging pendulum—a marvelous creation. But, if we're going to claim a silly appendage is essential to being god-like, then an octopus really should replace the church's patriarchal leader. Having eight appendages that *regenerate* seems extra holy, and both males and females have them. Why hasn't anyone thought of this? I'll bet octopuses have.

Jesus has humor, just like the animals, and probably owns the same Nativity "It's a Girl!" shirt as me, just to be ironic. People use religion to justify everything from hate, domestic violence, and child and animal abuse. Spirituality is about unity. People need unity to show more love to all animals and people, not just the ones we like.

Much like the nun's accidental dating advice, the patriarchy inadvertently inspired me to claim my power and let my witchy magic out. Questioning authority, and challenging traditions (a word often used to justify oppression) created new rules to govern my life. My life, my voice, my body, my choice. I empowered myself for adventures aligned with my soul and discarded degrading distractions.

Animals don't limit themselves by "tradition," so why do people? A big part of my work involves challenging people to challenge their core beliefs and see if they're open to adopting healthier ones for themselves and their pets.

The tradition in my house is I prepare the dogs' dinners. But, if I suddenly let them take charge, I guarantee they wouldn't say, "Nah, we should stick to tradition. We're just dogs and shouldn't be allowed to have control of the kitchen." They'd fire up the grill, get cooking, and tell me to quit begging!

Proverb James 2:19 (often paired with a mighty lion's face) states: "When the right spirit enters the room, the wrong spirits get nervous." My presence tends to trigger people. Even when I'm silent, my energy is talking for me, like how a lion's energy speaks, even when asleep. If a lion were snoozing in the corner of your Rotary Club meeting, people would be excited, or terrified when they notice THERE'S A LION IN THE ROOM!

My lioness self sees right through people and removes their societal masks. This can be inviting or threatening. Depending on where they're at spiritually, they'll either want to marry, or murder me. Once, while speaking on animal communication to a women's group, I began my talk by stating, "I don't believe pets go to Heaven." The room filled with tension and silent death threats toward me. I followed with, "I don't *BELIEVE* animals go to Heaven. I *KNOW* they do, and there's a big difference between believing and knowing."

Those who'd been plotting to slash my tires put their salad knives down and breathed a sigh of relief. I continued, "Belief is hope. Knowing is sacred, unshakable. There are few things I know for sure: I know our lives and animals' lives continue after death, and I know I can't live without animals or chocolate." Most of the audience was with me now, but some were still skeptical about me, my topic, and why I had a bodyguard next to my dessert.

I playfully asked the audience, "How many people believe a middle-aged white lady who claims she can talk to animals is likely crazy, but if a Native American male elder were discussing his conversations with animals, that would feel a lot more normal?" Laughter filled the room because as people, we make many silly assumptions and judgments about what's possible for people and animals based on species, race, age, and gender.

Challenge stereotypes about what you and animals can do. You already successfully communicate with your pets through facial expressions, sounds, and body language with no spoken words. Animals and people can smile with our eyes, and give the evil eye. Animals can understand, feel, express, and teach way more than people know. And so can I, as the weird guest speaker at your next luncheon! Loudly howl or meow if you're with me.

The good news is when people are ready for me, I can help them feel significantly better, and inspire them to rediscover their power too. I won't tame myself to put jealous or petty people at ease. My inner lioness is on the hunt to educate, inspire, and entertain people into being kinder to animals. That often happens when people learn to be kinder to themselves first. When people remember their own souls, they're more likely to see the beautiful, innocent souls in animals too. Animals are counting on people to WAKE UP, LISTEN, AND LOVE THEM!

As much as I listen to my pets, I can always pay closer attention to their wisdom. One of my dogs pressed "send" on an email I was obsessing over. I howled in horror. Later, it brought good fortune! I have to wonder how much more success I'd enjoy if dogs made all my life decisions. These furry geniuses and comedic jesters are who I trust with my heart, so why not everything else too? Ok, maybe not the grocery shopping, bill paying, or driving, but, *Mayor Puppypants can definitely be the entertainer at your bachelorette party.*

Animals often ask me to light a fire under their people, to take action on their behalf to create a happier, healthier family for all species members. Most often, everyone needs to get off the couch and let themselves out to play. Joy is the best wellness plan for all species. My conversations with animals lead to some of the best life, love, business, dating, and medical advice people ever receive. And, sometimes pet readings lead to people having sex. (No extra charge.)

My client Jenny's dogs, Archie and Veronica, got along well for years, but now she and her husband Lou were terrified because their sweet dogs were literally at each other's throats, fighting to the death. Archie and Veronica had LOTS to say, most of which matched Mom's complaints. Formerly playmates, they'd become fierce adversaries. Their parents kept them separated, one muzzled at all times, never unsupervised. It was no way for a family to live.

Animals are practical, bottom-line thinkers who show integrity of intentions and provide honest information, often confessing their bad behavior. They can also be both super silly and serious soothsayers. Jenny's pups were exhausted, unhappy, and now relieved to have me as an ally. Things had spiraled out of control for years.

The pups were acting out marital discord. Both pups admitted to liking each other, but their intense anger from being unable to manage their parents' silent rage towards each other was tragically being played out through them.

Jenny was motivated to do whatever was necessary to create harmony for her family, but she'd made the situation worse by overfeeding two already underactive pets. She and Lou were also obese. A self-aware client will always be more successful, as people often want to blame pets when it's a people problem hurting the animals. Food isn't love, and denial is an insidious thief of peace and joy. They were all hungry for happiness, but no amount of treats compensated for the lack of joy.

Veronica and Archie said Mom was mad at Dad a lot. Jenny downplayed her resentment towards Lou. The dogs, however, showed Jenny doing all the work while Lou watched TV, and Jenny's head as an exploding tea kettle, while Lou sucked on a pacifier (immaturity and codependency). Jenny laughed, "YEP, that's us!"

Jenny was in therapy but was only half the problem. "Baby-Daddy" saw no need to improve himself. The dogs' spirits were aligned in solidarity to help their people, but their physical selves had chosen sides in the human war. Archie slept with Mom, and Veronica with Dad in separate rooms building animosity.

Jenny was heartbroken at how stressed her dogs were, but still selfishly overfed them to manage her guilt and food anxiety. The dogs missed being active. Of course, they loved treats; they'd take as many given as any addict would. But, they disliked being fat and their souls craved balance for themselves and their people.

The dogs shared ideas to manage their fighting, but this hostile household needed its people on pet parole until the dogs were free from mental and physical confinement. Trainers can provide behavioral strategies and pet psychics can fill in missing puzzle pieces with hidden insights and solutions by asking the animals directly WTF (What the fluff) is happening?

Jenny's spirits perked up seeing how much her dogs cared. The two chatty dogs still had a secret solution to reveal. They showed staging romance in the bedroom, with rose petals and champagne, along with a "Do Not Disturb" sign, and giggled at the idea of their parents having SEX. Lack of intimacy caused both species to fight. Not much makes me blush, but I was a little nervous about offending my client by talking about her sex life in a pet reading!

I followed the dogs' guidance and relayed her dogs' message: "If Jenny doesn't get laid soon, she's going to murder that s.o.b!" Jenny burst out laughing, "OMG THEY SAID THAT? The dogs know we haven't had sex?" I nodded, "Yep." These furry therapists were acting out the sexual tension but stopped short of putting a sock on the bedroom door handle. Jenny and I laughed, and she was relieved to have the problem named (boredom and frustration) with a sexy solution.

Lou saw a new Jenny unwilling to tolerate or complain about his selfish behavior. She stopped cleaning up after him and began spending her free time enjoying her hobbies. Lou was confused and worried by his wife's new confidence. He began acting like an adult again and stopped taking her for granted. A few days after our reading, Jenny sent me one of the funniest updates I've ever received. "LOU AND I HAD SEX! AND THE DOGS WERE SO HAPPY WE 'DID IT' THEY DID ZOOMIES FOR LIKE AN HOUR AFTER!" Rekindled human romance led to a happy dog dance.

All was well for about a year when she messaged saying, "The dogs are back at it again—fighting." Uh-oh. I knew the dogs would tell me WTNF (what the no fuck) was happening and any possible solution. We met via Zoom, and her dogs showed me the family sleeping apart again. I described the image and Jenny said, "No, we sleep in the same bed. I swear."

I believed her, and also the dogs who again showed images of mom and dad happily swapping rooms and dogs. Animals don't lie, so I had to dive deeper into their message beyond the image. I joked, "Archie and Veronica must be secret sex swingers!"

Jenny gasped and slapped her face in disbelief. "Ahahaha!" she laughed. "Lou and I used to swing with other couples regularly in our old neighborhood, and I miss it. Lou's not sure he wants to share me again." (Luckily, she spared me details on the next update!) Separate bedrooms can save marriages by offering space and a good night's sleep. Rekindled intimacy and communication put the cherry and whipped cream on top of this reading, and the dogs at ease.

Success to me is how many animals call me their friend. And they do call, telepathically, all hours of the day when they need me or just to laugh. I answer with my heart, attention, and comedy too. Helping animals be happier and healthier is my mission. Some animals choose to help one person or many people as their mission by giving unconditional love, patience, and understanding. They hope their people will choose to heal and love themselves as the animals love them.

Any animal can choose to assist us, no animal should be forced to do so. Animal Communication can help facilitate discussion with an animal's higher self. What if their wishes determined their destiny, not their breed or a human's imposed will? This happens to animals ALL the time, only they're much less likely to escape their oppression as I did mine. It took many painful years to undo my conditioning of people trying to force me to be who I'm not.

What if animals who've been mistreated remembered, OMG I'M

A FLIPPIN' ELEPHANT...I'M A POWERHOUSE...NOT A SELFIE SHOT. I'M A WILD DOLPHIN, MY HOME IS THE OCEAN, NOT YOUR CONCRETE TANK. I'M A BIRD BORN TO FLY, NOT STARE AT YOU FROM A CAGE. And sometimes, I'm a dog or a cat and I'm not lost... I'm exploring.

It's not my belief that animals are born to serve us, or that ALL animals have a mission to help people. Animals can laser in on our hearts and intentions, and make a conscious choice about who, when, and how they'd like to help. I think there's a reason stories abound about the abused circus and aquatic animals maiming or killing "their person."

Perhaps animals that don't flip the script possess extraordinary forgiveness, or are too depressed or riddled with Stockholm syndrome to fight back. I've seen animals and people lose the light in their eyes because someone trained them not to see their inherent magnificent strength.

Once, while in the ocean, a few kids swarmed me asking whether mermaids are real. I smiled and said, "Well, you can see me, right?" Their eyes filled with excitement. Merging my energy with the sea created more wonder and laughter—the ingredients of magic. I waved to their parents on shore and invited the kids to imagine all that's around us we're not *yet* seeing.

Before swimming off, I reassured them that math really is useless. They cheered, "YES!" (It was the least I could do as their first mermaid friend.) I also confessed I wasn't a good swimmer, but was still allowed in the Mermaid club, because I have other skills that help the sea, like kindness. They were most surprised to hear a mermaid has dogs, but I told them life is full of surprises, including my getting to meet such awesome kids, whereas just a moment before I'd been alone in a sea of people.

To my knowledge, I'm not a mermaid, just an honorary one saying what I know a mermaid would say. My having legs didn't faze them. Kids seem to know a being can be more than one thing. Like a soul having a human body or a middle-aged woman having magic and a math disability, why don't I psychically know the answers? No idea.

I enjoy sharing animal communication experiences with my students because kids are open-minded. They're still connected to a wise, innocent part of themselves that knows "reality" can't always be proven, but is still real. I know I loved Teddy and still do. How can I prove this? Because I have a photo of him in a frame? Or that I cried when he died? Can you prove you love someone? Love means different things to different people and in different cultures. So does God.

Too often, we let others decide what our truths are without questioning those truths. Maybe those kids were mermaids testing me to see if I had any magic left as an adult. Animals are the perfect guides to call forth our magic. A part of our soul is already receptive to divine inspiration, intervention, miracles, and talking animals. People who live more colorfully and dance with deities are often perceived as crazy. Or witches. #CrazyWitchesGetMoreCandy!

The truly crazy thing is that more people aren't aware of the metaphorical *"rabbit hole,"* and that alternative realities are real. Crayola needs to invent a *Rabbit Hole* crayon for beige people that draws their minds out of the matrix. I often tell clients I wish I could screen-shot the scenes their animals and people in Spirit show me, and the Hollywood-production-like portals I enter with special effects created out of this world.

These spiritual portals are where I experience the unconditional love in Teddy's eyes and every other animal I've come to love throughout my life. Cows, tigers, bears, and everyone in between have been friends, clients, and mentors. Even a pack of pesky mosquitoes, my archenemies, once threw me a metaphorical bone, but still relentlessly bite me.

While sitting on the toilet, a mosquito incessantly buzzed by, and then...BIT MY LABIA...TWICE! The mosquito must've just gotten braces because the wounds swelled like mini coconuts. I laid with an ice pack on my vag for two hours trying to reframe my opinions of these perverted little sociopaths while asking my default question of God…"Really?"

I wanted to call a meeting with their tribal elders to settle our feud. I asked the collective mosquito species if there was anything I could do to be less tasty. I swear I heard them cackle while spiking their venom. Mosquitoes have a proboscis, a needle-like mouth-sickle they use to suck your blood to help them have babies, using *our* protein. So, weirdly, while not having human children, I've helped create hundreds of mosquito babies carrying droplets of my DNA. Happy Mother's Day, Shannon!

After laughing at my plea, they finally showed me a giant chocolate bar the size of the Eiffel Tower. I cherish chocolate, so I was hopeful eating it could somehow act like an anti-parasite bodyguard, but realized this improbability given how much chocolate I consumed, and yet still served as an unwilling blood donor to mosquito babies.

Mosquitoes weren't totally messing with me after all. Research showed if I were to slather myself in cocoa powder, this would actually deter them. So, I'd have to *wear* chocolate, not eat it. Their suggestion was, of course, passive-aggressive. Since I'm already pretty high on the weirdo scale, walking around covered in cocoa powder licking myself mumbling, "Blood bank is closed you little fuckers!" was not ideal.

While the animals have made me a much better person, I still swat mosquitoes because I'm not a saint. They always have the last laugh, including when I just typed the word mosquito and a disgusting emoji of them appeared on my screen. I began frantically slapping my IPAD until I realized I was trying to kill an emoji. Some animal communicators make peace and "send them love." I think that's just malaria taking over.

Whether or not you *believe* or *know* my stories to be true, or think they're all insane (who lies about labia bites?), it will not affect my reality. I do hope it affects yours because once you realize "the *rabbit hole*" is real, your life will never be the same in all the best ways.

Quite often, once I shared some of my more unbelievable stories, my students would share their "unbelievable" stories too. They'd confide hearing a deceased relative lovingly whisper to them before falling asleep at night. Or excitedly share they still see their *deceased* cat or dog playing in their backyard. Who am I to question their reality? Who are you to question mine? (In fairness, you did buy my book.) My point still stands though, no one can take away someone else's experiences, only judge them through their filter. Magical experiences aren't negotiable.

More people are waking up to their own experiences with "unexplainable" phenomena, and understanding that animals they previously misjudged as insignificant are wildly intelligent, lovable creatures. The documentary, *My Octopus Teacher,* certainly shows octopuses are more than just odd-looking aliens. At least one human was able to deeply connect, cry, and even fall in love with this mysterious creature deep in the ocean.

My inner teacher assigns everyone this documentary as homework. The first time I watched it I fell asleep because it's so relaxing. The second time I was glued to the screen, and cheering for the octopus to survive. Aren't we all on the "wanting creatures to survive team"? (Not you, mosquitoes.) Maybe it's time we stop saying animals don't talk, and just start listening.

Animals are always listening to us. They're trained experts on our thoughts and feelings, and do all kinds of crazy things to get our attention, protect, teach, support and humor us. Silence and unspoken words are equally valuable. Pay attention to the signs all around us, some of which literally drop out of the sky upon us.

My dog, Jack, and I are seriously picky eaters. My tastebuds are sweet like "Buddy the Elf." Jack's ideal chef is Homer Simpson—pizza and donuts. In college, my friend Kim's mom graciously gave us chicken salad sandwiches she'd made to take to the beach. I hated chicken salad, even though I'd never eaten it. It just sounded gross, and once my mind decides something is gross, it most assuredly will taste vile. Unlike Jack, I can't publicly retch it up.

The sandwich taunted me on how I was going to play this. I had to eat it, or I'd hurt Kim's feelings. Being a vegan didn't factor back then. Maybe if I had enough water I could just swallow it whole. Just as I mustered courage to bite it, a heroic seagull swooped in and stole it right out of my hands! My arm was a drive-thru window. I disguised my delight at my good fortune, but my wingman felt my gratitude. People broadcast emotions to animals, and my luncheon-lighthouse signaled HELP. Kim frowned. "That sucks! But at least you still have your chips."

But, as "luck" had it, when God takes away one sandwich, She opens a Ziplock bag with a new one. A mom and her young kids sitting next to us witnessed the seagull's drive-through-hoagie-heist. "Oh, you poor thing! That naughty bird stole your sandwich. What kind was it?" I hesitantly answered, "Yes, naughty bird...it was a chicken salad sandwich."

Beach mom became overjoyed. "Oh my gosh! It's your lucky day! I just so happen to have (reaching into a bottomless basket) an EXTRA CHICKEN SALAD SANDWICH!" (Where was my bird savior now?) "Oh wow! That is...lucky...thank you."

Beach mom hoped her kindness would rectify the bird's crime and proudly watched as I took a bite. My feathered hero flipped his beak in disbelief. He gobbled up the first, but couldn't finish in time for seconds. Do I think that seagull stole my sandwich to help me out? Absolutely. He could've lunch-jacked anyone, but being a world class improv player, he played, "Here comes the airplane" with me. I ate her sandwich with gratitude for two new friends of different species with the same goal—solve the sandwich crisis.

Everything is energy being sent and received throughout the world and beyond. Animals everywhere listen, and hope we hear their hearts' messages (and lunch orders too). Are we paying attention to their energetic invitations to befriend and assist them? Fast Eddie the Fish is just the dude who can explain the importance of paying attention to small signals from beings with the biggest dreams. Put your fins together and welcome FAST EDDIE to the stage!

I felt a WHOOSH of energy (the kind rom-com stars feel when they first make eye contact), when I entered a grooming shop to distribute my flyers. I was facing straight ahead when the WHOOSH took over, demanding I turn to the left, and acknowledge this force of nature frantically calling me. An electric blue fish (Jack Dempsey breed, I'd later learn) had spotted a lifeline through me.

I approached his filthy tank, fascinated that this little fish, so BIG in energy, was able to cut through my busy brain's thoughts, luring me over to chat. I hollered towards the back of the store, "What's the fish's name?" The groomer answered distractedly: "He doesn't have one." Having worked with thousands of animals, I know names matter, and this little dude didn't even have one. He was just a decoration they'd imprisoned in a stinky tank.

I gazed lovingly at my new finned friend. "Well, you deserve a name. What would you like to be called?" I watched him swim, absorbed his awesome energy, and heard "FAST EDDIE!" So, I repeated aloud, "Fast Eddie! Perfect name for a cool fish like you!" Immediately, he swam like Nemo was out of a job—excited for earning a name.

His formerly sad face now free-styled with pride; this little superstar swam like he'd just met himself for the first time (no baptism needed, as he was already under water). It was impossible to deny what was happening...we were becoming friends...we were falling in love.

I silently wondered how to free this captive wild man when the groomer called out, "He's up for adoption." I laughed in deep appreciation for what was happening. Fast Eddie was not "up for adoption" like rescuers promote. She knew he'd been neglected, and sensed what I was thinking, staring at his filthy tank. She was really saying she'd be happy if I took him off her hands. Whichever way you filet her words, this clever fish was catching a release for himself. And I love a clever soul!

I headed to the back to meet the groomer, who could've been another fish for all I knew at this point. Spirit loves to surprise me and keep my improv skills fresh. I introduced myself and my work. We talked about the hopeful fish who'd reeled me in with puckered lips. She said she'd ask the shop owner how much he wanted for "the fish."

I wanted to yell, "Say his name! His name is Fast Eddie!" But, once in a while, I can just be normal. So, I thanked her and said "See you later" to my blue...boyfriend? (I didn't know our status, but things were definitely moving fast.)

Once home, I told Fast Eddie I'd be happy to help free him from that dump, but he'd need to be very clear in his wishes. I relayed a picture of what life would be like if I did "adopt" him. He'd have a wonderful screened porch to chill out on with a great view of nature, but he'd also have four drooling mutts staring at him sometimes. I assured him I'd be back.

A few days later, I returned with a friend, excited to introduce her to this feisty fish I'd fallen in love with. My friend was excited too, as I'm contagiously enthusiastic. But, when we approached his tank, he wasn't the same little Olympian swimmer. He looked at us sadly with a vacant stare. Telepathically, he held a sign reading: "Help!" We've all been in situations we can't bear for a moment longer. He needed out...NOW!

The groomer said she was still waiting to hear back on the price from the owner. My friend and I left to go eat lunch next door, so I telepathically told him to "Just keep swimming, I'll be back!" I knew he understood, although his spirits didn't brighten. He needed a life preserver.

After lunch, I sat on my porch surrounded by four mutt sleuths who knew something was up. I checked in with Fast Eddie and said, "Ok, so which is it? Would you like to be my pet and live here with me and these furry goofs? Or would you rather be a free man in wild waters? Instantly, I loudly heard the freedom song, "BORN TO BE WILD"!

It was the most fun game of "Go Fish" I'd ever played. Feeling him relieved and thrilled at the idea of wind in his gills gave me chills. It's impossible not to feel joy when you bring it to another soul. His freedom was imminent, and his excitement and gratitude permeated my core.

I returned to the store the next day with a fish carrier and a crisp $20 bill. I walked right up to the now-present owner like I was a hero who needed no introduction. "I'll give you $20, and take this creature off your hands right now." The owner, mistaking me for a fool, tried to sell me his toxic tank for $200, and I said, "No thanks. His new home is waiting for him."

I scooped out my strong-willed boyfriend (he was definitely a boyfriend now), and put him in the carrier of fresh water. Fast Eddie and I headed out like newlyweds, although we'd be spending our honeymoon apart. He rode shotgun in my red Subaru. Today was the first day of the rest of his life, and I joyfully escorted him safely to his new home in the lake.

I drove with one hand on the wheel, and the other with the back of my hand resting against his tank. There was a similar WHOOSH of energy like when we first met, but of pride, not desperation. My inner reality show producer awakened and was certain that Subaru should feature us in their next commercial where cute Golden Retrievers had dominated for so long. Wasn't it time an adventurous interspecies couple represented the fun family values their brand promotes? #Challengefishystereotypes.

In the brief time we shared, I became enamored with this macho blue beauty's mighty spirit. Ten minutes later, we arrived at our destination—a gorgeous nature preserve that presented a Catch-22. I carried him gently in his carrier like a newborn baby, but respected him as a grown-ass man. No doubt he'd be a catch for the ladies of his species who'd challenge me to a swim-off if I dove in after him. They'd blow bubbles at me as I flashed my Mermaid Club card.

When we reached the lake, I saw there wasn't a good place to release him. The water was murky, and he wouldn't be able to see. The only other option was to pour him out over a small bridge, a violent beginning to his happy ending. So, I coached him. My one and only gig as a swim coach, for a professional swimmer!

I coached, "Hey, Fast Eddie, I'm going to release you on the side here, and it's going to be very dark, but only for a minute. Then, as long as you just keep swimming, you'll be a free man out in the open to go wherever you choose. I gently poured him into the darkness and cheered him on to find the light. My heart butterfly stroked.

With tears in my eyes, I wished him well. I told him to stay in touch, and thanked him for his faith in me to set him free. It was a true honor to help him escape a lonely life and restore his dignity. When else in life can we change someone's entire life for $20—not a part of it, but the whole thing? Fast Eddie kept his promise to me too, and he swam back into my consciousness just a few weeks later.

While Fast Eddie was finally home, I still felt like a fish out of water in my human world. Nobody I know could change my life for $20. I went for a reiki session to realign my chakras. The reiki lady was working some energy on me to release stress, when she stopped cold. Some might say, cold-blooded. Fast Eddie whooshed into our session.

I'd been somewhere off in LALA Land, seeing calm, blue waters, when Jill hesitantly said, "Umm...Shannon, this is going to sound weird, but...." Nothing sounds weird to me, so I encouraged, "Go on..."

Jill continued, "This is going to sound weird, but there's umm...a fish...he's here and he wants to thank you. He says things were very dark, but he made it to the light. I thought you'd want to know." Jill's *imagining* a fish talking to her was real.

Fast Eddie had worked his magic and swam into her subconscious to impress me with his gold medal skills—making quite a splash. "Fast Eddie!" I called out, as if he was standing at the door, ready to now drive me in his Subaru, somewhere to be released. Confused, but amused, Jill said, "So, you know this fish?"

I answered, as if I'd accepted his fin in marriage, "Yes, I do. That's Fast Eddie. He and I are old friends." Jill smiled and continued the session. I smiled, knowing what I said was true. This special fish and I were old friends—from which world, and in what species forms I didn't know. I do know it was the best $20 I had ever spent.

6

SALEM THE SORCERESS CAT

You're only given one little spark of madness, you mustn't lose it.
Robin Williams

As a kid, I was acutely aware that childhood is a magical, fleeting time and adulthood is overrated. Long before *Toy Story* hit theaters, I was convinced my stuffed animals talked as soon as I left the room. I'd stand outside my door and listen, then quickly open the door when I thought I heard talking, only to be met with smiling, silent faces. It seemed implausible that my dolls didn't talk, given how many conversations I'd had with them.

Despite my rough childhood, I'd squirreled away playful energy for the impending doom of adulthood. Magic somehow survived the war. Am I saying stuffed animals (and other things) *can come to life and talk? Yep.* Thankfully, in my house, in a Christmas joy, not creepy horror movie way. When we believe in magic, unseen magical beings and phenomena can make themselves seen, and combine creative forces with us.

Nature, animals, and spirits can send signs, make things come to life, and make us laugh. I discovered the 1990s *Sabrina The Teenage Witch* sitcom starring comedian, Caroline Rhea in 2021. It's made for tweens. Luckily, my inner tween is alive and well. I binge-watched this quirky comedy after falling in love with its wise-cracking, irreverent black cat, Salem.

According to the show's storyline, Salem was formerly a human man who misbehaved excessively in his lifetime and was karmically sentenced to reincarnate as a cat. It takes a lot to make me fall off my sofa laughing, and Salem did it every time with his inappropriate remarks and total disrespect for authority.

When Christmas arrived, I unwrapped a stuffed Salem doll—a gift from my dogs. *(Technically bought by me, because dogs don't have credit cards...at least not in this world.)* About a month later, while I was reading next to Kermit the Dog, I heard a distinctive "MEOW, MEOW, MEOW!" right behind us on my headboard where Salem lounges. Windows were closed, and electronics were off, and *dogs don't meow...at least not in this world.*

I've had enough weird experiences to know what was happening. The non-mechanical stuffed cat was talking! Kermit was excitedly wagging his tail when another sassy chorus rang out: "MEOW, MEOW, MEOW!" It was an after-Christmas miracle, and I was thrilled by the surprise feline cabaret. (My dogs always know just what to get me.)

Thankfully, this toy cat, named after the famous town of witches in Salem, MA, came to life in my bedroom when I didn't have company to run screaming into the street. Nor did I have to play a game of opening and closing my door, secretly listening for purring sounds and meowing mischief. This comical, Spirit-infused toy cat brought the magic of Christmas to Puppypants Town.

Much like a normal cat, Salem won't meow on command. He's nobody's fool like that. He only meows rarely, randomly, and for what seems like no particular reason. Next time he's feeling chatty, I'll ask him what inspires his visits. That same afternoon, a mysterious bag of cat food was left at my doorstep, and my dog Grover *meowed* upon seeing it! One weird guttural meow that came through him, but not from him. It's always mysterious when an ordinary day will catapult us into hilarious hijinks and disprove an absolute truth, such as dogs don't meow.

Ducky, now in Spirit, later took credit for Salem's mysterious meowing. Our loved ones of all species can find sentimental or silly ways to reach us. When I adopted Ducky from the Atlanta Humane Society, I'd only gone there to donate blankets. But, when I saw her tiny, shiny, black body, I asked to hold her. The savvy employee immediately hung a sign on her cage congratulating, "I'm being adopted!" Even I know that dogs can't read, but I can, and the love I felt in those words sealed the deal.

Ducky went home to her new big sisters, Lucy and Stormy, who wagged their tails at first sight. In return, she curled her lip in a brave display of PUPPY POWER! The two gentle Goldens were amused, and they all became fast friends. Ducky was pure ninja—special ops trained in fence scaling, balancing like a gymnast. And then as if Superman himself gave her his cape...she'd FLY! Ducky was a cat in dog form.

I hesitated sharing this talking Salem cat toy story with my online students, but traveling farther down the *rabbit hole* is always a trip I'm willing to take, and so are kids. During the next creative writing class, I began as usual with fun prompts to inspire imaginative writing, but quickly became Buddy the Elf—unable to contain my Christmas joy.

I held up Salem and mused, "What if your toy cat came to life? Would you be excited? Scared? Speechless? What would your toy cat say?" One of my savvier students paused with a wry smile. "Wait, did that REALLY happen?" I posed his question to the class, "What do you think everyone, did this stuffed cat talk?" It was all I could do to stop myself from jumping up and down squealing, "SANTA IS REAL!"

Finally, a few brave students said they believed it really did happen. That here at "Puppypants Town" (the namesake of my magical, furry cottage), somehow we had a talking stuffed cat. Other students stopped typing, and weighed the credibility of my claim, along with the students who'd dared to dive into the *rabbit hole* too. I knew like his sitcom self, Salem would be quiet as a mouse until everyone left. A marvelously maddening character!

I asked my students, "Why do you think this is real and not just a creative prompt?" Ellie answered, "Because it's you, Ms. Spring, and you're really nice to animals. So even the "non real" ones want to talk to you too!" An enchanted exchange. Whatever students believe, as long as it's said with respect is welcome. We must first trust in ourselves.

Fairy doors everywhere crack open for fun when another special soul's magic journey has begun. Ellie's intuition understood creative, non scientific truths; things can be real without proof. I was relieved that all parents listening off camera didn't yell, "Off with her head!" (at me) fearing I was teaching witchcraft, or breeding sorceress cats. Salem Spring's got a nice ring.

I'm sure some parents thought I was just playing, and others had their own Hogwarts-like secrets. Speaking of Hogwarts, I attended a mediumship training to advance my skills. I made a new friend, Tammy, who has a laugh that makes me laugh just thinking about it. The intense week-long training was taught by a famous medium, who while very talented, lacked the warm, fuzzy side I crave in mentors. Most students treated her as a demigod. I reserve hero worship for animals and Muppets.

Our mentor inspired me to look forward to all I'd continue to experience, including magic that makes human brains burst from its magnitude. It's unlimited MAGIC within the Spirit world and ourselves...worlds within worlds. The intense skills training was mentally and emotionally taxing, and involved mediums giving readings to each other to advance our craft.

It was Friday, and while classmates had given me psychic readings, no one had brought through my family on the other side. I felt like the only kid without a Valentine. (In fairness, at the time, my loved ones in Spirit were mostly dogs, and these were people-mediums.)

Finally, Tammy (then a stranger) and I partnered. She excitedly shared, "I have a LUCY here...do you know a LUCY?" I felt like a dog being asked, "WANNA GO FOR A WALK?" Lucy is my beloved Golden Retriever in Spirit—the one who gently asked me to break free from toxic love. She came to deliver me a Valentine. "YES! I KNOW LUCY! Thank you for coming to say hello. I love you!"

Tammy beamed, and shared, "Lucy wants to thank you for the ice cream you gave her." (Lucy was the only dog I gave ice cream to.) Tammy and I smiled with joyful tears in our eyes. Reunions like this happen every day, but we're often unaware our loved ones are right here. Lucy made me feel so loved back when she was physically "here," and now from Spirit.

It made sense Lucy chose Tammy, a fellow red-haired loving soul, and fierce advocate for the underdog—both human and animal. It's a rare person I feel understands me, and Lucy knew Tammy would. My furry angel in Heaven gifted me a laughing angel friend on Earth.

A few years later I stayed the weekend at Tammy's house to attend a metaphysical conference at the Edgar Cayce Center in Virginia Beach. Being away from my breathing, talking furry security blankets was a big deal. Tammy, however, is a fun host and packed her house with sugary treats for me, and gifted me an adorable stuffed animal to make me feel at home.

She was temporarily without pets, and has since adopted two rescue cat siblings. Tammy's kindness is like an animal's—genuine, warm, fuzzy, and funny. It's nice when a special person comes along who makes up for a lot of the icky ones. When I packed my suitcase to go home, there wasn't room for the new stuffed animal. So, I left it behind with the promise to visit again.

A few months passed since our visit when one afternoon I tried to take a nap, but couldn't fall asleep. I opened my eyes, and floating in front of me was an image of this stuffed animal, now called Herbie. Instantly, I knew it came to deliver a message for Tammy. The floating Herbie doll then passed the mic to an adorable hamster.

I texted Tammy: "Did you ever have a hamster?" I didn't preface my message with "This is going to sound weird, but..." because Tammy knows I'm weird. She instantly texted me back: "YES! I HAD A HAMSTER...HERBIE...50 YEARS AGO! WHY?" *(What follows next might have skeptics spinning on their own hamster wheels.)*

I asked Herbie, her childhood pet who'd stayed by her all these years, what he wanted to say. He wanted Tammy to know he was proud of her, always by her side, and not to worry about her medical test results. There was nothing to fear. She excitedly texted back she couldn't believe this was happening. Her childhood hamster was ALIVE, and she was headed to her doctor's office! We were in awe of Herbie's divine timing. No need for a nap, I was wide awake.

Herbie and I chatted a bit, and I asked him what he's up to now in Heaven. He showed himself with his tiny little hands making hamster furniture and clothes for all his friends in his hamster village. When I shared what he's doing with his "free time" as a Spirit, Tammy said she nearly fell over in disbelief. At that very moment, she was standing in a craft shop in front of tiny doll furniture! "WHAT?!" I texted back jumping in uncontrollable joy.

Right before I texted Tammy, a woman in the shop insisted Tammy "go look at the tiny fairy furniture." And so, when Herbie floated into my space right when I messaged Tammy, she was admiring a tangible fairy model of Herbie's handiwork! Fairies love creating playful mischief, and visiting people who are childlike at heart, who breathe in sunshine and share it with others, especially animals.

Just as she and I were laughing at this surreal moment, the other shopper called out to Tammy, "I LOVE YOU!" then smiled and left. Why would a stranger say this? Because Herbie spoke through her, teamed up with the faerie realm and I to work his magic delivering his message to prove he's alive, well, and Rodent of the Year or...Lifetime! He could host "Heavenly Hamster Home Makeover" shows in Spirit; his craftsmanship is exceptional.

This clever little rodent turned an ordinary afternoon into a virtual Alice in Wonderland tea party. "It's always tea time" in the Spirit World. Faeries are something I'd stopped believing in, but they never stopped believing in me. They're the creatures that adults feel silly believing in along with other concepts considered "child's play."

Since Herbie's nap-crashing appearance, I now see faeries regularly. Always brightly colored, laughing, dancing, playing, bike-riding, flying in through windows, fairy doors, plants, and even paintings, like the vibrant flower one above my bed—the perfect portal for them to enter.

Faeries appear in a flash, and can make you wonder if you really saw one. I've learned to interact with them, and they reciprocate. Worlds within worlds are all around us, and if we seem like the kind of soul open to faeries and other fun creatures visiting, they'll joyfully fly in unannounced with a happiness bouquet. The more I trust what I see, the more they visit, even slowing down and backing up for me to see them in detail, often laughing and waving.

I see entire film strips play on my ceiling, previewing things to come, or answering life's questions. Other times, numbers or words will rapidly flash, and I can ask them to slow down too, so I can experience and process them. Trust in myself is paramount to all of this. Imagine being a ghost, fairy or angel. Would you rather visit someone who knows you're real, or someone who needs the validation of others?

While in the dog park one day, I accused my dogs of "staring at nothing" when in fact, a mountain lion was just over the fence where I was chucking wild mushrooms accidentally right onto his head! Granted, my dogs probably smelled him too, but animals and kids see all kinds of things most people, especially adults, don't see. I apologized to the lion who was growling from the bushes and backed away slowly, vowing to always take my dogs' word for it, that they know something I don't!

Mystical experiences have a wide range of what people can (or want to) experience, largely based on what we're open to seeing, hearing and feeling. Some people don't want any part of this fun. Some are afraid. And some will never believe it's real, even if it's happening to them directly. Enjoy the party anyway, and let them RSVP in their own time.

Religious zealots often refer to metaphysics as "the devil's work," and tell people hiring mediums to "read the Bible and accept Jesus." I've got Jesus on speed dial. Believing in God and what I do aren't mutually exclusive. I believe more in God now because of animals and deceased loved ones of total strangers who comfort their loved ones and me. What possible evil lies in my speaking with my beloved pets and friends who've passed? NONE. If anything, Jesus helps me make a clear connection, always five bars.

When Jesus pops in on me and in my sessions, it's always with LOVE, never fear or judgment. Since He knows not to turn water into wine in my house, I wonder if He'd be open to turning water into chocolate? Miracles do happen. Although, I imagine somewhere on my soul's chart it mentions my candy addiction, so it's more likely it'll turn to vegetables here. Not all prayers are answered as we wish, but as we need.

The Bible (which ironically has themes that get other books banned), says a lot of weird shit that gets used to hurt people. I've written a relatable new testament centered on common sense and compassion. Can I get a witness? *Be kind to animals and each other. No one race, gender, or sexual preference is better than another. Act in the name of LOVE. Stop using God's name to hurt each other. Life continues once the body dies. Thou shalt always let pets sleep in thy bed. Eat your vegetables, Shannon.*

Much like we see in children's fantasy movies, you truly do have to believe in magic to harness it. Sometimes we experience magic, but dismiss it as a coincidence or losing our minds. I'd rather have a candy-coated, colorful mind that explodes in wonder, than one full of hate shrinking in fear. I'd rather be off the deep end splashing in joy, than shivering in righteousness on the shore.

One day, after reading stories about fairies, I went shopping at a fairy themed store. When I returned home, right in the center of my freshly made bed (something that's rare with four furry beasts) were two sparkling blue beads I'd never seen before. They were perfectly placed side by side...glistening...impossible for me to miss.

I stood there in amazement not knowing where they'd come from. Aha! This magic came from reading about spirits who add, rearrange or remove objects from homes. I smiled in delight that they'd gifted me these beads. (An incentive to make my bed more often!) Then, for just a moment, doubt crept in.

I went to the bathroom, and my practical side (yes, I do have one) began to try to solve the puzzle of where these two beads came from. Did the dogs somehow place them there? No, not possible, not with their perfect positioning and delicate size. Had they fallen off some pair of shoes or purse? Nope, nothing I owned had blue beads like that. When I returned back to my bedroom, one of the beads was GONE!

Instantly I received a karmic consequence (the spiritual middle finger) for doubting my intuition. I quickly placed the remaining bead in my jewelry box and locked it shut. I apologized for my doubt (to no one in particular). I should know to trust my experiences, however weird or impossible they might seem to the "rational" mind. I promised myself never to doubt again, a valuable lesson and serious challenge for humans. Luckily, I'm only part human.

Miracles do happen, and great forces unite to manifest them for us. Spirit really can and does move mountains to get our attention to let us know we're loved and never alone. It should've been easy for me to celebrate, and validate the two bright blue beads magically appearing without doubt spoiling the party. Who invited doubt anyway? Doubt's an opportunistic party crasher who plants seeds that blessings are for other people, and I need to find something to worry about. Like the world running out of chocolate.

About a month later, the second blue bead was gone, which also wasn't possible given where it'd been kept, and yet, it was gone. Rather than being sad, I took it as a sign to trust more magic would manifest, and just enjoy it without fear. Trusting and enjoying magic and miracles creates room for more. #BeautyandtheBeads.

There are many ways to invite mystical creatures into your life, from the animal kingdom, nature spirits, and human loved ones to the embodiment of the creations of alchemist minds like Jim Henson, J.K. Rowling, C.S. Lewis, Lewis Carroll, Steven Spielberg and Walt Disney. Creativity is energy, and energy is around us—both seen and unseen. Tapping into it can take great focus, or sneak up on us like a tap on the shoulder saying, "Made ya look!"

If you ever sense a pair of invisible, magical pants whooshing by you, I hope you remember who it is! (Have you been keeping track of the dogs?)

Whimsical hamsters, flirty fish, mischievous dogs, lusty tigers and all species of animals can positively manipulate humans to be their messengers, just as humans can communicate through them when needed. Inter-dimensional and interspecies reciprocity are the best "friends and family plans" relying on 5D, not 5G.

These "fairy tails" I share are real experiences, and the reason I stand by my statement that *imagination is real.* Not all imagination is brought into reality, but the possibility exists. *(I'll keep you posted if my womb ever births a kitten or puppy. I'd love to send that update to Boston College alumni magazine.)* I never asked The Mad Hatter if I'd gone mad. I knew he'd tell me that like Alice, I'm "entirely bonkers—the secret to being one of the best people."

Animals partner with people and other animals to deliver their messages. Diamond, the Guinea pig, was one of the most resourceful creatures I had met when it came to alerting me that his human sister, Amy (both names changed), was in danger. Diamond began her communication in a most unusual way—through a fish when Mayor Puppypants and I were lunching at a fishing pier restaurant on Anna Maria Island.

I heard great excitement from the pier and wandered down to check it out. A group of fishermen were admiring their superior catch—a huge whatchamacallit (no clue on breed)—and diners gathered to admire "it" too. The fish was laid out on the wooden dock, gasping for air. I knew I was there to witness this for many reasons, but the biggest reason was baiting me.

I'm not delusional enough (not yet anyway) to think I'll convert fishermen to seeing fish as individual beings with a will to live. No doubt some already know this, while others don't care. Maybe some will one day be lucky enough to meet their own Fast Eddie.

For now, I debated what I could do while watching this fish suffer without even water to help her breathe until she died. The energy felt toxic with entitled, drinking, smoking, and littering fishermen. Let me clear the air on this. Smoking in nature, which harms animals, the air, and people, is a great way to advertise being an asshole. #Don'tBeAButthead.

Fish are yanked from their homes, tossed aside and used as bait in Tinder selfies, which no woman I've ever met finds sexy. Fish want to know if these losers get laid, and if it's like fucking a dead fish. For now, my focus was on how I could help this one beautiful fish. I could grab the fish and release her back in the ocean, but one of these men would jump in to retrieve her. She was now their property, despite being plucked against her will from her peaceful home.

Also, the fish's survival odds were small, given how long she'd been writhing on the dock. I searched for a bucket to fill with water to comfort her, but no luck. I debated whether to appeal to one fisherman's compassion, and ask for mercy, but I knew he'd say no.

Even if I managed to rescue the fish, I'd be in a dangerous situation. There wasn't a clear escape with all the men surrounding the pier. There's a reason for the expression "Florida Man." Provoking a gun-happy-good-ole-boy whose temper guarded his taste buds wasn't wise. Nor did I want these wannabe gator wrestlers practicing on Puppypants. (Also, I don't think all fishermen are bad. Bears, for example, I like them. And the fishermen who feed my fish-eating dogs. Being human is riddled with hypocrisy, but we can always strive for kindness in this, too.)

I could only make sure this fish's suffering wouldn't be in vain, or her life forgotten. And of course, thank God, I don't *believe* animals go to Heaven. I *know* they do. Her spirit would teach my debate-class students about when and how to speak up for animals, and how to deal with the bigger issue at hand—millions of fish are treated like this. This fish's tragedy could help create change to help all fish just keep swimming for as long as possible. My students were eager to debate how to handle this issue on a bigger scale. #BiggerFishermenToFry.

Most students said to push the fish back into the water. But, as always happens in debate class, kids quickly learn that we can't always do what our hearts tell us. Often we can, but not always, and so we debate all sides of an issue. They agreed this fish wouldn't have survived, and the men could've become physically aggressive with me and my little dog too.

There are ways to educate and inspire that can capitalize on an opponent's self-interest, and advance the cause of kindness to animals, what we call playing the long game. As we continued the discussion, the class concluded it would be best to ask any businesses or overseers of fishing areas to ask fishermen to please be humane in their "hunt," and perhaps even provide buckets for the fish to be placed in while they wait to become someone's lunch or dinner.

If this idea upsets you, it upsets us too, but sometimes letting a small fish go leads to catching bigger ones. Animals, thankfully, always see the bigger picture. Each smaller picture frame shows my face stifling a scream. I've always believed patience is overrated. Sometimes, many small screams lead to big relief. (Other times, just high blood pressure.)

Witnessing "Anna Maria Fish" lose her life so mercilessly, and debating with kids how to help her inspired one of my students to speak up about something weighing on her own heart. Amy said another teacher taught her about how fish and all animals have feelings, which made her sad and her dad angry. He made the family eat meat and fish, regardless of Amy's compassion for animals. Amy then introduced us to Diamond, her pet Guinea pig, and said she couldn't imagine eating her or seeing her captured.

Amy thought Diamond was pregnant, but Diamond told me she had a severe bellyache, and laughed at the idea of pregnancy. (It did seem implausible given she was a solo Guinea pig and not on Tinder.) She said she desperately wanted fresh air and veggies, more play time, and the shavings in her cage were making her itchy. Thankfully, Amy got her parents to take Diamond to the vet. The vet confirmed Diamond had a severe belly infection, wasn't properly digesting food, and wasn't pregnant. Diamond was a boy!

Amy wasn't thrilled about his non-sex change sex change, but still loved him the same. She asked the class to please keep pretending he's a girl, so we did. After all, animals aren't concerned with gender identity. I've only met a handful of animals out of the thousands I've spoken with that preferred to be thought of as macho or girly. Just ask my overly confident Mutt Mayor; he thinks he looks good in ANYTHING. Stereotypes don't stop him.

After class, Diamond the Guinea pig dropped in on me telepathically, as I sat reading a book about trans Guinea pigs. (No, not really, just a book.) She told me Amy was being abused by her dad, and needed my help protecting her. I wasn't surprised; Amy's dad had a temper. His energy poisoned the air the few times he lurked in the background.

Diamond let me know there was sexual abuse too, and my heart sank. I knew it was dangerous to get involved, and would possibly cost me my part-time teaching job. But I knew this is why animals chose me for these jobs. I'll always speak up, and consider it an honor to be so trusted. I've never been a cowardly lion, and animals smell my pride in that.

I was teaching the debate class through an online educational company. Amy wasn't even "my" student. Diamond, along with Anna Maria Fish, were asking me to not only tell Amy's mom that I'm a pet psychic, but that a rodent told me her husband is abusing their daughter. Exactly how does that conversation start?

Pet Psychics are already kind of the weirdest of the psychics. But, I was all Diamond and Amy had, which isn't a bad start. Remember what I said about having unshakable confidence in my conversations with animals, and how much I trust my ability to receive the most subtle of signals? My hard work pays off Heavenly in these moments. I know the souls of my animal friends, as they know mine.

I had to speak the truth—Diamond and Amy's truth. Of course, some people can't tell the truth to themselves, let alone hear ours. I emailed Amy's mom asking her to call me to discuss debate class. On the call, I delicately explained my work with animals, and hoped she wouldn't hang up. While I don't care who thinks I'm weird, this was different.

I needed Amy's mom to trust my character and abilities. I have a Master's degree in Education and a PHD-og in Animal. Fortunately, Amy had already told her mom I was "the greatest teacher ever!" Mom was thankfully receptive to why I called. She seemed to already know of her husband's behavior, but not the extent. Once their Guinea pig spoke truth through a "stranger," it became real to her mom. She said she'd share our concerns with their family therapist.

For the next two classes, Amy's dad demanded she keep her door open, and that we not discuss "animal rights" anymore. The patriarch and I have a centuries old feud. They wish to control my body with no rightful ownership, and need to keep it in their pants around children.

Animal rights, like feminism, are triggering terms for many who wrongly equate freedom from suffering for innocent souls with extremist violence, but ironically aren't triggered by the violence happening to women and animals around the world.

Imagine Diamond saying of herself, she's not an animal rights activist. How silly! And yet, that's no different than a woman being uncomfortable advocating for her quality of life and safety as a feminist, or ya know, human being. Amy's dad had no idea the Guinea pig, whose food he buys, ratted him out. But, his own intuition kicked in alerting him I was a threat. Amy wasn't allowed to come to our final class.

I'd gotten to know and love Amy, and taught her many skills to advocate for herself and all species. In my heart, I know she knows I stood up for her. The last class Amy attended she was heartbroken because Diamond had passed away (days after she'd helped Amy through me). I assured Amy their connection was alive, and one day she'd see her furry hero again. I even told her she could look me up when she's older, so we could talk to Diamond together. Because of the trust we'd built, she seemed comforted and hopeful that Diamond, much like her teacher, would always be alive in her heart and protect her.

Gratitude overtook me when I made the connection on how a "random" fish and Guinea pig in two different states collaborated to help a little human girl feel loved. They were her voice, and I was theirs.

I do my best to protect my students and animal friends while making life and learning fun too. Amy was now without a pet, and that's no place for a kid to be. But, she'd learned how to advocate for animals which transfers to advocating for herself too. Her dad was exposed, and last I heard was kicked out of the family.

I wondered how child predators are welcomed into Spirit. Spirit answered in a calm, spooky voice, "Tough love, Shannon. They'll be welcomed home with tough love."

I was twelve years old and without a pet for two years when my family moved to a very boring suburb in Connecticut where everything was named after a farm. While I was very sad to leave my friends behind, I wasn't worried that by leaving Teddy's body behind, I'd be leaving him. His spirit is everywhere, most especially inside me. We'd continue to grow up together.

A cat once perfectly explained through me to his grieving dad why he shouldn't worry about leaving his cat's scattered ashes behind. The cat asked, "Dad, when you enjoy a nice campfire with your family and friends, where you share laughs and memories, do you scoop up the ashes from the fireplace?" Dad answered through teary eyes, "No." The cat gently continued, "Your memories of those happy times are in your heart and soul, not those ashes. The love is always alive wherever you go. It's not possible to leave me or any loved one behind. We aren't those ashes or bodies. We are spirits free to travel wherever we wish, and so are you. You're free to start a new life, and I'll be right there with you."

Dad's face softened with relief, and I praised the cat for the incredible imagery. He added lightness to a "grave subject." We can see how silly it would be to scoop up fireplace ashes after a fun family reunion roasting s'mores. We can never leave, lose or be abandoned by our loved ones in Spirit. One client was meticulously protecting her deceased marine husband's dress uniform, and asked if he was pleased by this. He answered, "You can cut it up and make dog clothes out of it, or fingerpaint on it. Doesn't matter. That uniform isn't me, stop worrying about it!" His wife gasped and then burst out laughing in joyful surprise and relief.

People become preoccupied with bodies and material possessions and mistake our identities for them. Set yourself free. Trust that objects including ashes and bodies aren't your beloved pets or people. The marine husband even encouraged his wife to start dating, and offered his opinion on which of the two men she'd received gifts from would be a better lover for her! We're meant to enjoy our lives, just like our Spirit loved ones are right now. New life doesn't replace old memories.

My family finally adopted Hellion, a stunning Golden Retriever with black freckles on her tongue and a heart murmur. Hellion was named by and given away by a breeder because of her heart. There was no telling how it would affect her or how long she'd live. Such an absurd name for such a sweet dog who later earned the nickname, Smelly. (Not much better!) I haven't seen Hellion in 29 years, and as I type this, my heart fills up with love and sadness. I'll ask her to visit and trust she will.

Helly-Smelly once brought home a whole deer leg, and laid it on the porch. Grossed out, but wanting her to feel appreciated, I thanked her before relocating the carcass to a farm upstate where limbs run free. Smelly ran free throughout the woods chasing and joyfully rolling around in putrid smelling things. I saw her wrestle a skunk by the neck. "No, no...Hellion...Let go! ARGH!" Hellion was in it to win it though, and wouldn't let go.

Our neighborhood was eau de stinky for a month after that skunk smack down. Hellion was elated thinking she'd protected her family. Fortunately, my next skunk encounter was only telepathic.

Susan wanted to know how her dog Sparkles felt about her boyfriend. Sparkles showed me a skunk image, and then held her nose and waved her paw to indicate this was a stinky relationship! Sparkles had enough of Susan dating the same types of men who treated Susan badly, and needed her to see the stinky pattern.

Sparkles asked, *"Have you smelled this skunk before?"* I let the question linger without explanation. Susan's eyes lit up, understanding what Sparkles meant. She'd been settling for scraps and begging for love. Animals, of course, know that's no way to live. Sparkles feverishly wagged her tail, feeling Susan's energy awaken and shift, and proclaimed: "Susan's 'Prince Charming' will shower her with roses, not make us plug our noses."

Sometimes the right question gives a life changing perspective. Susan broke up with the man the next day, vowing to never settle for a "skunk" again. Skunks take no offense, as they'd never settle for most humans! When have you "smelled this skunk before," what can you do to remove a stinky person or situation from your life? Sparkles invites you to freshen your pawspective and smell the roses already.

Hellion, like Teddy #1, became the focal point for the family. One thing we did really well was not limit her by her heart murmur. It never slowed her down, and it would've been wrong to limit her quality of life because of it. Many species live long lives with heart and other issues. While it's something to be aware of, dwelling on it isn't healthy. No pet wants to live in a protective bubble, preserved like a collector's toy in a box, unable to play. Animals, like people, are born to play.

Animals are always practical, and unlike people who sometimes go to Frankenstein-like lengths to live, including pig heart transplants, would choose one wild and silly year (or day) of freedom and fun over a lifetime of being treated as broken and too fragile to play. We treated Hellion like a normal dog and she relished the freedom we allowed her.

For my final high school field hockey game on a cool, fall, Connecticut day, I dressed Hellion in one of my team shirts. She was excited to cheer me on. Coach Martha gave me the evil eye and later punished me for it. Who in their right bleeping mind gets mad at a Golden Retriever smiling in a $5 polyester shirt? Martha, that's who. Martha was also my math teacher—a real-life word problem that made me scream. #GoPuckYourself.

I often sat on the bench at my field hockey games, not because I didn't have the potential to be good, but because potential remains only potential when you're never given a chance to play—something that still stings all these years later. Put me in, Coach. Benching kids who want to play teaches the opposite of sportsmanship. If you're never going to put kids in the game, you don't have a team, you have a business.

This prep school cared about stats, not kids, and required us to "play" three sports. Instead of developing athletic skills, I developed depression. I showed up with team spirit, but eventually did what I could to get out of practice, earning a reputation as a slacker. It was cruel.

Hellion, however, always picked me to be on her team, and taught me to put myself in the game of life. Speak up, raise my hand, take risks, and spin the wheel of fortune in my favor. Animals know the point of any game is to have fun. The thrill of victory is short lived, but the joy of playing for fun can last forever. Never let any "Martha" bench you from your own life. Play!

Pets play for the joy, not the win. I've watched Kermit the Dog slow down in a game of chase to let tiny "Coach Grover" with his little legs catch up. Kermit evens up the playing field, letting Grover play and the game continue. Hellion cheers for all of us here on Team Puppypants. She served as a wonderful big sister to puppy Rowdy. I love you, Smelly. Thanks for being the first sister who happily played with me.

About ten years after Hellion died, I chose a random day to spread her ashes in the ocean. Holding onto a tin of her ashes through so many moves didn't feel right. Hellion wasn't in there. Hellion was running free, and rolling in snow with Teddy #1. There's no greater silence in a home than when a pet dies. When the furry mediator and comedian is gone, and it's just dysfunctional humans, the emptiness grows into deafening silence.

Hellion comes in dreams, and it's a rare treat, as high school is a time I'd rather not remember except for her. I see Hellion light up with a smile, sharing:

"I remember you, Shannon, as the silly sister you were then. I've watched you grow up and I'm so proud. Nanny is with me and walks me, and we stay busy watching and loving you. Just like the teenage you is alive inside you, the young dog is alive in me. We are the same as we were, and we are us as we are now. We are a dog and her girl, and a dog and her woman—still a kid inside.

There's no death, only growth, releasing whatever we need to let go of—in my case smelling like skunks and deer, and in your case, self-doubt and fear. I love you, Shannon, I love you so very much. Thank you for remembering me and honoring me as you have, by still speaking my name, seeing me alive and happy, for that's what I am.

I am ALIVE and smiling, always. I am not those ashes, and I am most certainly not dead. You know this, and for that I am so grateful. You know with certainty that we're all around you. I've met my many brothers and sisters since I lived with you. Each one makes Heaven a little brighter, and each one speaks of you with such love and devotion. We will be with you until the day you leave behind your body too. Oh, how free you'll be...keep setting yourself free now!

That's the trick, that's the game. Set yourself free now...walk unleashed through life. Smile, knowing it's all temporary. Smile knowing it really is as easy as going to sleep and waking up at your own surprise-welcome-home-birthday party. Yes, we are eating cake in your honor, because we know you'd think this is funny, that we eat cake. And we play. Play more, Shannon.

When we see you're having a bad day, we gather close and we form a circle of love and light, and we shine our love upon you, strong and bright.

We shelter you and we heal your heart, so that every day you have a fresh start—a day closer to joining us here, where there's ONLY laughter, never fear.

Shannon, we are sorry your heart breaks so much. Sit quietly, feel our furry, warm touch. Go on now, continue writing this book. We just ran out of the lake, and upon you shook Heaven's healing waters and our golden light. Feel it each day, feel it each night. We'll see you soon at a time not far away, because for us, it's all the same, and yet a new day."

- Love, Hellion

(P.S. I've met the skunk from your murder mystery case. We shared a good laugh together. Keep up your psychic detective work. It'll pay off.)

The murder mystery skunk case Hellion's referring to was a crazy "Who dunnit?" episode involving a dog mom of five who asked if I could tell her which of her dogs had killed the local skunk who visited her property. She knew the answer, but let me test out my psychic detective skills. So, I telepathically called in all five dogs (the cutest suspects ever), and began my interview to identify the guilty stinker.

After chit chatting with the pups, my telepathic detective hat on, I asked the first dog, "Did you murder the skunk?" He sang the song, *"WASN'T ME"* by Shaggy. His denial was sincere. "Hmm, okay, fair enough. You're free to go." The next two dogs were partners in crime, cheering spectators, but not the actual murderer (nor Good Samaritans). "Dismissed!" I told them, while mentally rubbing their bellies.

The fourth dog appeared chewing a bone, "Nah, I'm too smart for that charade...skunks spray, ya know." And so, we were down to one suspect who proudly introduced his furry self as "The BMOC"—The Big Man on Campus. He reveled in his prowess, and would've shared every gory detail had I let him. "AHA! The killer!" I announced, as I wagged my own tail in satisfaction. "Case closed."

I awaited the secret envelope with the murderer's photo and paw print from their mom who witnessed the whole party/crime first-hand. "Well done, Detective Spring! Indeed, it was Bubbles, the ringleader, who killed *that poor skunk.*" Skunkerella (name assigned postmortem) *"that poor skunk,"* materialized onto this scene...laughing! Surprised by her giddiness, given she'd died a violent death, I asked, "What's so funny?"

Seeing her death replay in my mind's eye, Skunkerella replied, "I did die in a not so favorable way. BUT, while I've been *'dead'* for weeks, my smell lives on!" Sweet revenge and a smelly last laugh. Overall, animals consider life and death cycles, however they happen, as nature, not tragedy. The circle of life. (A smelly last laugh is a heck of an epitaph!)

7
NARNIA IS REAL

You know what the issue is with the world? Everyone wants a magical solution to their problem, and everyone refuses to believe in magic.
Alice, from *Alice in Wonderland* by Lewis Carroll

Our favorite childhood books become so for a reason—they speak to our souls, and often reveal our nature and purpose. Mine was *The Lion, The Witch and The Wardrobe* by C.S. Lewis. It's a story about a brave little girl named Lucy, who upon stepping into a magic wardrobe enters Narnia—Land of the talking animals!

Imagine adults telling their therapist they've discovered a magical wardrobe, and can now talk to animals. They'd be labeled cuckoo puffs and either pitied, medicated or institutionalized. I don't have to imagine this because I lived it.

When kids speak of magic, talking animals or imaginary friends, it's "play." Adults are labeled mentally ill, or if you're lucky, eccentric. But, what if I could somehow *prove* the magical wardrobe leading to NARNIA is real? The *Rabbit Hole* is real. That's exactly what I've done—handed people keys to open their own wardrobes to experience other realms where their loved ones live. Afterwards, going back to life as we'd once lived it is unimaginable. Losing our fear of death gives us more freedom to live!

Adulthood can hijack our special gifts and childhood dreams, making us unrecognizable to ourselves. Who stole recess from our inner child? Sometimes we steal our own joy and magic by clipping our wings, or letting frenemies pluck our wings rather than growing their own. Balancing limitless childhood imagination with practical adult wisdom is a powerful potion for a happy life.

One day Spirit whispered to me to see a hypnotherapist, and even though she'd later betray me, the process was transformative. Roses with thorns in our paths can open our senses and remind us we ultimately heal ourselves. In the first session, I subconsciously experienced myself chained in a dungeon with my head hanging down, shoulders slumped. How long had I been locked away?

Many sessions later I learned I'd been hunted and persecuted for my gifts in many lifetimes leading to my suffering and death, and these soul-crushing chains still pertained to this lifetime. Outside the dungeon, through a tiny window, I could see a magnificent tiger lounging in a beautiful garden. He was energetically supporting me by showing a different reality that could be mine. Tiger-like confidence is available to all of us. Hypnosis helped me locate and call forth my inner tiger...a very happy reunion.

While I'd gone through hell, my inner tiger was unscathed. He was peacefully sunbathing, content in his majestic form when he looked at me in recognition. He was who I once was and would become again—fierce, fearless, and never changing my stripes to make others feel comfortable in their own skin. (Tigers also have striped skin!)

Rather than joining me in the dungeon, this mighty tiger-spirit-guide playfully invited me to join him in the garden to play, then walked me up the dungeon stairs to start facing my fears. Play empowers, but pity diminishes. I'd feared my own power. Being powerful scared people away, but trying to be "normal" created more loneliness—a true beast of burden.

Animals are comfortable in their own skin, a powerful feeling people will go to great lengths to achieve. Playing, especially with animals, shakes up the brain and soul with fun, not fear. Metaphysical practices and my own creative games were creating rapid shifts. I was becoming an unselfconscious 5-year-old in a tiger swimsuit. Look out...CANNONBALL...SHANNONBALL!

Only by living my divine mission could I fix what was broken at my core. No amount of counseling (or drugs) can help when you're an inherent mismatch with your lifestyle, job, or romantic partner. Our inner spiritual Sleeping Beauty won't wake up until it has met its match. My "happily ever after" came when I followed a tiger, and started kissing frogs, without wishing they'd be anything but frogs. Happily ever after isn't a wedding day, it's a way of life.

It was the second hypnosis session while in a light trance exercise, I visualized a hallway with doors on both sides, and the hypnotherapist asked, "Which door do you choose?" Without hesitation, I answered, "The last door on the right." The hypnotherapist replied, "What do you see when you open it?" In an otherworldly voice, I unleashed a loud whisper, "NARNIA!"

In disbelief and delight, I realized I'd opened the magic wardrobe's door and entered Narnia—land of talking animals from my favorite childhood book! I entered a winter wonderland with brambles I needed to push through, and glimpsed the White Witch who represented everyone who'd sabotaged, attacked, or stood in my way. She was almost foaming at the mouth waiting for this battle with me.

The Witch wanted to destroy me and usurp my powers. Of course, it doesn't work that way. Killing a lion makes one cowardly, not brave, and the lion's powers don't transfer to its killer. (If you behead someone, you have their head, not their soul.) I knew the plot of my life had epically thickened. It was time to become Aslan the Lion, King of Narnia, and defeat the witch! Aslan protects all the animals, trees, and FREEDOM. Many people act like lions and tigers, but few ever achieve their essence.

The hypnotherapist was clueless what NARNIA was, but could see it was a BFD for me. Soon after opening this door in my mind, my abilities to communicate with animals, angels, nature, and many other Light beings exploded. No dynamite-carrying-cartoon-coyote was needed for this part of my soul's excavation. BOOM! I was unchained (in this area of my life).

Aslan's love creates endless Springtime and freedom. Live and let live. But the Witch's ego demands endless winter and slavery of all creatures—War. The irony that a Christian book reawakened my witchy gifts didn't escape me. The White Witches of the world weren't going to steal my life force anymore. #GetYourOwnMagic!

Narnia waited a long time for fearless warriors to reconnect to magic and remain fiercely committed to help free the animals, regardless of ridicule. We're all born alchemists, but our powers are useless if we forget we have them or we fear activating them. The older I got, though, it became a bigger battle to be a colorful soul in a world of people seeking to camouflage.

My hypnosis sessions brought forth animals of all species, fairies, fairy tales, cartoon characters, Jesus, comedians, poets, athletes, celebrities, mediums... Anyone who spoke my soul's language changed my life's game with renewed strength and powers.

The character, "Shannon," in my life's video game was being awarded new challenges and gifts upon mastering levels ranging from laughter-filled to terrifying. Feeling the animal kingdom's love, along with Spirit's joy, is a blissful adventure. My subconscious mind rested and played in higher dimensions, but always had to return to the hard, human world—hitting concrete after an exhilarating ride down a magical slide.

Whatever we're running from will eventually hunt us down and save, or kill us. In my case, a little of both. The entire Animal Kingdom and Glinda, the Angel-Witch, had chased and assisted me with relentless determination, patience, and humor. I couldn't outrun them. They'd been running alongside me, but the noise around me had drowned them out. Had I slowed down earlier, rather than broken down later, I might've sensed their presence sooner, and not run at all.

Glinda had assured, "You're right on time, Shannon." Spirit has its own nonlinear time table. My pain during "the lost years" was repurposed into pain relief for the animals I was serving. I felt like the luckiest person with my secret initiation into Narnia, a childhood dream brought to life with no doubt help from my beloved Lucy-Goosey-Pants in Heaven.

Through hypnosis, I experienced myself as a rapid river with a black leopard racing alongside me, keeping pace with my rapidly transforming spirit. The leopard's intensely focused energy, familiarity, and loyalty comforted me—a rare friend so natural to be with. Suddenly, I became the leopard and felt incredible peace and power—a divine combination.

As the leopard, I ran with exhilaration, but when I stopped and looked into the river, I'd become human again, and cried at my reflection. As a river and a leopard, I was wild and free, but as a human I felt trapped. How could I be free like the leopard and river while in this human form? Could I get a permanent pass from human responsibilities if diagnosed with "Species Identity Disorder?"

I'd have to unlearn the conditioning of the human experience, but still be amongst them. I've often told my dogs never to select Human as their chosen mission. There are too many arbitrary rules from people who haven't a clue what they're doing. Luckily, unlike the character in the comedy *Office Space* (that inspired me to become self-employed), I've created a life I don't need to be hypnotized into believing is some better alternate reality. My life *is* an alternate reality of funny, shape-shifting adventures—albeit with an occasional "Case of the Mondays."

The subconscious only reveals what's already real in other dimensions. Narnia is the party I'd been looking for, and I was awake exploring new worlds where life is a funny, furry (and sometimes ferocious) fairy tale. We come into this world in a dream-like state, forgetting we come from divine Light. I often want to shout to random people, "IT DOESN'T HAVE TO BE THIS WAY! WE CAN CREATE OUR OWN REALITIES!"

Hypnosis is a fast track to healing for humans, and animal communication speeds healing for animals by listening to and implementing their instinctive knowledge about their own wellness. Animals, fairy tale characters, and a few actual people showed up in my subconscious to help me write a new life story.

Any "real" or "fictional" characters who appear are parts of ourselves fighting to be made real, or given a voice, previously silenced. Some spirit allies represent gifts and strengths we need to develop or align our energy with, such as Muhammad Ali and his champion fighting spirit, Robin Williams to lighten up, or The Cheshire Cat for life changing secrets and magic. If a superhero shows up, rescue yourself and step into your power.

Developing a mystical mind opens a new way of life and old ways of being become insufferable. Albert Einstein said, "Imagination is more important than knowledge." Without imagination and creativity, nothing comes to life. Most often it's those lacking imagination deciding which color crayons everyone else must play with to be considered sane. I've warned friends that if they ever see me in beige, call 911...I'm dying.

We are empowered, magical creatures, as long as we maintain our ability to think, feel, and create for ourselves. We become victims when we let someone else write our story, or control us through fear while the White Witch invades. Many fairy tales demonstrate a quantum physics principle that we're all connected through energy. If we can manage our own energy, we can change our destiny, and maybe turn a prince into a frog with a kiss, or vice versa. Set a clear intention on that one!

Anyone who benefits from the status quo of your being addicted, depressed, poor and disempowered, without dreams or boundaries, will not want you to become enlightened and awaken your gifts. They'd rather you fall asleep under a spell in a field of poppies like The Wicked Witch did to Dorothy in *The Wizard of Oz*. They'll keep you plugged into mind machines, like in *The Matrix*, where people think they're living their lives, unaware they're controlled by a software program.

NARNIA is real. It's a state of awareness, an energetic connection, a magic wardrobe in our souls. Narnia is nature itself. Nature and animals have always communicated, whether or not people were aware or listened to the rivers and lions. In fact, had we listened we'd be breathing in the most beautiful clean air, the kind bouncing off waterfalls. Life itself.

Instead, we've dominated nature, exploited animals, and created mass pollution. It doesn't have to be this way. Aslan's Spring provides health and harmony, but disconnected souls choose the White Witch's winter and war.

Christians embrace *The Lion, The Witch and The Wardrobe* for its message of resurrection, and good triumphing over evil, and yet often malign metaphysics and witchcraft. Jesus performed all kinds of magic and healing spells. The book's underlying theme is the epic battle of moral choices, and whether to align with a loving Lion or a narcissistic Witch.

SPOILER ALERT...After the White Witch humiliates and kills the mighty Aslan, he comes back to life because of a "deeper magic" involving his nobility. Aslan is resurrected! A miracle, that while different from reincarnation, embodies the continuation of life after death. Resurrection is where the body is reunited with the soul after death, whereas reincarnation is the soul living on in different bodies. Whatever you believe, there are many more similarities than differences in various religious doctrines, with most heralding an afterlife.

In some religions, we take our ruby slippers with us (our bodies), in others, we get new shoes (spirit forms and/or new bodies). In my view, we go barefoot dancing full speed into our animals' arms, as if no time has passed. My belief is we all fly different airlines, watch different in-flight movies and still arrive at the same general destination. BUT, our personal afterlife experiences differ greatly based on how we treated animals and people while in body.

I've been shown a variety of afterlife scenarios from various human spirits I've communicated with. Some are doing hobbies they once enjoyed while in their bodies. Some are in "spirit school" studying to help those on Earth. Others are still struggling to learn their karmic lessons, and while loved by Spirit, remain stubborn by nature—denied access to higher level amenities until they learn. They can hear the fun, but they have to learn to play nicely before they can join in all the reindeer games. I like to imagine freshly baked cookies for pure hearts and flea-sized crumbs for heartless, human-mosquitoes. The afterlife is as varied as the human experience, but everyone is guided by loving beings helping them grow.

Animals simply run through the "gates." Cats, of course, love to ask for the password despite there not being a password. Humor is alive and well in animals, whatever form they're in. Open Mic transcends worlds and all of their jokes are funny. If you're ever writing comedy, ask your animal guides to assist you.

While doing a reading for Sushi, a cat, I asked him, "What are you up to now in the afterlife?" Sushi replied, "I work the Wheel of Karma." Curiosity consumed me. "How does that work? Are you spinning for consequences?" Sushi grinned. "I spin people who never learned their lessons, and I keep spinning until they do!" That's when I asked Sushi to show me who was on his wheel right now. I saw a chubby, bald man in suspenders yelling insincerely, "I'M SORRY...OKAY?" Sushi yelled back, "I CAN'T HEAR YOU..."

When I described the man to my client, her eyes widened in delirious gratitude. "THAT'S MY EX-HUSBAND!" Now, whether this was actually happening, or Sushi simply knew this would make her laugh, I don't know. I do know she laughed A LOT, and the cat provided stellar evidence of his time with Mom. That accountability is part of the afterlife's curriculum.

Sushi showed images that Hubby was a collector of wheels,

including steering wheels, in his lifetime. Sushi's mom confirmed he was a control freak who never let anyone take the wheel. Spirit Justice took the wheel and spun him karmic catitude delivered by his former cat beloved by his ex-wife, disrespected by him.

The storylines animals show me in the afterlife usually match themes from their time in bodies and their person's life "now," and any new passions. A Wheel of Karma seems reasonable—it's both funny and effective. I hear Jesus joke He has "no problem with this cat's methods, and there's nothing in the rule book against it." Well played, Sushi. WWJD? He'd look the other way when Sushi is serving up some fishy justice.

People who talk with animals are in divine harmony with nature. The Narnia children restored light where darkness prevailed by listening to and honoring animals. In the human world, some fearful followers of Christianity and other religions view this same concept as dark magic. Not everything fun is bad for us, so spay and neuter your judgment, and go split a sundae with a feral cat who might one day decide your fate.

I facilitate two-way conversation between worlds, and offer evidence it's really your loved ones. I answer quality-of-life questions for living people and animals, bring through memories and humor, and help heal emotional wounds for all species in the family. Our pets are always around us, even when invisible to our eyes. Having an unshakable faith that life continues makes me receptive to afterlife signs. A loving heart, clear conscience, and desire to serve Spirit keep me emceeing this otherworldly Open Mic.

You don't need an Animal Communicator or Medium for your pets and people in Spirit to hear your thoughts. Trust they always hear you and know what's in your heart. Cleaning up your own litter box makes connecting with Spirit easier. Working with professional mediums is a great way to get support and insights and takes the pressure off of you. Mediums seek counsel with other mediums, too. All of us need to get out of our own heads and hearts sometimes to re enter them with a lighter energy, fresh ideas, and answers from objective experts.

Spirit guides, including animal ones, can be permanent or transitional, depending on what we need help with—projects, relationships, inspiration, protection, wisdom, or humor through a challenging or triumphant time. We're all connected through energy, whatever our species or the time we arrived on earth through physical birth.

Since linear time doesn't exist in the afterlife, beings of any kind across timelines can assist us. A dinosaur from prehistoric ages? Of course. Your childhood pet? Woof, yes! A dolphin in the wild? Echolocation underway! A loving grandparent, child, or spouse in Spirit? Heaven, yes! A "fictional" character from your favorite book? YES...watch their energy come to life.

The themes of *Alice in Wonderland*, *The Wizard of Oz*, and *Narnia*, among many fairy tales like *Snow White*, *Cinderella*, *Frozen*, and *Maleficent*, played out through me in this *human* "reality" show, which I learned isn't so real. Spiritual connections feel light. Heavy feelings are our human side. Our loved ones who've passed exist in both our memories AND in other realms, alive on their own, regardless of our beliefs or emotional states. Love is a creation larger than our human minds and lives. It transcends death—an eternal shameless flame that whispers, "I'm still here."

Animals and spirits can access anything from our past or present, joyful or tragic, to communicate what they're thinking and feeling to facilitate healing, connection, love, and laughter. My transparency enables all species here and in the afterlife to trust that my integrity and talents will lead to successful communication. With nothing to hide, I offer my best, albeit still imperfect, self.

Setting ourselves free through honest introspection and mature action accelerates spiritual growth that, while often challenging in process, has the sweetest rewards. Fake happiness vs. genuine joy. This transformative soul recovery process requires courage and transparency. If you're still playing Hide and Seek with yourself, you're going to miss out on the magic.

In one particularly transformative hypnosis session, I was in a funny debate with Jesus and Elsa from the Disney movie, *Frozen*. I asked Jesus where my next soulmate was, when Elsa cut me in line! I wanted to throttle her like Homer Simpson does to Bart. Then Jesus smiled. "Shannon, she's you...you're her. Elsa's here to help you unfreeze your love life." I burst out laughing. I was ready to murder a cartoon character...in front of Jesus!

Indeed, I'd been frozen in fear. Elsa sang "Let it Go!" and was speaking with Jesus on my behalf while coaching me to let go of my fears, and trust in divine timing—something I've always found painfully slow. Real and "imaginary" people and animals from the arts, history, and religion were healing me and helping me unfreeze my dreams and make them real.

Soon after entering these Narnia-Wonderland-Oz worlds and other mystical places, mega magic flew out of my soul, turning up all around me, including my front doorstep. Later that day, having now integrated my Elsa-like powers, I opened the door to my home and stepped outside to see a smiling little boy on a scooter. He waved at me, turned around, and joyfully exclaimed, "Look, Mom, it's ELSA!" Mic drop. This kid whom I'd never met just tapped into my "being" Elsa. Magic at play. Belief creates manifestation. Spirit decides the details.

Opening spiritual gifts requires humility (a strong sense of humor helps), along with trust in one's experiences. Validation is nice, but not needed. As I often tell my clients, "If you think it's a sign, it's a sign." Don't overthink it, or let someone who hasn't experienced magic stop your happy dance. Animals, angels (and your inner Elsa), are inviting you to play. Let go and step into your power.

As William Butler Yeats said, "The world is full of magic things, patiently waiting for your senses to grow sharper." Animals, kids, and spirits play puppeteers planting seeds in my head as to who needs my help and how best to reach them. I work for them. My innate silly sense of humor—my feral side—is a receptive antenna. Soul work shouldn't be all serious. If you can't laugh at yourself, don't RSVP to my party.

Being playful *and* reverential separates me from many mediums who take themselves too seriously and miss the laughter that animals and spirits are dying for their people to feel, especially in their grief. Mediums should remember to be sensitive because a real person is receiving the messages.

 I've been to mediums who are so obsessed with evidence that they forget to deliver the spirit's message or disregard my needs. I don't need to relive death details. I want to experience the aliveness of their spirit through their words to me.

It's a tremendous responsibility to connect someone with their beloved pets and people. The Spirit World knows how each medium works and who's best suited for their loved ones to facilitate connection. Listen to your heart above all else when choosing. My soul's resume is well known, and my virtual business card gets passed around the Animal Kingdom and Spirit world. Celestial networking is a powerful referral system, and just needs a sweet rewards program for every soul I serve. #UnlimitedAngel/Devil's-Food Cake.

"Narnia's Lion King" left me feeling like an enthusiastic gameshow host playing "Who's knocking on my Spirit door?" I was receptive to receiving all creatures of light, but one ghost wasn't welcome. I'm not sure if I moved into his space or he into mine, but

I'm definitely not the roommate type (unless you have paws or a human penis).

While I don't mind ghosts, I didn't care for this snarky heckler. Most of us don't just sit around feeling good about ourselves, but on this particular day that's exactly what I was doing. I was excited for my life again, and knew my gifts would spread much joy. Kermit, Puppypants and I were lounging on the sofa staring out the window when I heard a crackly static noise coming from behind the TV that was turned off. A man's voice sounding like an old radio station scanning for reception angrily spoke, "Who the hell do you think you are?"

His voice grew louder, repeating its angry investigative journalism. "WHO THE HELL DO YOU THINK YOU ARE?" The ghost was asking me the same question countless passive aggressive people had asked me in various ways. This bitter ghost wanted me to feel as bad about myself as he did about himself for whatever dark things he'd done while alive. Maybe he was a shitty pet parent. I didn't ask.

Being a Ghost Whisperer was never my goal, nor cohabitating with one. I asked Archangel Michael to send this spirit into the Light. I'd read this works wonders. Well, apparently this ghost had read the same books I did, and wasn't going to fall for my ghost-busting-for-dummies hacks. Ghost Grouch dug his translucent heels into his wall space, and raised his voice at me like a scolding principal once did for "hijacking the social studies lesson to talk about your dogs again."

I realized he wasn't going anywhere until I gave him what he wanted—an answer to his rude question. I assertively announced, "I AM SHANNON SPRING. I live in the Love and Light. I'm protected by angels and am safe. I do good work in this world, and have the right to be here. Go now into the Light and leave this house. You are worthy of love, but not welcome here. Go now." Poof! The ghost disappeared.

Negative entities can attach to our pain, and since I'd recently dropped some negative entity dead weight, the ghost couldn't feast off my pain anymore, and he was hangry. Who the hell was I to feel happy when he felt like shit, even after he died? Much like the living, he needed some tough love to take action and get off the couch (or walls in his case).

With my Narnia crown secured, and this freeloading ghost evicted, it was time to set up shop as a Professional Animal Communicator, and let my magic out—unfiltered, uncensored, extra fur and slobber. Who the hell do I think I am? I'm an animal in human form—Shannon Aslan Spring. BOO!

8

GIRL, LET YOUR MAGIC OUT!

Use what talents you possess; the woods would be very silent if no birds sang there except those that sang best.
Henry Van Dyke

My first clients were Gloria, an open-minded teacher from a school where the Mayor and I presented, and her dog Rascal. I was excited and grateful for the chance to help them. I take people's trust in me very seriously. Gloria wanted to know if Rascal was happy, why he disliked other dogs, and why he seemed so agitated lately.

With clients of all species, I ask open-ended questions and listen closely with all my senses while they share what's on their minds. We address the person's goals, and the pet's needs, and focus on any behavioral or medical challenges, including life-threatening emergencies. The first thing Rascal showed me was an image of a skull and bones—a universal sign for poison. Rascal added, "It's in my food, my food is toxic. Lethal."

When I relayed Rascal's message, Gloria confessed he was eating the brand, "Ole Boy," one of the worst pet foods, and was on the pet food recall list for containing phenobarbital, the euthanasia drug! (Many pet parents think all pet foods are the same and buy the cheap stuff. Or, wrongly assume the most expensive one is best.) Pets have varied diet needs like people. Please educate yourself on how to prepare properly balanced meals for your animal children.

Rascal summarizes, "Fresh food is music to the soul, kibble's a pain in the butt hole." Question why your vet pimps a certain food. Most aren't pet nutrition experts. *Forever Dog*, written by veterinarian Dr. Karen Becker, is a brilliant book questioning traditional wisdom and providing in-depth research from well-vetted sources on how to help dogs live longer, healthier lives.

As Rascal and I chatted, I heard in my mind a song I hadn't heard in years. John Denver's "Sunshine On My Shoulders." Rascal said he missed soaking in the sunshine and was cooped up inside and bored. Gloria confirmed neither of them had been outside much since she'd been sick in bed for weeks, and Rascal's favorite thing to do was sunbathe. Rascal wagged his tail and smiled. As always, animals up the weird factor; Rascal showed applying sunscreen to his nipples!

Instantly, I pondered, "Do boy dogs have nipples?" Sure enough, they do. Gloria burst out laughing as she had just begun applying dog sunscreen to him, and "His nipples are the only area besides his ween I didn't protect." Animals can have a sophisticated, sarcastic, or silly sense of humor too. Nipples are practical, sexy, shameful, or funny—species depending! A deer you'll meet soon helped me free mine.

Making Shannon blush is an ongoing prize that animals covet. Sunscreen for a pet's ween would be weird even for me, and no doubt, word will spread and pets worldwide will start demanding ween sunscreen. I'll often get a few cases in a row with similar themes, and even jokes that play off each other across species and continents.

When I asked Rascal about his mom's concern that he didn't like other dogs, his response was, "I'm too cool for school," a fitting expression for his teacher-mom. Rascal added, "I'm content being a lone wolf. Please assure Mom I don't need dog friends. I'm happy being like 'Oscar The Grouch.' Grouchiness can be fun." Gloria laughed in relief and I breathed better too because grouchiness can be a sign of medical illness or an unhappy household.

Rascal said he felt "mostly okay" when I asked him if he had any pain. I ran a telepathic body scan on him to see if I felt any pain. While his grouchy attitude was normal for him, Gloria said he seemed unexplainably more agitated. I saw many tiny skulls floating in his bloodstream. Rascal admitted blood poisoning but said he'd be fine after flushing his system out and named some homeopathic remedies.

Natural cures are preferable when possible, but western medicine is often needed, or a combination of both. Western medicine, relaxation techniques and a stuffed animal are what got me through eye surgery. Whatever the procedure or the patient's age, regardless if they have paws, claws, or hands, don't underestimate the healing powers of love and a teddy bear with proper medical protocol.

A telepathic scan is when (with permission) I merge my energy with the animal's body to see if I feel pain anywhere and to what degree. I'll then ask the animal for any clarification I need. I often feel their person's pain too. Animals will send me sensory snapshots of what they're feeling for me to experience without me getting the illness or being left in pain.

I do multiple cross checks to make sure I've accurately understood their situation from *their* perspective. Sometimes they'll play a game show with me to make receiving information fun. It's a great way to help me process, remember and convey their situation.

If they play "Family Feud," they'll flip over the top three answers on the board. It might be their top three food requests in preference order, or new name ideas or diagnoses of what ails them. (I'm not a vet or a game show host, but I love playing game shows through my *Just Humor Me*™ programs.)

Rascal finished by offering his mom some creative ways to handle classroom management issues. He loved being her virtual co-teacher. I often tell clients don't be surprised if your pets give you the best life, love, business or medical advice. Their wisdom and wit are unlimited.

How can animals possibly have advice for us? Because they deeply understand our strengths and struggles, and have a keen sense of the energetic communication that goes on in our lives. They are self-aware, aware of our needs and wants, where we self sabotage, and how we can get unstuck. They know who we like, what drives us crazy, and how many snacks we're hiding.

Animals, like straight-shooting bartenders, invite us to spill our guts while they listen without agenda or judgment. They'll offer a clever solution in a one-liner that we might not like, but know is right. Then we tip or treat them for their tough love. The sooner we listen, the faster we can get back to having fun. Gloria needed to accept she'd been letting her students run the show, and Rascal, the self-appointed School Resource Officer, was ready to set those kids straight.

Gloria and Rascal thanked me, and I was thrilled to be of service. Gloria stated she'd buy him new food, just as soon as she used up the rest of the current (toxic) bag! Even the most educated people are often in severe denial about how serious an issue their pet is experiencing. (Don't wait for it to manifest as an emergency or death.) I have to be willing to be disliked. (You're killing your pet. Throw the food out!) Animals need authoritative advocates.

The human mind has a remarkably dangerous capacity to dissociate from negative reality. Animals tolerate all kinds of threats to their physical and mental health because of people. Much harder decisions have to be made when denial is your deity.

Gloria couldn't accept she'd unwittingly poisoned Rascal, and continuing to feed lethal food to not waste food was wasting Rascal's health. It wasn't until I said, "While Rascal's still alive, poison is attacking his system and can KILL him anytime. Saving food money will be canceled out by thousands in vet bills, or a dead dog. Please take him to the vet." Sometimes clients need love, and sometimes bootcamp. In being direct, I'm being the best possible compassionate communicator for all species involved. Being nice isn't kind. Being truthful is my job.

Gloria emailed me weeks later with a positive update: "Rascal is much happier and calmer, and getting plenty of sunshine. He has more energy and life now with the new food. It's incredible to know what he's feeling, and how much he loves me. He really connected with you, and your kindness and skills saved him. Thank you for caring."

Everyone deserves to have their voice heard. Rascal was lucky he didn't die from his daily dose of poison and that his mom had an open mind to animal communication and made immediate changes. So many animals are waiting to take the mic to let their parents know how to help them. Minor fixes to diet and lifestyle save lives. Hearing animals' voices reduces heartbreak and costly vet bills. Don't let fear of what they'll say cost them precious days. Facing the truth is much easier than living with regret. Animals also provide great comic relief through the readings.

Testing out my skills as a professional Animal Communicator was FUN. I felt alive in brand new ways as the voice for my greatest heroes and new employers, the Animal Kingdom. Being new in the "psychic business," I knew I'd have to prove myself. Rightfully so.

Psychics can be seen as frauds. Fair enough, although there are good and bad people in every field. There are corrupt doctors, cops, ministers, politicians and, arguably, hair stylists—as evidenced in photos from the 1980s where everyone looks electrocuted. It's particularly evil, though, when the *helping* professions exploit a suffering soul's trust.

Being transparent makes life easy and enables animals to know they're in good paws with me. I poke fun at myself for being a pet psychic. I get it. Sometimes things that are totally natural are seen as silly or spooky. Humans judge; animals simply want to join in the fun.

If I didn't have the confidence, credentials and competence to back up my interspecies and inter-worlds conversations, I'd probably be on some kind of cuckoo bird watchlist. Maybe I already am... here's hoping! I have to have a sense of humor about this, or I'd miss the joy in this work, or suffer from delusional infallibility like I've seen in many mediums whose egos go awry. Animals keep me in check, cheer me on, and count on me to relentlessly pursue their rights to life (or death), liberty, and happiness. Mediums don't know everything, we're not perfect, and we can't fix bad people, only educate them and love animals.

The "Ms. Enchanted Paws" genie on my website whose crystal ball globally predicts: "I see fur and slobber in your future," is always right. Sometimes even haters regrettably find themselves laughing with me. This is always particularly rewarding. Unselfconsciousness and laughter go a long way towards a healthy perspective. Whether I'm the teacher or student, my goal is always to laugh and learn in my own way, not take over someone else's show. (That's Puppypants!)

I don't let people bulldoze my workshops with disrespect either. When people are learning, and having a good time while following rules and doing the activities, that's a success. I create a safe space to learn and play by having rules and recess. Even kids know rules make recess more fun, like don't hog the ball or hit anyone.

Being a great leader is a lot of work, and so is being an asshole. Lack of leadership causes problems, and so does rigidity. Set and enforce rules, and give permission to play whatever the students' ages. My Laugh and Lunches have a simple rule: NO SAD STORIES/NEGATIVITY. Check your problems at the door and bring your best self in to play. Everyone's welcome to reclaim their baggage when they leave. Animals do all of this naturally. They'll never tell you their sad story before playing chase. People need resiliency resources, stress relief and to have fun while learning new tricks, just like animals.

My cheerleader puppet once caused trouble in an online mediumship training with Anita, a British medium whose mentor had emphasized the importance of creativity in our craft. I used the peppy puppet to add levity to a very stressful class and introduce myself creatively: "This is Shannon Spring. She's not small…She's not large…She's the Medium…in Charge! Gooo Shannon!" Penelope bopped her pom poms and I bowed.

Never before have I seen someone want to murder a puppet, except maybe another puppet. But Anita looked at Peppy Penelope, then looked at me, and by process of elimination I deduced I'd be taking the rap for both of us.

Anita exploded, "Are you mentally ill, Shannon?" she mocked. I let her question hang in the air to let its cruelty breathe. My spirit had irritated her demons.

Fun made Anita uncomfortable *(although the word contained two of her favorite letters)*. Rather than kindly ask me (and Penelope) to be more serious, she tried to pass her pain onto me like a hot potato. She was ice cold and I felt panicky. I do much better "performing" when I CAN JUST BE MYSELF. Conformity stifles creativity, and creativity is where the magic happens. Anita's puppet rage was alarming. *(If you or anyone you love is experiencing puppet rage, eat a cookie and take a nap.)*

Penelope is always a huge hit at humor retreats. It's virtually impossible not to smile when she's excited about something. I've taught humor and creativity classes from K-corporate for decades and always rewarded students for courage, team spirit, and silliness. I once had a sales team of grown men in business suits working out their conflicts through puppets in their boardroom. Playing creates powerful magic, including sales. Penelope both landed me a lucrative client and exposed a bully, and that's equally worth cheering for.

People who disdain play and laughter won't have much luck befriending animals, let alone becoming animal communicators. You don't have to play with puppets, but it helps to be unselfconsciously silly. Just moments before Anita poo poohed Penelope, I was the only student to acknowledge a bird breezing by her, her deceased mom's sign she was present. My puppet taught Anita more about her own wounds than Anita could ever teach me about mediumship.

While studying animal communication, I visited the beautiful land of Findhorn, Scotland where my ancestors once pondered the pros and cons of creating me generations later. They rolled the dice and here I am. Luckily, this land does physically exist outside children's books and movies and is locatable on a human map. Just for fun, call the airlines...ask to fly to Narnia. If they call you crazy, thank them. You're one step closer to opening the same Magic Wardrobe portal Lucy and I did.

I marinated in Findhorn's magic, which hosts many big-name metaphysical speakers and authors. The forests of Findhorn are known for being alive with Spirit, fairies and a deep, mystical feeling of connection. Its air is crisp and healing, with fresh lavender blooming. I flew to Findhorn, leaving behind Puppypants and Kermit who share British heritage with me, being respectively part beagle and part Jack Russell Terrier. Muttopia's matriarch was on an unchaperoned adventure.

The Nature and Animal Communication class was led by two humorless instructors, Betty and Wilma, who abhorred my American "attitude," aka confidence and free spirit. My student label varies from Teacher's Pet to Teacher's Threat. These two party-poopers flagged me as a high threat. They cringed at my Golden-Retriever-like enthusiasm while holding invisible "No Dogs Allowed" signs whenever I appeared.

"Laughter equals learning" and "There's no excuse for a boring teacher" are my mottos as an Educator. Coloring within the lines is not virtuous, and daydreaming isn't a crime. Playful minds manifest magical transformations. Controlling minds build walls.

One of our assignments at Findhorn was to choose an animal to "become one with" in a fluorescent lit conference room rather than outside in...NATURE! Still, I was eager to participate and chose to "become" a deer. Betty and Wilma began guiding the students scattered around the room with our eyes closed. They asked us questions such as, "What does it feel like to be this animal? How do they move? Are they fast or slow? What do they eat?"

I resisted the urge to eat the candy in my pockets because deer don't have pockets, and opening the wrapper would make a noise that'd scare off a deer. Getting into character, I became uncomfortable in my bra. (Real deer only wear bras for Halloween.) I released my boob handcuffs through my armhole, free, but not yet buck naked. Braless and barefoot, but no *Buck-buddy*.

Afterwards, we were summoned to the circle to share our experiences as animals. Betty and Wilma listened as each student shared a moving tribute to their animal counterparts. With hesitancy, our stone-faced leaders called upon my smiling face.

I held up my bra, explaining the first step in becoming a deer. "Free the nipple!" My classmates roared with laughter. Threatened by a deer with headlights, Betty and Wilma stopped my reindeer games in their tracks. *(FREE THE NIPPLE is a brilliant documentary on Netflix.)*

They didn't appreciate my commitment to character acting. I really did move more like a deer, and having fun and making fun are two different animals. Insecure people are a lot of work in life and an improv scene. My deer had a profound message: Free your body, and your mind will follow. It's not like I removed Betty and Wilma's undergarments!

We entered the forest where we were instructed to sit solo, close our eyes in silence and "become one with Nature's creatures." I wish I could tell you Señor Sapo and Esteban stepped out of a portal here, but it was just me and nature. I didn't feel like sitting, so I walked off peacefully by myself for my own adventure, as classmates found their spots and closed their eyes.

Like the white rabbit once did, waiting by a stream for me, I stood with my eyes wide open waiting...for what, I didn't know. And then he appeared! A handsome, Scottish man came skipping down the path. Shame he wasn't wearing a kilt given the skipping. He sported nice muscles and bright orange headphones while singing like the proudest songbird in all the land. He intrigued me.

My whole body tuned into his contagious joy bouncing my way. He danced up to me, looked straight through my soul with his wolf-like eyes, and commanded, "GIRL, LET YOUR MAGIC OUT!" Entranced, I didn't care whether he meant to sing along or strip down and mate right there (as was my custom in foreign lands). I grinned then howled, "YES! I WILL LET MY MAGIC OUT!"

Like feral Cheshire Cats, we high-fived each other's souls. The woodland creature I was supposed to experience becoming one with was a man. A wolf-human-angel in one. A hybrid I've never seen before or since. They should definitely make a puppet with his looks and personality. He skipped and sang down the path leaving me mesmerized.

I floated back to the group, my cheeks glowing of honeymoon sex, despite my rendezvous not being even one of the fifty shades of gray. A magical moment in a wrinkle in time between two free spirits. Not even first names were exchanged this time. It was an animalistic play-bow, a celebratory sniffing of an old friend I'd just met.

Humans and animals aren't the only beings that LOL. Things were about to get weirder in the most wonderful ways. I met many wonderful people from around the world who were studying animal and nature communication at beautiful Findhorn, including my three delightful roommates from Britain, Japan, and Romania. We had separate rooms in a tiny cottage surrounded by gorgeous gardens.

After Betty and Wilma led a fascinating discussion about how trees communicate, my mind was blown. How could I have known so little about trees? They literally keep us alive! Trees are ALIVE beings with rich inner lives possessing self-awareness, and caring for each other through a community of support sending nutrients across various tree species. They're sensitive to the energetic patterns of people walking amongst them. Our emotional states and how we walk through nature impact them.

Kindness makes plants grow, and negative energy makes them wilt. Nature responds to our loving thoughts and actions and dies from our indifference and neglect of the very "things" that allow us to BREATHE. I knew so little about nature, like many humans. I learned how trees have incredible abilities through their underground root network, and even a natural instinct to protect their fallen tree comrades.

These discoveries led to many more questions about trees' inherent magic. I raised my hand and asked, "Do trees laugh?" Betty and Wilma simply nodded and mumbled, "Yes." They didn't elaborate on this freakishly fantastic fact. Umm…excuse me…Yes? All you're going to say is Yes, without any fun facts or stories to illustrate that trees can LAUGH? WTF! (What the forest!)

That's like a child asking where babies come from, and an adult pointing at their stomach with no further explanation. They're missing the good part! It was time for our mid-day break though, so I returned to the cabin for a nap. It was the nap of a lifetime—far, far down the *rabbit hole*. (Can you hear the echo in this sentence?)

In a lucid, trance-like state, I began laughing in my sleep. Joy overcame my body, and I… couldn't…stop…LAUGHING! I was "asleep," yet awake "somewhere else." It felt as if my cells, my blood, my bones were LAUGHING! In this state, I was sure my Japanese roommate, Noriko, was laughing in her room. The wall between our rooms seemed to vibrate with laughter.

At one point, I saw the spirits of baby raccoons laughing and dancing up and down my chest. When I awakened, my face and eyes looked translucent. I felt full of giddy fairies, kindred spirits, the perfect playmates. I asked aloud to the collective baby raccoon spirits why they'd come, what they wanted me to know. They energetically infused me with wisdom, *"We want you to know you are no longer the student, you are the master."* What? OMG! How cool is that?!

The raccoons let me know that my gifts ran deeper than I knew.

No wonder Betty and Wilma were unnerved by me. A woman who knows her worth gives off a primal scent, a fearless fortitude. My Light was causing their groundhog shadows to see themselves.

While blissfully walking back to class, I waved to Noriko who smiled seeing the joy on my face. Still high on laughter, I asked, "Ahahaha, were you just laughing as hard as I was?" She laughed along with me, but had no idea what the forest I was talking about.

Noriko wasn't floating on the same divine cloud, out-of-body experience I was. But, in whatever fairy-tale world I'd entered, I was sure she was. Noriko's bright inner light didn't judge my giddiness. She just shared my joy magnifying it even more.

It was then I understood it was Noriko's spirit that'd been with me, not her human self. Similar to how spirits travel and visit us in dreams, or humans, through heartfelt connections. The experience is real in an alternate reality. We walked back together to class. I was grateful for nice roommates, and rascally awesome raccoons.

My Golden Retriever-like enthusiasm (tolerant of rejection), inspired me to try to share my experience with Betty and Wilma. Perhaps they might have insights or be amazed. Nope. They nodded dismissively and told me to take a seat. (Joy jealousy is a real affliction.) And while it's true, "You can't talk Butterfly language with Caterpillar people," I do believe in planting seeds, no matter how dry the desert.

Luckily, an Australian student overheard my life-changing, unexplainable full-body laughterpalooza, and knowingly smiled. "Shannon, do you know what just happened? (I felt like a dude who just got his first woody. A laughter orgasm happened!) You just got an answer to your question before the break, 'Do trees laugh?'" My jaw dropped as I processed the wonder, the miracle of what the trees so generously gifted me. LAUGHTER, just what I always wanted! I thanked my classmate and felt the love of the trees envelop me, a human sapling.

The trees rewarded my playful nature by *showing* me through my own body that TREES CAN LAUGH! The second my classmate said this I knew it was true. What I'd felt was exactly what it would feel like *if* trees could laugh, which they definitely do. It all made sense... the otherworldly giddiness, the peace, and wild sensations I'd never felt.

Feeling the collective trees' breeze laced with the laughter of babies of all species through my body made me want to laugh even more. I was in love with trees, and wanted to learn about and protect them. They're not disposable resources. They're friends.

Upon returning, I created "The Receiving Tree" puppet show about giving back to trees, as too often we take and also this poem:

I'll hug trees and talk to squirrels.
And teach all I can to young boys and girls.
I hope one day they'll wonder too...
Can trees laugh like me and you?
And may the trees celebrate another has awakened...
To give back to nature who's been so forsaken.
The magical forest gave me sweet relief.
Living truths some label childish beliefs.
I've laughed with the trees.
Flown with birds, and spoken with bees.
Worlds within worlds, the lucky few enter.
Where hearts expand, revealing a soul's center.
Narnia's wardrobe opened ever wider for me.
I sang, I danced, and set myself FREE.
I was the child, she was me, reunited, together. Finally.
Fairies were real, and oh so much more.
Like The Cheshire Cat who flew right through my door!

Girl, my magic was out...way out! Meow...

9
TOUGH LOVE FROM A TIGER

My reality is just different than yours.
The Cheshire Cat, from *Alice in Wonderland* by Lewis Carroll

Back from Scotland, my dogs and I daydreamed out the window. I felt weirdly sentimental looking at my Jeep and thanked it for its service. The next day I totaled it by pulling into oncoming traffic, mistaking it for the turn lane. No fairies or laughing trees were in sight. Just a sexist cop and an Amish truck driver.

The messiness of the matrix is heavy. I needed to keep the forest magic alive. After I handled the claims, I looked at the dogs and announced, "Boys, I need a man!"

Forest life was now behind.
Reality, though is just a state of mind.
I felt the passion of the Woodland creature.
I needed sex...perhaps a double feature.

Here I was speaking in rhymes.
An empty rabbit-hole's a serious crime!
It was time for a lover in my life.
All work, no play, madness- silly strife.

The next thing I knew, The Cheshire Cat in orb form was floating in front of me. I'd summoned him! A totally sober, trippy experience now that I was no longer taking magic killers— antidepressant/anxiety prescriptions. It was like I'd accumulated enough points in a secret spiritual rewards program from surviving the mental macarena of recovery to finally be feeling authentic joy. This feline alchemist winked at me signaling LET THE GAMES BEGIN!

I felt like Samantha from *Bewitched* who wiggled her nose and anything from a cake to a genie would appear. As a kid, I spent hours wiggling my nose to no avail, and spinning around jumping off furniture trying to transform into Wonder Woman. Spirit proved magic would find me when I'm just being myself.

I set clear, assertive, playful intentions (get laid) and let go, trusting it'll show up. The Cheshire Cat materialized to grant my wish. While he's more of a voyeur than a romantic, he's a mischievous, maniacal matchmaker!

I wondered- where could a sexy man be?
Then craved chocolate cake quite suddenly.
And what to my wondrous eyes did appear?
The Cheshire Cat HIMSELF...he was here!
Shamelessly grinning majestically- he ordered me-
  "GO EAT CAKE...don't hesitate!
Eating cake will change your fate.
Again he repeated with pressure:
"GO EAT CAKE, IT WILL BRING YOU PLEASURE!"
Craving a quick sugar fix,
I obeyed Cheshire Cat's mysterious tricks.

Under his spell, I sped to the corner store.
Cheshire cheered, "God Speed, you ravenous whore!"
I arrived grinning, on my hot pink bike.
And there was DESSERT...a man named Mike!
I'd met Mike just once before,
when I'd sashayed my mutts past his door.
He grinned and did a double take.
What brings you here for goodness sake?
I purred: "I'm here for chocolate cake."
Mike drooled like I was a juicy steak.
We ordered two slices and took it to go...
Mike, himself...a ravenous ho.
We had our cake, and we ate it too.
Grown-ass adults know what to do.
The Cheshire Cat had cast a spell:
Two feral cats mating. Ask me...I'll tell.
Relief! I'd scratched a lusty itch.
Chakras aligned for this pink and purple witch.
Alas, Mike's ego demanded too much room.
He'd always be a bridesmaid, never my groom.
I said goodbye to Mr.-Right-for-now.
My dogs said it too...Buh-bye, Bow-Wow.
A new adventure- a move was on its way.
But, Cheshire Cat always has more to say.
He visits often but never to stay.
Free Spirits, it's how we roll- it's just our way.
Only men of courage and authenticity,
  shall have cake in bed naked with me.
Now concludes this playful rhyme.
On with the story...we'll have cake again another time.

Cheshire Cat loves to play "Tag," often making a cameo when I share a story about him. He'll sometimes magnetize himself to the listener working magic on them too. My dogs and I were regulars at the market where I met Mike. I dared the employees in my adult "Show and Tell" to "Guess which one of your customers I'm sleeping with!"

They eagerly offered up a few suspects, regular customers, some of whom they scanned to see if their faces glowed like mine. I told them how it all transpired with the "make-believe" Cat appearing before me like a fairy godmother. They shouted, "No way!" many times, but my familiar grin was evidence I'd fallen under his truth spell. Contagious cerebral catnip.

About a week later, the manager waved me over upon entering. She looked spooked, but amused and whispered, "Do you remember the Cheshire Cat story you told me? Well...umm...he's now with ME!" She excitedly confessed how weird, funny things were now happening to her. Carla looked radiant and confirmed it was the magical cat because his face appeared right before or after "something good but strange" occurred. She felt "on fire with creativity and couldn't stop laughing. You weren't kidding, he's really real!" I laughed knowing it gets weirder...it always does with this grinning "imaginary friend."

Another cat, this one just as confident as the mythical one, but wilder in her own magical way, Charlene Tigress was about to help me earn some more stripes of my own. Charlene lives at an animal sanctuary in Tampa. She was my first "big cat" reading, and her sheer genius changed the game for me. I'd gotten too comfortable in my ways and forgotten good manners, like introducing myself. I laid in bed gazing at her photo, skipped the small talk and asked my questions.

Charlene commanded, "SIT UP STRAIGHT GIRL, SHOW RESPECT. I AIN'T NO ORDINARY HOUSE-CAT!" Whoa! That's an understatement! Her fierce energy pulsed through me like lightning. She was right, and I immediately loved her.

Charlene had many devoted caretakers, including Haley, who wanted me to check on Charlene's overall happiness and health. Tigers are one of my major animal guides, so I was especially excited to speak with a tiger so close to Puppypants Town. Animals can use anything they wish to communicate with me to illustrate their thoughts and feelings. It's difficult for people to understand how animals know they'd like a certain food, vet, activity, other animal or city if they haven't experienced these things.

One way to explain it is that every species is energetically connected to ALL information stored in our personal and universal energetic clouds, like computers with digital memories and data. Information, resources, feelings, thoughts, experiences, EVERYTHING is accessible through "the cloud" for us to virtually experience. Charlene, an opinionated cat like myself, had many purrspectives to share.

She began mocking Mike who'd strayed back through my door again, cake-less. (In fairness, he did bring dog treats.) Charlene telepathically appeared dressed as actor Sharon Stone's character from the movie *Basic Instinct*—an ultra-sexy, dangerous sociopath who thrives on mind games, flirts shamelessly, smokes, drinks, and flashes her "kitty" to police detectives questioning her as a homicide suspect.

Charlene's a naughty egomaniac who marinates in her own power. It's intoxicating to bathe in her unshakable confidence where doubts cower and confidence roars. Cue "Damn It Feels Good To Be A Gangsta!" She inhaled a huge puff of her long fake cigarette, showed me Mike's face and huskily exhaled, "Shannon, a tiger cannot date a non-tiger. Mike's not good enough for you. He's so...(big inhale)...BASIC. He'll bore you to death. He lacks the fire inside you crave...you need. A tiger cannot date a non-tiger. It'll never work!"

Best dating advice since Sister Catherine's: "When the bridge's open, boys will look." Everything about Charlene was an open bridge. I knew she was right. She simply speaks truth. No sense arguing unless you enjoy hearing "Told ya so!" when she has the last laugh.

Later that day Mike arrived. Within a few minutes, we were kissing when he spotted her glamorous photo on my wall. He felt nervous and self conscious. "Umm...Shannon, this is going to sound weird, but...I feel like that tiger on your wall is umm... making fun of me?" I roared in laughter, "OMG! That's not weird at all. SHE'S BEEN MAKING FUN OF YOU ALL MORNING! Hilarious!"

Mike, having never been insulted by a tiger before, raised his eyebrows and cautiously asked, "Wow, what did she say?" Charlene engaged Mike in her dance. He wondered if a tiger had mocked him for what's in his pants. While down there he was fine, his overall game was outta line. She told him, "Shannon's no average lady, clean up your act, stop being shady! Turned off by your addictive fix (vaping), Shannon needs a man with comedy tricks. Unlike your ex-girlfriends who settled for less, she'll hold you accountable, go clean up your mess."

Charlene spoke directly, rhythmically, and unapologetically. Mike loved a challenge and took it in stride. Pheromones, farewell mating, one last ride. This sociopathic tiger's wisdom spoke to my soul...don't waste time on ANY asshole.

I thanked her and she shared her story with me. She was grateful for the proper care she received and made a few requests to help caretakers win her favor. She requested the Halloween monster-themed cereal, "Boo Berry." It was funny and freaky when Haley confirmed one of the regular volunteers "used to snack on that stuff and must've used it to reward Charlene."

When I asked the Publix manager if he could "score me some Boo Berry for my tiger," he nearly sharted himself. I calmly elaborated, "She's not my pet tiger. Shame on Tiger King. She's at a sanctuary and has a very sharp sweet tooth." He was calmer but still uneasy, perhaps energetically feeling her tail swishing between us, fearing losing his mind.

I asked Charlene my standard question "What do you need to be happier and healthier?" She spritzed herself with Obsession and Chanel No.5 perfumes. (Tigers love perfumes with natural civetone, a pheromone released by the perineal glands in civets, a small carnivorous animal.) The sanctuary gave tigers perfume scented paper towel rolls to enjoy and mark their territory while smelling butt bouquets. Everyone needs romance!

Charlene spoke passionately about herself, friends and foes, like her fiercest rival, Princess—voted prettiest Big Cat a few times. Charlene is definitely not a runner-up beauty pageant contestant or a second fiddle feline. Their rivalry embodied a game day fight song.

Charlene, like all animals, knows everything about everyone in their world, including that I'm an outspoken animal rights advocate. "Education through animation," she purred, then roared with confidence knowing I'd relay her message. Haley nearly burst an eyeball at hearing me share confidential info only staff knew.

"Education through animation...OMG!" Haley cheered, then shared that producers from Game of Thrones had been filming Princess all week to capture a tiger's essence and create her likeness into an animated character for educational films! Charlene's direct view of producers fawning over her rival made her stripes boil.

Charlene felt snubbed, but adamant this opportunity brought awareness to animal welfare and respect for wildlife, including "The Big Cat Protection Act" which was signed into law December 20, 2022. It prevents private ownership of big cats as pets and prohibits public exhibition contact with big cats and cubs. Sadly, most animal welfare laws operate in slow-motion with years of humans hijacking animals' liberties for entertainment and greed.

Charlene sashayed and sang, "Single Ladies," announcing, "I'M THE REAL BEYONCÉ!" Unbeknownst to me, a sanctuary volunteer had rewritten the lyrics to "Single Ladies" with resident diva Princess as her muse! How does Charlene know Princess was nominated as Queen? Because Charlene never misses a beat and makes a powerful spokes-tiger. Eventually, Princess was relocated at the sanctuary and Charlene was happier.

Charlene's requests for entertainment were "creative." Like, stringing me up on a clothesline, remote control whipping me around at warp speed for her amusement. I was her Peppy Penelope puppet. Charlene slyly grinned knowing I have a no censorship policy. She relished envisioning me relay her request. Wild animals are my friends and clients, but still wild animals, and behave as such. Charlene's animated "hunger games" showed the odds wouldn't be ever in my favor.

Even though Charlene and I share a love of sugar, attention, and mocking enemies, she'd still eat me for lunch if opportunity struck. She won't modify her wild nature, any more than I'll change my human stripes. Her nature is to be a tiger, and mine is to be the kind in humankind, and spread her messages of respect, education, and dating worthy, tiger-spirited men.

Feeling the rush of a tiger's magnificent strength and prowess inside me is hard to define beyond, I FELT LIKE A TIGER! She's right, "a tiger cannot date a non-tiger." Many people settle for any dance partner, forgetting the point of dancing is to HAVE FUN, not just move your feet. Charlene would never settle for a tiger who didn't light her fire. I also needed someone who made my tail swish.

Charlene and Cheshire are a formidable life-coaching team. As muses, they give great advice and change my luck whether in business or a good ole fashioned duck. They made their first duo debut while I was in a meeting discussing offering my humor classes to a college.

The meeting was fueled by unbridled energy, creativity, laughter, and a hint of sexual tension—the perfect portal for their entrance. Laughter-laced, mischievous, cocky prowess and wanderlust souls are the Cheshire Cat's and Charlene's favorite elixirs. For me, it's an Italian New Yorker with a wicked sense of humor, unshakable confidence, and a kiss that I'd give up garlic for.

When the director asked me a question about my teaching philosophy, I grinned knowing I had a perfect, but wildly inappropriate response for a biz meeting. Immediately, the Cat appeared as an orb only I could see. He mischievously encouraged me to speak freely, roll the dice, see what happens. I tested the waters and told the man (let's call him Dan) I'd have to break business etiquette in order to paint the picture of how my talents can add fun and MAGIC to their curriculum while still being practical and educationally valuable.

Dan was intrigued. He smiled and said, "Oh I definitely want to hear THIS story!" The Cheshire Cat winked; he knew Dan wanted to play. I said I'll edit my story so it's still polite… he'd have to read between the lines to understand it right. Charlene licked her lips at the sexual energy in the air. She was high on pheromones without a care. My inner tiger, purring for me to go in for the kill, played uncensored…what a thrill! Cheshire knew I'd succumb to his will.

Trust them, lighten up…that's courage overflowing in my cup. Break the rules, I'm sure to win, my *rabbit hole's* wearing a grin.

I told Dan manifesting fun is a game I play. When I'd once mused aloud about "needing company," the *Alice in Wonderland* Cat ordered me to go get cake. And in pursuing "a slice of cake," I met a man who likes "desserts," too, and we "forked each other some sugar."

Dan's eyes widened. I'd made him blush…
Sex is always so hush hush!
Dan exclaimed, "I love cake too!" and Cheshire Cat knew what to do.
A mysterious knock rapped on Dan's door.
A man holding a CAKE! Our jaws dropped to the floor!
We'd summoned the Cat, in all his glory.
We kept our clothes on, though; this is a workplace story.
Say yes to magic, that's the trick.
Playful, clever souls…ooh, they're rare.
Dan made me an offer. I'd told the truth, he took the dare.

10

TURTLE CITY

Laughter is timeless, imagination has no age, dreams are forever... It's kind of fun to do the impossible.
Walt Disney

The time came to start over again and close a life's chapter. Things came full circle from arriving in St. Pete. From addicted and terrified to a kundalini spiritual awakening, sobriety, and my dog becoming the Mayor! In the past when making big decisions, my left brain made pros and cons lists, but the results were poop emojis.

My right brain deserves center stage to intuitively ask my heart what it feels rather than my brain what it thinks. My pets' hearts would certainly guide us to our version of The Emerald City that should host our life's show. Kermit and Puppypants cast their votes in a game.

I wrote city names on four sticky notes, then tossed them into the air and called Kermit over. The first note his paw touched voted...

Sarasota. The Mayor voted next after I'd shuffled and tossed the papers up again. His tiny paw also chose Sarasota—a Pawnanimous decision! For fun, I pulled a tarot card, the Wisdom card that features a tiny cottage and a little white dog. Wow.

My heart was peaceful knowing my dogs' paws held great wisdom. I walked Kermit down to the bay just after a storm, and as we sat looking out on the water, the biggest, brightest rainbow from out of this world spanned the sky. I've never seen colors that vivid in this world, each stripe vibrantly defined. Kermit and I had the park all to ourselves, but I still looked to see if anyone else saw the magic.

I heard a quiet, gentle Maya Angelou voice. "This is for you and Kermit, Shannon. You don't need to share it or give it away. Just enjoy." I felt deeply grateful and knew the rainbow was a divine sign. While soaking in its radiance, a double rainbow just as brilliant appeared. Gratitude multiplies! I smiled at my baby wolf. "This is for us, Kermit. Thanks for being you," and smooched his fluffy head.

I thanked God and half joked, "How about a TRIPLE RAINBOW?" And my wish was granted! (Maybe Bob Ross's spirit was painting miracles for us. Playfully painting my mistakes into beautiful rainbows.)

I lamented not having a camera, but recalled I rarely take pics like this. They take me out of the very moment I wish to capture, and I'd rather experience magic than document it, so we continued to capture the moment in our hearts. The triple rainbow ribbon sky needed me present to believe my own eyes. A magical memory that Kermit keeps alive in his heart too.

I told this story to a guy I dated and he refused to believe it without a photo, stating the unlikely odds I'd seen a triple rainbow. He became instantly unsexy. I pitied him missing out on joy living that way. The Spring family is too magical for a magic-less man. If you need photos to document miracles, you'll often miss the moment and always miss the point.

After Hurricane Irma, we downsized our things, including my

designer shoes and Mayor Puppypants' super gross tennis ball collection. I'd become obsessed with tiny homes, and creating a simple lifestyle centered around freedom and helping animals. Less things meant more freedom. I'd moved around more times than there are addresses. Renting your roots is its own special kind of hell. Landlords were a perpetual pile of poop on the soles of my ruby slippers.

I'd searched desperately for HOME, internally and externally seeking where I belonged, but never finding my people because "my people" are animals. A happy soul, unlike lots of stuff, will never weigh me down. Being happy with less always feels like more. Animal friends to laugh with and love are the purest form of health and wealth.

A local vet posted on Facebook a goofy little Shih Tzu mix in bad shape that a kind stranger had rescued as a stray. They wanted to find a family and spare him shelter life. I connected with his HAPPY face, and adopted a tiny, scruffy, street-smart Grover. His maniacal joy is infectious and his bros welcomed him home.

Grover lives up to his Muppet namesake's innocence, love for kids, and delicate self-esteem. The Mayor and he share a tennis ball obsession and Kermit worked through his jealousy issues and embraced Grover's silliness. No one is a misfit in a soul family. Pawtender, pour me a double shot of fur and slobber, stirred, shaken and wild. Celebrate the family you choose.

Now that I was home in my heart, the animal kingdom led me to my very first home of my own where my pawspring and I set roots, marked our territory, and welcomed many more animals around the world into our family.

Before we bought the house, we moved into a Sarasota apartment complex with a dog park on the property and a shady management team I should've saged from existence. Psychics can't know everything, or we'd avoid every bad choice, including the ones leading to the miracles we pray for. Trying to outsmart Spirit is like trying to outrun a cheetah. Spirit often tells us where cheetahs are hiding. If we don't listen, cheetahs POUNCE, catch and chew us up. But, the healing has a painful lesson with a powerful gift we can use to thrive.

Spirit can't block us from major soul lessons, but it can lessen our pain and send support where and when we least expect it. Dance with the cheetah and re-emerge more powerful...with a few more spots. As long as we're human, we can't avoid suffering, or always make sense of it. We can and do find relief along the way, and eventually see Earth's crazy maze from a higher perspective. Pain transforms and peace prevails. May butterflies follow you along your trails.

A major influence in my success as an animal communicator was studying with Dr. Maia Kincaid, a pioneer and author in the animal communication field. Unlike previous teachers, she welcomed my humorous approach, encouraged my success, and led with her heart. The animal kingdom made a perfect human match. Maia guided me to become my best animal self.

Shortly after I'd moved to Sarasota, my "luxury" apartment went downhill to the dark side. The man in the apartment above had two beautiful huskies he neglected. I heard them howling in desperation for weeks, but couldn't access them. I reported him to management, police, and animal control who left notes on the door which did nothing for the dogs. Neglect is abuse, and yet management sympathized he "worked long hours and is a really good guy," despite his having left a bag of open kibble on the floor for a week of meals.

The dogs got so thirsty they turned the kitchen faucet on which eventually flooded my apartment through the ceiling, causing significant damage to my belongings. Finally, maintenance shut off his faucet and checked on the dogs! I named these gorgeous dogs Ponch and John after the two hot cops on the '80s show *Chips*.

If the millions of animal lovers united to demand strict animal welfare laws, maybe abusers would finally be nationally registered like child predators. Too many people post sad emojis on social media but don't take action in real life. Some are also abusive, like the apartment manager who also left her dog alone for inhumane lengths of time. Some people aren't sure how to help, but that's no excuse. Learn the laws, speak up to enforce or change them, and shine the spotlight on evildoers.

Ponch and John eventually found a new home, and so did the Spring family. But, first, more battles arose (you were expecting that, right?). Luckily, the triple rainbow connection before all of this ensured a pot of gold when the storms passed. I moved my beautiful (now water-damaged) desk into the breezeway to be tossed. A frog repurposed it as his crash pad. (One man's trash is another frog's treasure!) I cheered up when I spotted him and politely introduced myself. He had me at "Ribbit." My heart exploded, feeling his elation over a human acknowledging he's a real soul! Animals have deep expressions in their eyes, in their whole bodies, even little frogs.

The frog said how much he liked lounging and people-watching from his new frog mansion. ("Frog Mansion" would make a super cool reality show where people are butlers to frogs!) He smiled when I asked if I could call him Robin after Kermit the Frog's nephew. I also promised I'd bring him to Maia's class to meet a few people who love talking with animals. "Yippee!" he exclaimed, and leaped onto my chest, surprising me into a backward bounce, causing him to fall to the ground. I'd never been mounted by an amphibian, and while I didn't squeal, "EEK...Frog germs!" I may as well have.

Animals know our unspoken thoughts which is how they understand us, whatever language we speak. Emotions transcend language. Cute as they are, frogs are slimy and I'd never had one on my boobs! Robin fell to the ground with a bruised ego. I bent down to sincerely apologize. Our chat was going so well until...splat...then he retreated to his land lily pad.

I added Robin to our communicator's meeting agenda, but like a human ER, urgent cases warrant priority, including the neglected dogs who'd brought us together. His guest star appearance was delayed, and worse, I didn't see him for a while. I considered sketching him and posting flyers: "Have you seen this frog?"

I joked with Maia that Robin was going to be "hopping mad" that so many other animals cut ahead of his turn. Especially, when it's the first time in his life someone knows he can speak! After he was bumped for two weeks straight, this heartbroken frog was indeed hopping mad. I sensed he was plotting revenge, but I could handle whatever karma he was conjuring.

About a day before he was our headliner in class, he cleverly positioned himself atop the stairwell in the breezeway I had to walk under every day. I stood there, an unsuspecting fool while he telepathically hollered, "READY, AIM, FIRE!" then strategically slimed me with frog poop! It was an especially icky eww, but I laughed! He'd pooped his peace and cleared the air on my hair. Now, we could be friends again.

Finally, our class telepathically spoke to Robin. A classmate said she heard Robin say he preferred to be called Fred. Robin then said to me, "Fred Robbins, my name is Fred Robbins and I wear plaid trousers!" I shared his proclamation, and a communicator in India flipped out. "OMG, I SAW HIM WEARING PLAID TROUSERS TOO!" We cheered and laughed at the incredible "coincidence" that was of course, no coincidence at all. She even held up her notes showing she'd drawn a frog in plaid trousers!

How is it possible that two people on opposite sides of the world had the same communication experience with a frog? Because it's an energetic, telepathic process, and multiple people can talk with the same animal at the same time.

Communicator conversations can be very similar, or completely different experiences based on our own filters and personalities, as well as what animals feel comfortable sharing with us. As people, we might share our intimate stories with best friends, but only chat about the weather with coworkers. Conversational dynamics vary based on relationships, circumstances, and whether we feel we can trust, learn from or laugh with someone.

No billionaire can pay to rocket himself to "Frogtopia" (the magical land where frogs rule). You must stumble upon this portal honestly. There are frogs with tutus, parasols, snorkels (to be ironic), and so much more. Often, the "fantasies" we see in art are realities in other worlds that artists are simply bringing to life in our human world. *I wonder if animal artists paint us, are we all wearing trousers?*

Fred Robbins encouraged me to spread the ribbit and distribute my business cards in a wealthy neighborhood called Turtle Rock across the street. Somehow, I made it to adulthood without knowing it was illegal to put flyers in mailboxes. My dogs and I walked around breaking the law, wagging our tails, and leaving behind evidence in case someone wanted to hire...or report us. While spreading the ribbit, I opened a mailbox where three frogs were trapped inside, panicking.

My dogs thought the captive frogs were their good fortune—Christmas in July! Instead, I reminded them frogs are friends, not food, and assisted our thirsty, webbed friends to freedom. When we returned home, Frogtopia's esteemed mayor was waiting on the stairs again, but this time with gratitude, not revenge. I was now a frog hero! (Luckily, my flyer-felony went unpunished, as Florida's judicial system is swamped.)

I do my best to create a safe space for my animals, clients and students. I encourage my students to think independently and respectfully challenge me. "Don't believe me because you like me, believe something because it feels right to your soul." In one middle-school debate class, my student Meryl, who loved my animal communication stories and their funny life lessons, asked me to share more. But when I shared about a frog who wears telepathic plaid trousers and staged a coup, Meryl paused to examine her own beliefs about this story's validity.

"No offense, Ms. Spring, I believe you, but your stories *sound* fictional." I laughed and confessed, "To you and me both, sister...to you and me both!" I'd have a hard time believing me if I wasn't actually ME too. Meryl and the class laughed, knowing I can laugh at myself, and their opinions were valued. After hearing more details, Meryl concluded, "Wow, that's one crazy frog!" Indeed he is. Fred Robbins is one crazy little green dude, and so am I. (Crazy, not green. I've only been green once after drunkenly skinny-dipping in a freshly chlorinated pool. *Naked, Green and Afraid* was thankfully just one episode.)

Threatened people try to sabotage or discredit what they fear or covet, including, power, talent, freedom, wisdom, or wild adventures with frogs in plaid trousers. Meryl and her classmates simply want the facts and skills to make informed decisions. I want my students to trust their intuition and be open to magical experiences. Animals are a gateway drug to joy.

Our Turtle Rock adventure didn't send me an influx of pet parents, but it did foreshadow the next animal to cross my path, a turtle named Burp. His mom, Lynn, asked if I could read her turtle, a creature I'd not formally spoken with, and wrongly assumed wouldn't have much to say. Speciesism is the belief one species is superior to another. Burp was depressed, feeling speciesism from his mom. Lynn wanted to know how Burp felt about his five dog siblings, if he liked his food and enclosure, why he was sleeping so much, and anything else he wanted to share. Burp looked depressed in his photo, but I have to look past surface impressions. Sometimes animals can have RBF too, especially in photos.

I introduced myself to Burp through the world's free internet—telepathy. *(I'm working on how to telepathically stream everything; no more silly service fees.)* I told Burp my intention was to listen and help without judgment. We chatted like two old souls relieved to be reunited in this lifetime. Like many animals and people, he began experiencing some relief simply venting to someone who truly cares about his feelings, and Mom caring enough to hire a telepathic-turtle-talker.

Animals are funny, cheeky, creative, and even sarcastic and clever. But Burp was my first joke teller. When asked, "How do you feel about your food?" Burp showed himself bored, chewing a piece of lettuce. "Let-tuce (let us) have more variety." I snort-laughed. Lynn confirmed Burp had only been eating lettuce after she'd quit giving him his gourmet turtle food. Burp gave lettuce a one-star rating, and Lynn promised to pamper his palate again.

I asked Burp how he felt about his dog siblings. "We aren't treated equally. The dogs are the favorites and are way up here (gesturing his flipper as high as he could)." I expressed sympathy since dogs often steal the spotlight. "What do you need to be happier?" I asked my hard-shelled friend with a soft heart. Then, like a disco ball dropping down from the sky, a "BURP'S BIRTHDAY PARTY!" banner flew.

Balloons, streamers, presents and cake flooded my mind. This sweet, lonely turtle wanted a BIRTHDAY PARTY! Could that be right? Had my white rabbit tour guide shoved me too far down the *rabbit hole*? Or had I traveled somewhere over the rainbow and learned to understand animals of all species? My mind was fine; it was my heart breaking wide open, levitating with more love.

Burp was adamant he deserved a birthday party to make him happier. Lynn cried upon hearing his wish. "Oh My God, I can't believe it. I had no idea that his feelings would be hurt! And that HE KNEW IT WAS HIS BIRTHDAY!" Massive mic drop when Lynn shared, "Just a week ago I walked past Burp's room, uttering unenthusiastically, 'Well, I guess you're four-years-old now,' and a few weeks later I threw A HUGE BIRTHDAY PARTY FOR ALL 5 DOGS!"

Bittersweet sadness—empathy that Burp's feelings were hurt, and then honored by his magical messages. Lynn would make his dreams come true. Burp felt invisible while the dogs were celebrated like royalty. Turtles, like toddlers, can want birthday parties, praise and presents. Anticipating my next question, Burp wished for a "turtle tank," something I'd never heard of, but Lynn obviously knew. Her jaw dropped wide open.

Just days before our session, Lynn and her dad were chatting near Burp when Dad commented, "I'd like to build Burp a new turtle tank." Burp's dreams were manifesting; he'd planted the thought in

Grandpa's head. Grandpa could now customize it to Burp's liking. *(Some stores now have pet party registries! Now all the birthday animals can register their wishes through me!)*

I asked Burp why he was sleeping so much, Lynn's main concern. He answered two questions in one by telling me, "I need color! All of this brown is depressing. I want a happy, colorful home." Was I projecting? (I love vibrant colors.) Can turtles even see color? It almost didn't matter if this is what Burp wanted, but I was very excited to learn turtles can see MANY colors, and have a special tetra-chromatic gene, enabling his species to see colors humans can't! Was I beige compared to Burp? OMG!

As soon as Burp's mom transformed his boring, bleh, brown tank into a cornucopia of color, Burp was no longer hiding in his night shelter, but a dude ready to live la vida loca, enjoying activities again. He and Lynn have a beautiful new connection, and I love helping transform others' pain, and painting the world pinker one turtle tank (not shell) at a time. Never paint shells.

Burp's spirits brightened and he voiced one last wish. "I'd like a window seat please, NOT an aisle seat." Lynn had just moved his tank from a scenic window to against a kitchen wall! Every animal wishes for more nature time and scenic views, as well as love, freedom, healthy food, respect and bodily autonomy.

My home-life was about to get a powerful upgrade too. "Let-tuce stop renting!" I said to my pawspring in a nonsensical Burp inspired joke. Play is also prayer and my prayer was heard, thankfully not with snort laughter.

Turtle City is the fictional town symbolizing freedom in "How The Turtle Got His Shell," the childhood book I authored. Turtles were a main animal spirit guide for me as a child. They helped me become independent and create safe spaces. My story's main character, George Turtle (my feisty inner kid), was put behind prison bars by Evil Birds (long before "Angry Birds" games) because George couldn't afford the taxes on his shell. Birds ran the town and extorted turtles' money, charging rent on their own shells. (Imagine not owning the rights to your own body.)

Birds, of course have the power to fly, and escape evil. They're free to go anywhere with their own wings. Turtles are born with shells to protect themselves in life from predators. Their shells grow with their bodies—a solid piece of real estate unless someone else somehow owns *your* shell and you're forced to surrender it.

One day, while the evil birds were away, George clung to the prison bars, and had a powerful awakening. (Premonition of my real-life kundalini awakening.) He looked down and saw a tool belt around his waist he'd never seen before. Everything he needed to free himself was right at his flippers. George quickly set about tearing down his prison walls before the birds returned.

Once he activated his powers, he realized he could break free, and build his own shell out of the painful things that once imprisoned him. (A blueprint for my adult self.) The bars became a beautiful foundation to build his tiny home on his back. Once liberated, he led all the other shell-less turtles to build their own shells, and marched together to FREEDOM in Turtle City. (Shannon's Shawshank Redemption!)

My life has eerily mimicked this story's themes of isolation, getting stripped of my shell, fear, financial struggles, but then determination, spiritual power, compassion and leadership. My child-self was a caged lion managing powerful visions and feelings within a crazy family and world. I had great courage despite extreme sensitivity, and ached for my own home to feel safe.

When we don't feel safe inside ourselves, we radiate fear...catnip to predators. Teaching others how to free themselves is an honor and responsibility once you've orchestrated your own jailbreak. (My 5th grade self deserves a royalty check for the roadmap.) Decades later in the kundalini transformation, Spirit revealed why I named the heroic turtle George.

Saint George was known for his courage after being tortured for refusing to deny his faith in Christ. He survived countless battles...he just wouldn't die. (I survived decades of abuse and unsurvivable suicide attempts.) I also knew boys had more societal power. I made my turtle-self a boy, the way female authors once used male pen names to get published.

Roe v. My Shell. My Choice! Thankfully, the warrior girl turtle in me persisted. Purchasing my first home proved to be an epic battle, as predicted, including extortion from evil villains, imprisonment, and a powerful bird.

11

THE EAGLE FLIES HOME

There's no place like home.
Dorothy, *The Wizard of Oz* by L. Frank Baum

While driving on a sunny Sunday morning I heard an angel whisper, "Head straight through the traffic light." A miracle was underway. My very first home, just like the one I'd pasted on a vision board five years ago, was waiting for me, minutes from Frog Mansion! I'd lost faith this dream would come true and had thrown away the vision board (don't do that). Spirit keeps dreaming our dreams for us even when we give up.

My pawspring and I now own this magical cottage with palm trees and a huge yard. This home represents the final scene in "How The Turtle Got His Shell" (written the year Teddy #1 died). Most would've torn it down to build bigger, but I'd been dreaming of a tiny house, and this house wanted to live. It sprang on the market like a desperate wildflower hoping a human fairy would love it. (It was built the same year we moved away from my childhood home.)

Houses and land are alive (or dead) with the energy of their residents, and can thrive or fail accordingly. When in doubt, let animals in...show humans out. Darkness kept asking the same existential question the ghost in my St. Pete house had booed: "Who the hell do you think you are?" My answer was getting louder and prouder.

Bad people had owned this house, including a child predator forced to surrender it in a court battle, and a ruthless elderly couple who, along with their unscrupulous realtor, tried to extort me at closing. I signed a lease-purchase, something I'd negotiated to get out of the rent trap. A big deposit secured it with a promise to purchase by the deadline or forfeit funds and permanent roots.

As I'd often experienced, the greater the spiritual upgrade awaiting me, the bigger the spiritual battles tied to them. Dangerous people who popped up like a period and pimples on prom night were energetically attacking my home.

The apartment complex and its multi-billion dollar parent company stole my identity, created false debt in my name, and sent it to a collection agency with whom they criminally extorted consumers. I filed a police report and the embittered cop told me a detective would follow up with me. But, a call never came because the dirty cop buried this fraud case as a "domestic dispute." WTF (What the fraud!)

When I followed up, two male detectives tried to bully me into silence. I wondered if they'd been bribed by the apartment manager who used a waffle bar to bait new residents into leaving good reviews. The manager had a score to settle with me since the neglected huskies incident and my complaints on her. Her husband was a retired cop from another city.

It's terrifying how much damage corrupt people in power cause, confident in their impunity. (Satan's shell corp, an underground enemy of Santa's helpers, terrorized me financially, legally and emotionally.) These many obstacles represented the thick brambles like I'd seen in hypnosis when I opened the magic wardrobe to Narnia.

I needed to cut through them, and fight these White Witch(es) blocking my yellow brick road to happiness. They were especially hungry to fight someone smelling like a proud Lion. Self haters hate empowered free spirits. I've smelled skunks like these many times before, and I knew I couldn't back down.

Finally, horses told me to cut through bullies at the station, and find the animal lover who'd instantly sense the truth of my case. A female detective, a horse lover (horses symbolize freedom) with common sense responded to my plea for assistance. She didn't comment on her partners' corruption, but it clearly didn't surprise her. She re-filed the case as fraud, making the bogus debt invalid and my credit score soar. While the crooks escaped consequences, I was freed from their clutches and set down roots.

This home is Puppypants Town. It's our shell—a giant pair of angel arms, along with an eight-foot fence that shelters us from a crazy world. It's a respite, a magic portal, a colorful, comfy, hippie chick, whimsical *rabbit hole*. My front door sign warns: "Working from Home. Don't Disturb or Wicked Witch Will Drop This House on You!" It's effective.

Only if it were made of cupcakes and an invisibility cloak, hiding it from non-magical beings, would it be more perfect. The house had fought to keep its dignity from prior dark dwellers, and now was set free too to heal, love and thrive. Its location is unbeatable in a gorgeous city minutes from world famous beaches.

The first thing I did when we moved in was tell the dogs they could dig to their hearts' content in their very own yard. No more white walls, beige carpets, and creepy landlords or security deposits to worry over. I painted the walls pink and purple with beautiful animal art from artists around the world.

I was happy and busy with work helping ANY SPECIES, ANY CHALLENGE, ANYWHERE™. Kermit was maniacally landscaping, digging holes the size of planets, and chasing lounging lizards. Puppypants chased tennis balls and barked orders at me while Grover smiled a thousand sunshines, and humped squeaky toys.

We daydreamed and took turns marking our territory in the yard (yes, all of us). This tiny house represents big freedom of all kinds.

I'm free to run around topless singing, "My hills are alive with the sound of my own music!" Why should only men get to be topless in nature? Damn the patriarchy. It's hot in Florida!

We lived here for about a year before another NARNIA-like battle reared its savage human head, and threatened me to my core. Puppy-pants and Grover were brutally attacked by a breeder's dogs who'd (along with the owner) terrorized us many times when we walked by his corner property on the way to the water. My dogs despised his creepy smile and sinister energy the first time we saw him, and I noticed the deadness in his eyes.

The attack left me shell shocked and my babies with serious injuries, including a hematoma surgery for Grover, and a deep wound behind the Mayor's ear. It started off a beautiful day, and I was feeling truly grateful for how well life was going. The White Witch from Narnia seemed to smell my joy. The dead-eyed psycho opened his gate, sending his dogs to attack us, unleashing the war inside him upon us.

Life was spookily mirroring art, as his wife/co-breeder's last name is Winter. They refused to pay medical costs, so a lawsuit *SPRING VS WINTER* went to court. (They say you can't make this stuff up...I wish to Heaven I was.) In Narnia, Aslan the Lion created freedom and eternal SPRING, whereas the White Witch cursed Aslan's Land with endless WINTER (evil breeder).

This battle came fully equipped with a nefarious judge who showed favoritism to Winter (whose dogs attacked many others, all unreported), and the breeders' attorney named Ozark (like the serial killer show, but with a combover and desperate need to be relevant). He tried to leverage my psychic job title to humiliate me. Instead, he empowered me and made a fool of himself. They were all desperate for my attention, and their poor dogs desperate for my help.

A doofus ACO (animal control officer) reported: "Ms. Spring states her dogs are just fine." (Never said that, and their injuries proved this false.) He was friendly with the breeder and even tried to claim my dogs harmed each other! Psychos are often well connected and protected. Next, an inept, immature vet (whose name is a popular baby food) falsely stated on medical records that my dogs "were in a dog fight." My dogs weren't "in a fight," they were ambushed, brutalized, and defenseless, and certainly not "just fine."

If human kids are assaulted, they're documented as victims, not aggressors or willing participants. Misinformation can destroy their reputations and damage their futures. False facts on pets, mislabeling them as aggressive, causes unnecessary and costly problems that can even cost them their lives, health or happiness. Slander is serious, whatever your species.

When I asked the aggressive vet (who sneers at animal communication) to correct his mistakes, he filed another false report claiming I asked him to "falsify records" (what he'd done). Their clinic that shares a name with a candy bar has all five-star reviews because they threaten to sue anyone who reports the truth of their corruption.

Once reports are made, it's an uphill battle to hold corrupt people accountable. Sadly, false police, medical and animal reports are filed all the time by corrupt, incompetent or deep pocketed predators. I've smelled these skunks before. Mostly white men in blue uniforms, black robes and white coats abusing their power and protecting each other over integrity. They are frog poop.

I took a restroom break after typing the above, and the universe's wild sense of humor drew my attention to the name of my toilet's manufacturer—the same as the vet's last name. I've been pooping on his name for years! Spirit's toilet humor helped me flush that asshole for good.

People say I'm intimidating. I say I'm like a flasher without the trench coat with nothing to hide. Most people hide behind masks or screens. Authentic people make insecure people crumble inside. When a bright light shines on their darkness, they retaliate violently and abuse their power. Liars pray their pants really won't catch fire. (It's why the Supreme Court wears robes.)

Two of Winter's French bull dogs, attacking canine pastry puffs

"Baguette" and "Truffles" (yes, really), chomped down so hard on both my dogs' ears I had to pry them open, and Baguette bit me in the process. The only witness to the attack was their friend and neighbor Karen (yes, really), a local realtor and animal services volunteer for seven years, stood watching the torture. She and the breeders verbally harassed, stalked and filmed me for nearly a year after the lawsuit ended. Empty, black-holed humans Narnia would never welcome.

The case was settled in mediation at the recommendation of my attorney friend Amanda (a fellow animal rights supporter). Despite the defendants' culpability, the justice-impaired judge (who let them depose ME) was a white witch on a podium who'd only cost me more precious peace and playtime with my now four dogs. She could bang her shady gavel all she likes without the privilege of my presence.

I recouped minimal medical expenses only, and the breeders merely received citations for "dogs running at large" and expired rabies, once again escaping "dangerous dog" records. In the far more esteemed court of THE ANIMAL KINGDOM, they're all guilty AF. But, it was finally over. The only silver lining is the pastry puff dogs' vaginas are closed for business, no longer ATM machines reproducing more cruelty for their entitled owners.

After the flood, identity theft, dog attack and court case, my PTSD was intensifying. I begged Spirit for mercy. Amanda hadn't told me to forfeit a win, she'd simply advised I win a larger battle and let go of these losers. She's smelled these skunks before. The Spring family was one victory closer to OWNING our rainbow bridge home on Earth.

Amanda lost her dog Sara months afterwards. I thanked her with a pet reading and something amazing happened. My own beloved dog, "Be in Charge" Rowdy appeared as Sara's afterlife guide. They were in love. I laughed and cried at the magical connection.

I've worked with thousands of animals and have never seen such an adorable canine couple whose first date began in the afterlife. I joked with Amanda we'd be in-laws now. I felt a rainbow over both of us. I'd love to produce "Fluffily Ever After," a divine show where animals fall in love and throw squeaky toys instead of flowers at guests.

Sara's loving messages comforted Amanda, and I was honored to assist a fellow animal rights advocate through a dark time too. When sorrow weakened our hearts, the animal kingdom connected us in strength. We're all connected in ways we can't imagine. Rowdy and Sara sitting in a tree...K-I-S-S-I-N-G. Death introduced them, furever free.

Centuries-old spiritual battles were playing out through me in this lifetime. I was exhausted. According to multiple skilled shamans, I'd been chased out of town, hunted, hung and killed for my spiritual gifts.

It was time to close the deal on my tiny castle. The sellers tried to sabotage the sale and extort me at closing. Their realtor was drooling, hoping for a much larger commission from surging market prices. The unscrupulous characters in this final showcase showdown were knifing me in the back, charging me for the knife, at a profit, and claiming I stole it.

Family (who'd previously opened loans and credit cards in my name) agreed to send money needed for the purchase, backed out, then reveled in my struggle. A week before closing, I was a panicked shelter pet with a red line through my chart. I was about to lose my home, business headquarters, $10,000 deposit, owe money for damages, and we'd be thrown back into the rent trap—a financial and emotional coffin.

There wasn't even a place to rent for four dogs and a self employed person lacking the means to pay all the upfront costs I'd already spent on the cottage. Without a miracle, the kind where all the saints come marching in, we'd be homeless.

A tsunami rose inside my body. For the first time in my life, everything went BLACK...curtains closed...show's over. Hello darkness, my old frenemy. I took the dogs outside to play ball in the yard we love, and did my best to be a good mom despite the ominous atmosphere.

I asked Spirit for a sign Puppypants Town was safe. I knew the house needed me as much as I needed it. Poetic justice would be served by a survivor of childhood abuse owning this sweet home once lost in a court battle by a child predator. That's the fairy-tale ending this feisty princess fought for, and this house deserved. Otherwise, "Spring" would be lost forever.

It seemed I'd found "where the sidewalk ends" after all. I stared at my half drank glass of water, my empty porch swing rocking, and an open animal communication notebook with ideas for this book that'd go unwritten. If evil triumphed, my visions in hypnosis of the magic kingdom that awaited, and Aslan the Lion's/my dignity and lives being saved also wouldn't come true. All other visions had manifested, but was it all an illusion?

In my last hypnosis session a month before, Jesus dropped in to assure me that while some prayers wouldn't be answered, others would be. WTF (what the finances)! Jesus Christ, was the house mine or not? He also warned I'd have to let go of many people in order to move forward, including the hypnotherapist leading the session!

At the end of hypnosis, I saw "the magic kingdom" representing my cottage castle lit up in celebration. Victory for Puppypants Town and animal friends. How could physical "reality" be so opposite the reality of my subconscious—my gateway to wisdom and prophecies?

Unless my subconscious became a REAL ATM, I was stuck in the worst TO BE CONTINUED episode of my life (worse than breaks between Handmaid's Tale seasons)!

Bitchy Barbie, the greedy realtor, called to sarcastically express condolences: "I'm so sorry, Shannon. It looks like you've lost the house. What a shame...Bless your heart!"

I reached out to the hypnotherapist who had four years of insights into my PTSD and psychic powers. I told her I felt I was dying; I was scared to death. We briefly spoke on the phone where she tried cliches and then judgment. She couldn't empathize with my crippling terror, having just remodeled her million-dollar home, secure with a doting spouse, and nothing, let alone many things, threatening her survival.

My panic escalated and I said I needed to take a nap. I was very tired. PTSD is a bitch, but my subconscious was a worthy opponent. I wished my hypnotherapist invited me in for a session the next day and consulted the notes that documented my own predictions, all of which so far had been right. Instead, she called the cops, sadly not the strip-o-gram kind, as humor (or sex) would've been a much better solution. I needed an advocate, distraction, and nourishment, not armed officers, public humiliation and criminalized trauma.

Cops arrived to find me friendly, but stressed. I invited them in, knowing they were doing a wellness check. I explained the dire situation, and mentioned a scheduled call with an attorney I had in two days to buy more time. Despite being clearly sane, sober and articulate, "Officer Testosteroney" was eager to dominate the not so crazy, crazy lady. The female cop seemed compassionate, but with my defenses down, I fell for the textbook good cop/bad cop routine. Doh!

Unbeknownst to me, the hypnotherapist, knowing my ten year sobriety, told them, "I believe Shannon has taken drugs." Cops failed to apply direly needed critical thinking skills. There was NO EVIDENCE to support that claim. Perhaps a lunatic awaited behind the door with a sign threatening that a wicked witch would drop a house on them if they knocked, but when they POUNDED on my door, I invited them in where they were greeted by friendly dogs, too.

Cops asked me if I'd taken any drugs. Always the overly honest soul, I said, "I take Benadryl for sleep, along with Ashwagandha (a tasty, OTC adrenal support non-THC gummy) and blood pressure medication. (I didn't disclose that I talk to animals, trees, dead people, and a fictional cat who serves cake and gets me laid.)

The officers nodded, took notes and lied, promising they'd take me to a counselor who could review financial options to assist my housing situation. Seemed reasonable, although suspicious. I agreed and filled the dogs' water bowl, kissed them, and turned on nature music, planning to be back in a few hours. I had four days to come up with a f-load of cash. They asked if I was suicidal. I said, "No, but I'm scared to death of losing my home."

We walked outside and they handcuffed me. (Future lovers be forewarned...no handcuffs...trust issues.) Testosteroney wanted to collar a cuckoo bird. It didn't matter what I said, he needed a trophy. I was confused and now more terrified. He saw my shock and muttered, "It's procedure to cuff mental cases for the officer's safety." So, just to be clear, I hadn't taken any drugs, voluntarily let them in, politely answered their questions, explained that my four dogs and I were facing homelessness, and their solution was to ARREST ME. *And I'm the mental case?* Alrighty then.

While driving me to the hospital, Testosteroney confessed, "Oh hey, while you were using the restroom, I saw your uh, business poster, and thought it was so cool, yeah, like I didn't even know that was like a job. So I took a PHOTO of it so I could check it out." WTF! (What The Felony!) Taking photos of my private property for amusement is against the law.

He said "Benadryl" required him to hospitalize me, and delivered me to a doctor who drug tested me based on his badge of lies. (She was under no legal obligation to do this.) She held me for hours against my will, padded her fees, and later billed me $7,000 because she can, despite being uninsured and ironically there because of financial duress!

I tried reasoning with this militant extortionist. But, like cops, she had the privilege to abuse her power, keep her meter running indefinitely, and worsen my health. Testosteroney had written a fraudulent report stating: "Ms. Spring was found surrounded by multiple open bottles of medication." (Don't try to keep up with the WTFs.) I stayed freakishly calm—a Pit-bull being baited to fight, but refusing to feed society's stereotype. They needed me to be a crazy drug addict. Not a sober soul-whisperer challenging their integrity.

Two of the three "medications" are OTC, and blood pressure medicine won't make me the life...or death of any party. All bottles were full, closed, and in my bedroom, which neither cop entered. They also didn't suspect an overdose, or they'd have called in a medical emergency.

Ms. Spring was not, in fact, "found surrounded by open bottles of medication." Ms. Spring was awakened by two bounty hunters pounding on her door like mobsters. She greeted them alertly, then sat in her bear chair petting her calm dogs. The doctor threatened to hold me there indefinitely (cha-ching) unless I "permitted a uniformed cop to escort a neighbor into my house to retrieve your drugs." Perhaps *the doctor* should be drug tested.

Dr. Evil eyeball-tested me, and saw only the eyes of a mystic. I calmly explained she'd already blood tested me, proving my body only contained...BLOOD. The only thing crazy was I wasn't acting crazy given the first responders' first response was to perp-walk me and issue medical procedures against my will. Dr. Evil yelled, "The officer had no reason to lie!" and sent me to the looney bin in another cop car. (Liars don't need reasons, just qualified immunity.) The financial director of the hospital (with the ironic initials S.M.H.) plays The Grinch for their holiday party, and later tried with a vengeance to collect the ransom for their "care."

The mental health staff at "Not The Vacation You'd Hoped For" were way crazier than the patients, who were mostly just sad. Cafeteria staff accused me of having "contraband in my pants." Pretzels, actually. Fucking pretzels. I was saving a free snack for later...a BFD in Crazy Town. I calmly reminded them this was my first stay at their fine establishment, and salty snacks also aren't drugs, so please don't tase me.

I know my friend DJ, who passed from suicide a month later, would've sent me a bouquet of chocolate pretzels addressed to "June Spring" with a card: "Nolite te Bastardes." (Don't let the bastards grind you down. *Handmaid's Tale* wisdom.)

"WAKE UP NOW!" staff screamed after we slept under fluorescent lights on rock hard cots surrounded by miserable strangers. Being an empath made this particularly torturous. The one actual crazy girl spit on me, just as Aslan had been spit on when he was chained down and shaved before being murdered by a gang of jealous minions. So, thanks to her, my life stayed on storyline. I owe her some pretzels.

It was a prison labeled a mental health treatment center, accredited by hell. Back then it was governed by a former Chief of Police, a suspicious incentive for a wannabe like Testosteroney to deliver a trophy like me. I stayed cleverly calm knowing the shrink, who held everyone's freedom, could reason anyone facing homelessness with four dogs with now just two days left to save her home would naturally be STRESSED, not crazy, or criminal. The shrink diagnosed me as reasonable and released me back into the wild world.

I had no ride, a dead phone, and no wallet. Staff's apathy wasn't surprising, given they'd never even offered a smile or a listening ear. I walked down the city street and vowed to avenge myself by returning genuinely joyful and prosperous. I knew I would be a future speaker and trainer there and deliver justice with humor and hope. My mended *Maleficent*-like wings would earn me "Most Likely to Have the Last Laugh."

Luckily, a fellow medium (who'd once spent the night in a looney bin herself for panic disorder) retrieved my dogs, and they had fun. My boys knew I was okay and a miracle was underway. My medium friend normalized my pain which (take note, cops, docs) is VERY helpful. If you too experience normal human emotions, stash pretzels in your pants now, and watch videos on how to slip out of handcuffs.

My aptly named friend, Shepheard, made me laugh when I called from the clink. He acted like a true medicine man and treated my soul with his heart. No judgment, just laughter, love, and a humble request that I keep the faith. He'd been making calls on my behalf trying to get me a loan. A hugs, not drugs, type of guy.

This final battle was bigger than my tiny house. It was about living securely to tell animals' stories for the rest of my life, speaking their truths. Reclaiming their dignity and mine. Luckily, my visions had been right, and the animals who loved me and needed me to triumph had been busy protecting our home. While praying for signs of mercy and victory, an ENDANGERED BALD EAGLE flew up to my living room window.

This majestic eagle, fighting his own battle for survival, observed me in my nest, and looked me straight in my own eagle eyes emanating freedom, leadership, strength, and success. A twist on my childhood story, good birds have the power to fly too. The eagle introduced himself as "Barry White," pure LIGHT, the wind beneath my human wings.

I was stunned by his focus on me, and in awe of his massive "Size matters" wings. He gazed at me with such intensity; baby eaglet eggs formed from eye contact alone. Barry flew up to my roof after piercing me with love, then flew off to be free—how I aspire to be.

He had wrapped his wings around our house, a ceremonial gesture, a flying fuck. My dogs and I were safe under his watch. Barry White's showmanship was as smooth as his human namesake's voice. The next day, I stood in my yard, reliving the crystalized image of Barry's wise eyes. No miracle had occurred, and the closing date was closing in.

Again, I asked Spirit for a sign (immediate responses happen, but, more often I've been asked to be patient). This one was FAST!

Soaring in all his glory was Barry White, the real commander of the Space Force. He flew shockingly low diagonally over me, like a Navy's Blue Angels pilot performing a stunt. I stood in awesome gratitude.

Knowing it's both the animal that's significant, and the direction they cross your path that matters, I wondered aloud, "What does it mean when an eagle flies diagonal? What if he flew straight over me? Would that confirm all had been straightened out?" Like the triple rainbow, and laughing trees who'd heard my musings and wishes, Barry circled back and flew in a straight line directly over me! WTF (Wing The Freedom)!

A divine, magical messenger signaled my freedom. I was ecstatic by the magic, but he hadn't dropped cash from the sky. My bionic heart was hopeful, and anxious.

There's an epic scene in *The Lion, The Witch and The Wardrobe* where after the White Witch humiliates Aslan by chaining him down and shaving off his glorious mane, evil creatures spit upon him and he dies. The Witch celebrates Aslan's humiliation, and her victory over the kingdom of Narnia. BUT, what the witch didn't know was that a prophecy written on stone tablets long ago (a 5th grade turtle story in my case) decreed that any noble beast who died for his cause would be resurrected for all eternity. Perceived defeat was the illusion. The reality was Spring would win and winter would end. Animals and I would be free again. The sellers' extortion greed backfired and bought my attorney a time window, allowing human saints to come marching in. Simone, an animal lover on the other side of the world, generously wired the needed funds, and my mentor and animal hero, Maia, helped coordinate details.

They spoke to me in a way only angels can—to my soul, with only love. No judgment or cliches. The human equivalent of chocolate-covered pretzels. Together they protected my dignity, as Narnia characters once did for Aslan, praying by his slain body. Their compassion ended winter and let Spring bloom. My dogs and I won this final battle, the house, and our Narnia crowns.

Their divine generosity created a ripple effect that'll live on around the world through my work. A child's prophecy about a turtle foretold this story long ago. Each battle helped me grow up to be a lion, just like the one in my favorite book. A not so fictional tale of tails.

When just one person (including yourself) affirms your right to be free of harm, whatever your species, your freedom song is sung. Birds around the world will rise up to carry your tune to just the right angels, here or beyond. I had rescued myself and fought as bravely as I could, building my own shell out of what once imprisoned me, but this battle required a team.

Spirit sent fellow animal heroes to assist. It's been Light vs Dark since the beginning of time. Thank you to those who helped ensure my fairy tale's ending was sublime. Only *Alice in Wonderland's* Mad Hatter correctly diagnosed me as *Alice*. *"You,"* he said, *"are a terribly real thing in a terribly false world, and that, I believe, is why you are in so much pain."* That pain transformed in time.

Three years later, my dream of being an Avenger came true. Whereas my name was once scrawled on a recovery center's patient board as "Shannon S" (for privacy), my name would now be spelled out as an honored guest. My ironic "qualifications"—"former addict/mental case" are assets! I'm a peer to laugh and learn with—a relatable comedian having the last laugh. Imagine if my background check showed only an outstanding parking ticket...how embarrassing!

My scars are badges of courage. I once tried to take my own life because drugs couldn't kill my pain, but now I'm sober...and happy—those are inspiring credentials, too. Many wealthy board members raising funds for recovery don't understand how to share light with suffering souls. Fancy pamphlets with out-of-touch people don't create wellness. Status and money don't buy character, compassion, or sobriety.

Recovery happens when we treat ourselves the way we wish others would. My *Just Humor Me*™ LAUGHTER ON TAP KEYNOTE and HAHA RETREATS (Humor and Healing Adventures) are healing for staff and patients. An addict's mind is fierce and fragile, and the path to wellness lies in focusing on strengths, peace, and play. Addiction and depression don't discriminate. If you are fortunate to be spared, be grateful, not judgmental. Be the light that helps someone find their way home to themself. I became a lion roaring of freedom from addiction and depression. Transparent- nothing to hide. Fearless—like a bird who hitches a ride on an alligator's back. That bird might be crazy, but she can teach others how to float and how to FLY while the gator spares her life. Fearless joy- kryptonite to addictions. I am sharing my light, and sometimes, my pretzels.

12

JUST JACK: A VERY GOOD BOY

Humans will always tell you the story. Dogs can only tell you the truth.
Cesar Millan

Animals tell you the truth in their eyes. Have the courage to let them tell you about yourself.
Shannon Spring

Remember when I said keep up with the dogs, but not the boyfriends? Did you notice before that wild ride that a fourth dog snuck in without formal introduction? That's "Just Jack." He's the humility to the Mayor's bravado. Jack is a handsome wolf-looking mutt who landed at a rural shelter in Brooksville, FL.

The first time I saw Jack's sweet, humble face and compassionate brown eyes on a rescue post, I knew I needed to be his mom. He's much like his big Golden sister, "Love Yourself" Stormy in Heaven, who asked for nothing, but gave everything to anyone who'd pet her. Before we met, I asked Jack if he'd like a new name, and he joked, "No, I'm 'JUST JACK!'" (referencing flamboyant Jack McFarland from the TV show *Will and Grace*, the total opposite of his personality).

Jack Rabbit Spring makes me laugh, my favorite thing. He has a deep bark and a sensitive soul. His messages are soft, gentle, undemanding. Adopting senior pets will heal your heart with wisdom and a deep friendship centered on love and acceptance. An instant smile forms as I type how senior pets make me feel. I surrender to them completely and love them the same as if I'd known them my whole life. Jack is my heart on paws.

I brought the Mayor as our pack ambassador to meet Jack. Most rescues require a meet and greet to make sure all goes smoothly. We drove to adopt him on a stormy day, got lost and my phone died. My psychic senses embarrassingly fail as a back-up GPS. Eventually, we made our way there, frazzled, but determined. I saw Jack's beautiful face smiling across the parking lot. "It's ok, Shannon. It's ok. You're here." Getting lost freaks me out. Finding Jack made me feel like I was forgiven for every mistake I had ever made.

I calmed myself from the stressful drive, then walked over to meet Jack with his foster parents. Jack was already teaching me to be more like him, in a calm state, whatever's happening. His kind foster parents said he was a good boy and wasn't allowed on their furniture. Jack wasn't worried about their "no dogs on furniture rule," as he'd soon be replacing the guy I was dating and claiming his spot on my bed. I signed his adoption papers and Jack smiled, sightseeing out the windows on the long ride home.

Just a month before, I was walking my pups when I poked my nose out like a wolf sniffing fresh meat. I turned my head side to side, inhaled a big sniff and announced, "Boys, my next man is within sniffing distance. He's so close I can smell him!" The dogs enthusiastically wagged their tails and we walked on. Five days later, we met Jim just a block from where I'd sniffed him out. He looked like a fellow wolf with playful intent, and we began dating.

Sex was intoxicating, but the excitement fizzled, given he was conversationally limited outside the bedroom. Jim was like a broken Duo Lingo app stuck on PORN translation, Jim's native tongue. Presuming himself the alpha pack member, Jim complained, "You have too many dogs...get 'em off the bed." I yapped back, "Careful what you wish for. There's a lotta guys who'd trade places with you in a heartbeat." My dogs cheered, "Good one, Mom!"

Jack used his long legs to push tall Jim into being curled up like a newborn kitten. Jim was naked, afraid, and green with envy of my dogs' statuses.

In addition to not being "dog dad" material, he once criticized me for being "too confident." Skunks everywhere knew I'd smelled this guy before! He was used to women submitting and not prepared for my Cheshire Cat's grinning reply. "You know, Jim...it's going to be a lot easier for you to learn to like yourself more, rather than try to get me to like myself less." He was speechless. I'd offered an invitation, not an argument. My "DOGS OVER DUDES" mandate replaced Jim with Jack, a confident gentleman who encouraged me to believe in myself.

Jack snores like a jet engine, a sound so strangely soothing that recordings should play worldwide at spas for relaxation—"Just Jack's Snoozey-Tunes." He only speaks when he needs me, or when it's time to go for a WALK and acts like a puppy. I was thrilled when he finally barked three weeks after adoption, speaking up in this tiny house of big personalities.

Jack's a model citizen making his brothers look like hellions (no offense, Hellion). Jack values kindness over winning—perpetually pleasant even through Puppypants' power trips. As Bed Bouncer, Puppypants blocks entry and checks Jack's ID every single time he climbs the bed stairs. Jack smiles and forgives the Mayor's shenanigans. Jack loves him and knows they're all VIPs in my club. He's a perfect role model to let things roll off my back...and my plate.

Imagine how shelter pets feel when random strangers stand by their cage, judging if their life is worth saving. In most cases, pets can't choose their family. Some wait years to find love, some are only given days before death. They need time to decompress, learn, heal and thrive. Empathy, not expectations, and then reasonable goals. It's our job to protect them, although many animals choose and excel at protecting us physically and emotionally. Jack took on the role of Papa Bear. I felt safe; his heart was my home.

Jack knew he wasn't in high demand as far as shelter pets go, and wore that humble look on his face. Seniors like Jack have lowered expectations, but I encouraged him to raise his. Seniors deserve a baby shower welcoming them home. I let Jack know it's now his home, his yard, his things. He is family and it's ok to make mistakes. I assured him only Puppypants is expected to wear matching mother-son dresses, and he melted when I adorned him with his first bowtie. Jack is perfect, and I blush at how much I love him.

Animals can lead us to discover beautiful hidden treasures within ourselves and our world. They share their wisdom when playing, walking or snoozing. As family and friends, we love and guide each other, and understand what makes everyone feel safe and happy.

Don't rely on telepathic communication to protect them. It's great to send and receive love and information this way, but just like with human kids, create a safe space and be the responsible one. Remember, that while their "higher selves," aka spirits, might know chocolate and chasing cars are bad for them, taste buds and adventure can override good judgment.

Pay attention to what and who they trust or resist. Is a person, food or medicine toxic? Or are they acting stubborn? Pay attention to their wisdom before labeling them difficult. If they are being difficult, ask why, and see what you learn about yourself in the process. Be keenly observant of your animals' behavior. Calmly listen and receive their messages. Be willing to see them for who they are, not who you need them to be.

View situations from THEIR perspectives with compassion. Be willing to compromise. If you don't want them on your favorite chair, buy them their own chair and include them in the process. Maybe you can teach each other new tricks and a new way of being. Never force an animal to be your trophy in any way. Love should always be the reason for bringing an animal into your life. Anything else they bring is a bonus.

When interviewing a dog sitter, my dogs acted like rowdy frat boys. While they are playful, they do settle down, but not with her. They were screaming, "Noo!" through their behavior. It allowed me to see she wasn't playful or a leader. She confessed she only liked small dogs! Other animals might withdraw when uncomfortable. Studying animal body language, knowing your own pet's idiosyncrasies, learning to trust your gut, and honoring their needs, emotions and experiences are essential to being a great pet guardian.

Be sensitive to, but not rewarding of their fears. Don't praise panic or dismiss fears as "being silly." Maybe the groomer/vet/trainer is hurting them (intentionally or not). Not responding to a command isn't necessarily "being difficult." Be scrupulously honest about what your role is in any situation before judging them. Are you communicating clearly and consistently with leadership, not aggression? Is it rewarding or punishing for them to obey?

Many people project their issues or nonsensical theories onto animals that don't accurately reflect the animals' experience. Generalizing that your cat hates kids, and not just the brat who pulls her tail, is an example. Or, believing your cat hates walks or playing when it's an ill-fitting harness, or you're too rough when playing with them. Rescue pets are often mislabeled by staff or owners who misunderstand animals' behavior, emotions and intentions. People issues are most often the cause of pet issues. If Puppypants ever asks if he looks fat in his invisible pants, that's on me!

It's never funny to cause your pet frustration, or jeopardize their physical or emotional safety, like we see on social media. Animals need love, not Likes. Controlling through fear, or training a pet's personality out of them, is abuse, not friendship. An animal's personality and preferences should be honored, not fixed—assuming they're not endangering themselves or others.

Not every animal wants friends, or to hike, swim, or perform in competitions. Some crave all of those things. Ask what you can do for them, not how they can serve you. Pets LOVE to train us to be our best selves, and hopefully we let them. Jack trained me to pause more, LISTEN. The way he looks at me earned me my PHD-og.

Jack was 12 years old when he adopted me. I never let anyone call my dogs old. Usually the first thing people ask upon meeting pets is, "How old are they?" annoyingly followed by, "Oh, he's such an old man". Luckily, I carry a one-size-fits-all human muzzle to silence people who can't think of anything creative to say. Why draw attention to how limited our time is together?

Instead, saying, "Beautiful family!" creates wellness for everyone, including the stranger. Jack taught me to stay calm with whomever is annoying me. He possesses an inner peace even Buddha would bottle up and bootleg.

While speaking with Maggie, a senior Labrador at a pet fair, a passerby interrupted our conversation to pet her. "OH YOU'RE SUCH AN OLD GIRL. MY WHAT AN OLD LADY YOU ARE!" Before I could roll my eyes, Maggie retorted, "You ain't such a spring chicken yourself, lady!" I repeated Maggie's rascally retort exactly as she'd spoken it—a teaching moment for everyone.

The woman chuckled, realizing the dog had a point. I kindly explained how animals don't like being called old either. So, the old lady (see what I did there) complimented Maggie's shiny coat. Maggie said "Thank you," through me, and the woman beamed. Kindness is age defying.

Throughout the reading, Maggie's mom, Nancy, commented how all the messages "sounded like Maggie's personality, things she'd say," and confirmed facts about their life together. But, how could I "prove" Maggie's spring-chicken quip? What if I'm saying whatever I want with the pet as my ruse? The delivery of the message matters as much as the words. Maggie wanted to draw boundaries and enlighten, not hurt the unintentionally rude stranger.

All of us had a hearty laugh when Nancy showed us a picture of the Easter gift her husband bought her yesterday—a "Spring Chicken" sweatshirt! Maggie knew of the silly gift and used it to cleverly communicate her annoyance. Animals have unique humor styles that will resonate with their people, but still be the animals' own voices. They can pick up colloquialisms, ideas, or any knowledge, simply being in tune with life and downloading universal wisdom the way I download messages "out of thin air."

While I'm the creator of Peppy Penelope's cheers and zingers, I'm the messenger, not the creator for animals. Each session is special and evidence based from the animals' lives with their people that I have no way of knowing unless it came from the animals. (Yaaaay... evidence!) I can't recall a time an animal's or spirit's joke landed flat. I channel their personas. No one wants a hack wrecking their joke.

According to Nancy, Maggie seemed very sad and often hid when people visited. First, I validate an animal's feelings, then help their people understand the issue. Telepathic communication happens fast—questions and thoughts are exchanged, answered, and understood simultaneously.

Nancy experienced a tearful awakening when I shared Maggie's perspective: "I feel so unpretty. Everyone's always fawning over the puppies, and Mom's prized breeder dogs (aka The Bitches)." Maggie was terrified of being chosen to breed because she didn't want to lose her puppies to strangers or lose her status as mom's baby. She showed Nancy crying every time a puppy left with a customer.

Adding insult to injury, Maggie felt insecure and heartbroken, telling me she constantly heard Nancy complain: "Maggie's looks aren't the best" whenever someone asked why she didn't breed her. Nancy burst into tears admitting, "OMG...I didn't know she understood my feelings about her looks. I always say she's not pretty enough to breed! And she always sees me cry when I sell the puppies!"

While pets don't understand language the way humans do, they experience the emotions and images projected from our hearts and minds. Our thoughts can heal, humor or hurt them. (Don't mistake

Maggie wanting to be called beautiful with wanting to be bred.) Many people obsessed with an animal's looks are insecure about their own. Maggie's and her mom's low self-esteem resulted in mutual erratic emotions and behavior.

Maggie didn't want to be bred, and yet "the bitches" received all of Nancy's attention and praise. Nancy confessed how her mom also made her feel unattractive. Generational wounds can be passed onto pets too! Animals are great problem solvers, and don't stay stuck in self-pity or blame. They want change.

Maggie shared, "Animals love their people so much, we'd do anything for them. We need to know they'd do anything for us." Maggie suggested Nancy choose an activity that strengthened their bond and brought them both joy. Nancy smiled, hopefully. "Would Maggie like to start joining me at the senior center?" Maggie immediately wagged and barked, "YES!" in human speak. Maggie wanted a purpose, and asked Nancy to brush her, with each stroke appreciating her beauty inside and out.

While many animals are loving moms, it isn't because they craved being mothers. That's human projection. Animals naturally mate if they're in season, not because they dream about motherhood, or fantasize about gender reveal parties. Watching animals nurture their young is best done naturally. A mom's love and devotion is unmistakable across species, as are the challenges of abandonment and the power of a community becoming a family of caretakers.

Animals' bodily responses during telepathic communication vary from overtly reacting (wagging, dancing, purring) to what's being discussed to passively absorbing and considering their options (soaking in a belly rub while you do the emotional heavy lifting). They might respond with sound, movement, and facial expressions in approving, rejecting, empathic, or comical ways, or they'll listen and respond telepathically. I'm speaking with their soul.

Not all animals exhibit a flashy physical reaction like Fast Eddie the fish did to confirm I understood him and he liked my plan.

Animals often share the same message a few different ways for clarity. It's their version of "Can you hear me now?" Most animals are great examples of assertive, non aggressive communicators. Aggression (apart from a chemical imbalance or pain) is a result of being disrespected and ignored.

There are no stupid animals. They might be with the wrong person or situation, but animal intelligence is far greater than human ego often permits seeing. Not doing what you want doesn't make them stupid. Understanding who they are, what motivates them, and making learning fun creates a smart team. Animals are smart enough to sabotage a bad situation and try to secure their freedom and even risk death. Horses are often bought and sold by people who see dollar signs, not intelligent creatures, worthy of respect.

Horses can tell you if they want to race, retire, be a companion, or anything else you'd like to know to successfully kick off your relationship. Listen now so you're not kicking yourself or getting kicked later at both of your expense. Lead with your heart, not your ego or wallet. After hearing me speak on animal communication, a woman ran up to me and said, "I can't wait to give you my money. You're incredible! I need you to help my dogs." I sensed she had another animal in urgent need of my help.

The woman laughed and commented she owned an angry horse at a stable giving rides who wasn't really part of the family. "She's never been the same since we sewed up her vagina." I couldn't process her statement and asked why anyone would sew a horse's vagina. "It's common in the horse industry to increase racing speed." The horror of this horse's trauma showed on my face.

What veterinarians are engaging in this abuse? The same who dock tails, ears and declaw? Altering animals for cosmetic purposes, convenience or profit is cruelty. So is buying and trading them across countries with no thought as to the horses' needs and desires.

I suggested she include the horse in the family reading to see how we could assist her. She never hired me. It was heartbreaking to hear the horse cry for my help, but be unable to assist. Stripping a free-spirited beast of her dignity led to severe emotional and medical problems, and the person further assaulted her horse, silencing her from speaking through me to heal the wounds. The woman was afraid of having to feel even a second of shame for the lifetime of pain she'd caused.

Like Anna Maria Island fish, horses worldwide are exploited by a cruel industry. Influence whomever you can to see animals as equally worthy of freedom and joy. Their worth is inherent, independent of human standards. Imagine a group of judges holding up scorecards to sunrises and sunsets, ranking their beauty and performance. Small minds judging Creation. There's not a derby hat big enough to shield the fragile human ego from its blinding darkness.

Let horses race, ride or lounge on their own. Bet on who can win their hearts by asking nothing from them. Some would choose to compete, to carry us or run wild, and both species would be in harmony honoring souls, not filling human holes. The more people view themselves as inherently worthy, the less they subject animals and nature to humiliation and tragedy.

Animals draw boundaries for their peace and protection, and people ignore the signs. In general, cats and dogs don't bite when a growl or hiss suffices. The depth of animals' feelings and awareness goes well past primal emotions and instincts. Like an invisible crystal ball built into their DNA, they're instinctual *and* soulful creatures.

People broadcast emotions and energy received by animals and people alike. Animals read our faces and body language like other humans do, but they understand things more deeply, and don't suffer from analyzing, ignoring or combatting what they receive. People see the iced cake (public persona); animals see the ingredients (inner child and authentic self). Humans make things hard. Animals are easy.

Bears won't stop drinking a beer because "the bottle is gay."

They'll drink and roar "Cheers, honey!" Animals have too much common sense to act like people.

Science explains biological communication, like brains signaling bodies, echolocation, sonar, and avian flight patterns. Animal Communication concepts are beautifully illustrated in the movie *E.T.*, about an alien and a boy who understand each other. The boy didn't want to change or experiment on the alien, just know, love and help him. He turned on his heart-light and befriended a creature of another species. (Bring candy, and don't trust the government are other powerful takeaways!)

Animals don't question quantum physics or their innate abilities. They listen with all their senses, receive our thoughts and emotions, and send information out for us to receive. Pets are a lot like an "Elf on the Shelf" witnessing our lives and observing our joy and madness—experts on what makes us tick or ticked off.

A kitten named Smitten told me there's a book on her dad's shelf with a lizard in it that was going to help him ace a big interview. My client confirmed he owns the book and it has a tasseled lizard bookmark that Smitten kept swatting. While Smitten couldn't straighten dad's tie, she energetically supported him while preparing for, and during, the interview.

She knew her dad was a serious cat, and that his future employer needed to see his softer side. The bookmark mysteriously made it into his briefcase, prompting him to relax and mention he'd rescued a cat. The employer was a feline fanatic and sharing Smitten's sweet story landed him the job!

I've heard people use happy voices to call their pets fat or stupid while pets wag their tails. Pets might tolerate name calling, but it isn't healthy for either of you to speak negatively. Words carry energy. Besides, fat pets usually have parents who need exercise.

Some people or animals are indifferent to names or teasing, but most prefer praise and positivity. Ida lived in the apartment across from me, and everyday I'd hear her call Cesar old, and he'd hobble along accordingly. But Cesar came alive and played when he saw

Kermit and Puppypants. One day, I asked Ida to try an experiment. For two weeks she'd promise to call Cesar young, healthy, handsome and strong. She'd only speak of wellness and not call herself or him old.

Over the course of two weeks, both began to look noticeably happier and healthier. Cesar had an unmistakable spring in his step, and Ida had a new rosy glow. She knocked on my door looking like she'd won the lotto exclaiming, "You were right. I can't believe how puppyish he's become! We're having so much fun!" Everyone prefers compliments to criticism, and it's more fun to give and receive kindness. It's never too late to have a happy puppyhood.

A vet found Grover as a stray, with pounds of severely matted fur, and nicknamed him "Matt." (Insert my rolling eyeballs.) Luckily, they also loved on him, restored his dignity, and posted for an adopter to spare him shelter life. A few families were interested, but Grover chose me. Grover is wide-eyed and goofy with wild curly white fur. He's sensitive to shame from severe neglect and often lives in his own world, but is happy with his family, tennis balls and a *Lambchop* doll nearby.

Initially, Grover felt inferior to his two confident brothers and marked everything—peeing mostly on their monogrammed beds. His message: "Who the fluff do you think you are?" (A joyful, but insecure little dude.) When people shame and yell, it creates more fear. I gently spoke with Grover about this unwanted behavior, and how he's very special and his past doesn't define his worth. (Like mother, like son.)

I reassured Grover he's a mighty little dude, he'd find his place in the pack and had nothing to prove. About a week later, he relaxed. Sometimes when we just show forgiveness, animals feel safe and behavior improves. Sometimes they're testing to see how much they really matter to us. Other situations are multifaceted and require more understanding, patience, time, training, treats and personal growth.

Don't expect yourself or animals to be perfect. Celebrate small victories and laugh when you can. See if you and your furry buddy can partner on learning to work through bad habits together, and replace them with healthy ones. Whenever Grover felt uneasy and lifted his leg to pee graffiti, I'd make a wacky disapproving sound (like when someone reaches for my fries). He'd lower his leg, I'd praise him, and we'd play.

He needed a win and positive experiences. His sunny PUPPY POWER personality made him a natural at the kids' pet care camps we led. Grover thrived as a canine "Coach Ted Lasso". When I bestowed him the title "Coach," he developed a magnificent muttitide when he led our pack walks. His wild smile melts my heart, while his loud yapping drives me bonkers, but is the first thing I miss when he's not feeling well.

Grover's voice is his whistle: LET'S PLAY! Maybe animals don't need to always calm down. Maybe our inner Peppy Penelopes can cheer louder with more team spirit too. I say YES to as many fluffy invitations to play as I can.

We must speak kindly to ourselves along with our pets. Grover lovingly gazed at me, when I criticized myself. He howled in pain and sounded like someone stabbed him in the heart. Someone did…me. By bullying myself, I wounded him. I was hurting his best friend, and I apologized to both of us. Coach Super Grover beams now when I do Zumba. "Look how strong, healthy and beautiful I am! Thanks, Coach Grover!" Grover squeaks his toys and I feel great making him proud.

Most things animals need and want from us are cheap, easy or free. Focus on mutual wellness, choose loving thoughts and actions, and get busy being more animal and less human. I don't measure success anymore by society's definition of what my life should look like. Quality of life is how much my pets and I smile, and success is how many animals call me their friend.

My client, Beth, asked me to stop her dog Chip from peeing inside the house. Beth is a perfectionist obsessed with maintaining a "model home," and "hates fur" (somehow her own long hair isn't offensive, just dog fur). Chip was excited to talk and stop being in trouble all of the time. He felt shame over peeing inside, but was overwhelmed. The household energy was a pressure cooker. Beth needed to literally stop "pissing him off!" Neither could relax.

I asked the naturally happy go lucky Chip what it's like living there, and he said, "Everything's off limits. I can't go anywhere or do anything. I'm lonely and nervous." Beth denied his reality. "Well, that's not true. Chip has toys and plenty of space. And he gets attention, so I don't know what that's about."

I asked Beth, "Where can Chip run and play?" Warden Beth replied, "Well he can't be in the living room; we just put new floors down. He can't go in the bedrooms because of carpet; he can't go here or there because of blah, blah, blah." I ventured, "So, basically, everything's off limits, like Chip said?" Beth blushed, feeling Chip's hurt feelings for the first time. There's no law you have to have a pet. Paw printed homes are a privilege. Control freaks deny themselves the joy a pet brings.

Chip was treated like a problem (for being furry), then developed one—indoor peeing. Unwanted behavior does not make an animal bad. In fairness, Chip wasn't asking to have his buddies over to smoke cigars and play billiards. He just wanted to feel he was really family, not an unwelcome houseguest. I needed to help Chip, and shoot Beth like an 8 ball into the corner pocket for a time-out.

I felt an overwhelming urge to jump in their pool as we talked about her many grievances with Chip. She then confessed the pool was off limits to Chip. No wonder I was dying to swim! I was mentally going off the deep end, feeling his restlessness excluded from family fun. Swimming is also great exercise, and both he and Beth could've been water ballet besties.

I felt Beth's emptiness inside. Life spent only in the emotional shallow end or deep end is way out of balance. Her OCD was drowning their joy. We weren't talking about letting Chip use her shower, loofah, or personal massager, just to enjoy a nice doggy paddle in the pool. And, in fairness, dogs are the least likely to pee in the pool!

While I can't say it's emotionally abusive to ban your dog from your pool, it does raise my furry eyebrows. Without play and laughter, what's the point? People repeat and project self-deprivation and overindulgence onto their pets, creating an emotionally unstable environment. "I hate seeing fur!" Beth whined. I added, "You know what's worse? Not seeing fur."

A clean house is enjoyable and healthy, but a sterile house void of fun, fur, and slobber is sad. Count your furry blessings and muzzle your mental fur balls. People pay the mortgage, but pets make a house a home. Beth would faint just looking at my furry floors. Only serial killers have sterile homes (and my sister.) Furry floors are a small price to pay for UNCONDITIONAL LOVE (and keeping serial killers out).

Chip suggested Beth treat her OCD by learning vulnerability through art therapy. Draw pictures of her fears and feelings and have fun with her flaws. I knew this would be a tough sell; Beth crushes feelings into croutons. Chip's dream was to swim in the pool, and for Beth to lighten up. Most animals' dreams are this simple, but people poop on their party. Unstructured goofiness is a lifesaver that sets spirits of all species free. Cannonball your way to freedom.

Before "last resort, go to a pet psychic," Beth had taken Chip for long runs, hired a trainer, and used medications, but nothing worked. Too many pets are medicated for non-medical problems, or their people's subconscious issues, and it was Beth, not Chip, who needed a chill pill. Art and play therapy are all benefits, with no negative side effects like chill pills. Crayons and clay are over the counter!

Animals show me behavioral root causes, likely solutions, and their willingness to change. I followed up on "Chip's issues" a few weeks later. "Has Chip shown progress not peeing inside?" "Nope" was her reply. "Really...*NO* improvement?" I asked in disbelief. While improvements aren't guaranteed (animals have free will too), clients always experience *some* positive, if not many positive, signs of a happier, healthier pet (and self) after our session. Beth insisted, "No...he's exactly the same."

My poker face asked, "Did you do your session homework?" (Chip and I telepathically eye rolled, smelling a lie-whopper cooking.) "Yes," she casually lied. Then Chip tattled his tale. "Mom didn't do *any* of her homework, and yells about my fur being everywhere." This sensitive boy was sorely disappointed. Beth was still an out-of-control-control-freak...an ironic condition.

"Interesting...well, you and Chip better get your stories straight! Chip said you didn't do your homework, and yelled at him." Silence awaited Beth's confession. Beth squeaked, "Chip told you that?" Even though it was she who had betrayed Chip.

"Of course, I said. Animals have an honor code. They protect their people, but won't take the rap for you." Beth admitted, "I was skeptical the ideas would work and felt silly telling my dog my issues and coloring." She let fear of feeling silly sabotage their joy. Animals of all species are powerful healers who understand our issues from a higher perspective, and happily help us heal when we allow it.

Beth was choosing suffering over smiling, and in an obsessive relationship with her vacuum cleaner. It was time to unplug and let fur fly. She agreed to be honest and do her homework, which was play! Within the next two weeks, Chip only had one accident and was enjoying more space to run and play inside while being allowed in the pool on "fun Fridays." It was a start, but why do people think fun has to be a reward and not a right?

Remember, this plan worked for this family; it's not a catchall solution. Don't expect to sip wine and paint... and poof... your pup's now a perfect potty pup and pool guest. Calmer people create calmer pets, but each situation is unique, which is why animals deserve open mic nights. The innate wisdom of animals supersedes human judgment. Don't rule out fun as a fixer. Silliness succeeds where seriousness suffocates. Weird works, and happy people don't have time to waste *not* playing games! Art therapy is a healing mechanism that draws out pain, strength, solutions, and solace. (Our inner child is an extraordinary guide.)

Many people can't accept that animals are fellow souls, capable of deep awareness. How can creatures who eat their own vomit and hump furniture also be highly evolved beings? They wonder the same about us staring at "smart phones" and waxing our genitals. People self-identify as the highest species. Animals put people into perspective—comic material for their "Show and Tell." No trainer, marriage counselor, vet, or psychic can fix you or your pets if you're unwilling to do the work and play. Good-humored, self aware people make better animal friends. Fun creates transformation. "Relax, nothing's under control," is a bittersweet biscuit of truth.

13
A FAIRY PIG MOTHER

Someday you'll be old enough to read Fairy Tales again.
from *The Chronicles of Narnia* by C.S. Lewis

Animals tell and face the truth better than people. Hairball, the cat, was tussling with a cocktail of cantankerousness, and using his newly adopted sibling, Honey, as his scratching post. His desperate mom, Mara, contacted me. "No offense, Shannon. I have a hard time believing in what you do, but I'm desperate and hope you can help."

Hairball was terrorizing Honey, whom he judged guilty just for existing. He was ripping Honey's fur out, causing her to spend her days hiding and peeing everywhere but in the litter box. The shelter was lonely, but at least she'd been safe. At the same time, Hairball was miserable being the aggressor. My heart broke for both cats. Whatever the reason for a person or animal's pain, abusive behavior cannot be tolerated. Both cats deserved help. Human "hairballs" also deserve prison.

I sympathized with Mara's desire for a peaceful home. "I can definitely get answers from both cats on what's causing this and how to heal it, but animals, like people, have free will to either change their behavior or continue to suffer. My role is mediator, detective, guidance counselor, and always, friend."

In an emergency medical case, there's no time for small talk, and I immediately ask point blank questions like, "Did you eat the entire refrigerator or just what's inside?" Fortunately, here I had time to get to know the cats. I can often motivate animals to make healthier choices by showing love and empathy while discussing rewards and consequences for their behavior. I introduced myself to both kitties.

Hairball's energy was initially defensive and suspect of my intrusion into his business. I never make accusations like, "Why are you being aggressive?" I focus on gathering facts and feelings. After validating feelings, and demonstrating I care about them, however terrible their behavior, I address the issue. "The family is concerned for Honey's safety, and states you seem very angry and are physically harming her. Is this true?"

People often make excuses, break eye contact, lie, or blame the victim when confronted. Animals keep it simple with truthful answers and insights. Hairball replied with a slew of angry emojis about the family, but not Honey. I considered offering to trade my sister, Kelly, for his—problem solved. But Honey wasn't the problem and trapping Kelly would be dangerous.

I asked Hairball, "How do you feel about Honey?" Hairball shrugged. She was a toy to him, not even real, because he was blinded by rage and grief. After I shared things that made me angry (people, passwords, carrot cake), Hairball relaxed and opened up. "My family's behavior is unacceptable. They need a time-out!" The two young kids had been responsible for his last two cat best friends' tragedies—death and missing. Flower was hit by a car in front of Hairball after the kids left the door open. Heartbroken, Hairball lost his sweet heart along with his sweetheart.

The family adopted another cat—Leon, who went missing when

the kids left the door open again. Hairball became enraged, but knew he couldn't take his fury out on the people, so Honey became his target. Honey was depressed, anxious, and fragile—exhausted from the unrelenting assaults. Her first wish was to be rehomed as an only cat, so she could just decompress with love. "Hairball is the roommate from hell," she lamented. "The family's nice, but I'm miserable and scared all the time. My life is in danger."

I could relate. My former teenage sibling once threw a glass at my head when I asked her to turn the TV down. Kelly was an aspiring *The Real Housewives* star, way ahead of her time. She was sent to anger management therapy and came home angrier. I had once been Honey, and she needed relief...fast.

I sensed how much Hairball missed and respected Flower, so I called upon her to help him. She was already his angel on duty. "Tell my sweet friend I love him and I'm watching over him. He needs to remember his manners and be a good boy so I can be proud of him. I am displeased with his meanness to Honey." Overhearing this, Hairball stopped in his tracks and turned his head, as if seeing Flower in his rear-view mirror.

Even though animals can access each other anytime, my summoning Flower somehow shocked Hairball out of his dissociative behavior. I saw Flower's face through Hairball's eyes and felt the adoration, love, and devotion in his heart. His energy softened with love and relief and he transformed from angry to remorseful. Hairball had been so mired in grief, he was disconnected from Flower's presence. Like a person with headphones on who can't hear a loved one calling their name, Hairball was so tuned into pain, he couldn't feel her love that surrounded him. I helped him tune into Flower's frequency, the way animals do for me.

Hairball now had motivation to be kind to Honey. Flower's opinion mattered and he felt better. But just because our soul knows we need to do better, it doesn't mean our "human self" will do better. Hairball needed to integrate his enlightened mind with good behavior. When I asked him if he'd be kind to Honey, he showed me a traffic light highlighting yellow. He was being a stinker, but at least an honest one. He didn't greenlight "Yes," or redlight "No." He meowed an auspicious, "MAYBE."

Animals often come up with solutions for their own behavior challenges and could write their own self-help books (I'll write the forward). Hairball suggested that the kids make a two-week behavior chart for him and draw smiley, neutral, or negative faces, depending on whether he's being a good boy, average, or a full-blown cattywampus. They would display his chart on the fridge and review it in two weeks. If Hairball's behavior was still rotten, they would give *Honey* away. Flower rolled her eyes. Honey held her breath.

Mara was grateful for the insights and plan, and agreed to have a serious talk with her kids about pet care, too. We were cautiously optimistic, but even I wasn't prepared for Mara's update two weeks later. I opened my email to a photo of Hairball and Honey, sleeping side by side in the same cat bed—a furry falafel.

Hairball beamed with pride, sensing my joy at his beautiful transformation. He realized hurting an innocent cat made him feel worse, and chose to honor Flower by forgiving the family who stopped being #HUMANHAIRBALLS and improved their behavior. They made kitty playtime a priority, and gave Honey her own kitty castle to enjoy alone time. Flower's spirit glowed peacefully. Miracles happen when hands and paws help a sister or brother in need.

Mara thanked me. "I'm definitely a believer that you can talk with animals. They really listen to you. Our family is so much happier and everyone can be together because of your help. We learned a lot, and the cats are happy."

I had always been a skinny-mini until I got sober, which is a pretty sucky reward for doing something so hard. Chocolate really is life. It's healthy, delicious and cellulite worthy. But I needed a fierce body to match my fierce mind. What better friend to help me lose weight than a real piggy? Benny, the pig, and I met telepathically when his mom Rita was freezing fat off my belly. I was hoping for a quick fix to look fit while still enjoying my sugar fixes.

Weight gain and my inner Elsa wanting to freeze things led me to Benny. My "Go Eat Cake" lifestyle also led a sweet, lonely pig one step closer to tasting freedom! I'm fairly astute at finding the frosting in any bitter situation.

Rita hooked me up to the fat freezers while I watched Netflix and ate a donut. As Rita and I chatted, she mentioned her mother-in-law had a severely neglected pig living in her backyard. He was starving, depressed, and had skin wounds. She claimed he had become aggressive (hungry, lonely, in pain) and she was planning to kill him since she didn't want to pay for his care.

Rita saved Benny's life by caring for and sheltering him in her own backyard. This created a lot of stress as her dog couldn't use the yard, and her husband disliked Benny. Benny wasn't too fond of hubby either and sometimes charged him. Rita was distraught since Benny had nowhere to go and their chaotic situation was unsustainable.

But it was her lucky day! She was freezing/talking to an Animal Communicator—a Fairy Pigmother who'd sprinkle love on this muddy mess. A wave of joy came over me realizing Benny was born the year I tried to exit the world from suicide. My cumulative suffering—the broken road—led me straight to this curly tailed sweet soul whose suffering was about to end. As the fat froze, my mind freeze-framed flashbacks of being bedridden with depression, losing the will to live. How could I've known then that a baby pig would grow up to need a friend just like me?

I realized if I'd never gotten depressed and gained weight from drugs I never needed, I wouldn't currently be at a modern-day fat farm, eating a donut learning about his plight! Had so many wrongs made a right?

Rita was overjoyed I could help. I said hello to Benny, who was gentle, humble, friendly and desperate. He pointed at my donut. "I like your style, Shannon. You're unapologetically you." We both smiled, kid-like kindred spirits. Then Benny pleaded, "HELP! I need outta here. I'm lonely. I don't have any friends. Rita is kind, but terrified of me."

I expressed sympathy, having lived in lousy situations too. Animals get depressed and lose the will to live, too. They can also choose to run away, or manifest behavior or medical issues to escape bad situations. Quality of life over quantity is a most oinked about quest. Benny was head-butting his heartache out on the man who wanted him gone.

I emotionally triaged the situation and gave Rita some ways to keep Benny happier until our scheduled housecall. Benny's first concern: "STOP EATING PEPPERONI PIZZA!" Rita's jaw dropped. "I just ate that last night. Why? Is that bad?" Benny and I gave her a moment to catch up. Horror struck. "OMG...I FEEL SO BAD! I never made the connection."

I observed her wheels spinning. She'd saved his life, given him her backyard, endured marital strife on his behalf, and provided fresh fruits, and now she had to give up pepperoni? But, it's not pepperoni, it's BENNY. Her food has a face and feelings.

While studying at The Institute for Humane Education, I was assigned the book, *WHY WE LOVE DOGS, EAT PIGS AND WEAR*

COWS, by Melanie Joy. The title's inconvenient truth cut to my core, leading to profound self transformation. It's hypocritical to love some animals but harm others.

How can I advocate for kindness while supporting cruelty? How could I eat my friends...and clients? Lesson learned. #PourSomeVeganChocolateOnMe.

When I visited Rita's home, her sweet dog, Beau, greeted me. Beau liked Benny, although they were separated for their safety. Small, black, and wiry, Benny is not the Babealicious poster pig for kids' movies, but he's uniquely beautiful, and stole my heart with his trusting eyes. His loving, desperate expression was like looking in a mirror. I'd prayed similar prayers of being seen and rescued, but had to be my own Fairy Pigmother.

When we're depressed or have shaky self-esteem, it's hard to imagine our wishes will be granted, making us downgrade our desires or ditch our dreams. Benny deserved his perfect pigsty paradise and not this pig pen of pain.

Benny let me pet him and feed him cookies as he confided, "I really want friends...to be loved like someone's baby. I want to run free on a farm and live like storybook animals do with their families—happy, playing. LOVE." Benny had tremendous love to give, but was spending his days alone and bored. His life makeover became my mission.

I assured him I'd reach out to my animal peeps and see who might be looking for a dude just like him. I hadn't a clue how to make this happen, but Spirit did. If all people used their networks to make animals' dreams come true, the world would truly become more fairy tale, less factory farm. Animals ask for such simple things, and ALL of us have something to give that could change their lives. #BeAFairyTailHero.

I remembered an animal advocate in St Petersburg, a pig lover. I only knew she was a piggy lover because she'd once commented on a pig cartoon I'd posted years ago. Animals always know how to make magic happen, and cartoons are often involved because I love them. I messaged Valerie, "Do you know anyone who has a farm in Florida that could take in a sweet pig who's a good boy in a bad situation?"

Within a few hours she replied, "Yes! I do! I have a friend with a big farm and lots of animals who loves pigs." Woohoo! A week later, Rita drove Benny to his new farm family in the country. The before and after photos show a miraculous, energetic transformation. His new mom sent a celebratory update: "Benny fit right in and made fast friends with the cows and goats, and fell in love!" Benny wore sunglasses and a red feather boa, smiling next to his true love.

Loneliness cured and skin healed, Benny was a powerful piggy at play in his new life with a cute pink girlfriend. With love and understanding he moved on, he set sail. His past shame fell off his curly tail. Benny held his snout proudly in the air. His soul, honored...piggy people care.

My factory frozen fat had farmed his future. Healing hearts from depression. Eating sweets for swine...an answered prayer so divine. A fairy-tale ending for his life...and mine.

My conversations with animals provide insights and solutions directly from the horse, pig, cat, dog, bird's (you get the picture) mouth. Whether it's as serious as cancer, or as silly as humping stuffed animals, we'll have a parent/teacher conference with your little angel/stinker to get answers and results that often require change from you as well.

I can't *make* your dog stop chewing the sofa any more than I can force you to go to the gym, but I can save you time, stress and money and spare an animal's needless suffering. Maybe your sofa is really ugly and your future soulmate is at the gym. By destroying the sofa, Rowdy inspires your inner couch potato, helps you get in shape and fall in love. Good boy, Rowdy!

Many animals are unfairly labeled as "jerks, aggressive, psycho, assholes," etc. when they, or their people, are experiencing a serious environmental threat or emotional or medical issue. Other behavioral issues stem from lack of basic training, human irresponsibility, cruelty, a mismatch of temperament or lifestyle, or conflicts with other animals in the house. Successful relationships within and across species come from respect and mutual friendship, not one-sided demands.

Puppies or kittens labeled with behavior issues are most often just acting like babies—a birthright of all babies! Don't wish their precious babyhood away, and don't get a baby animal if you're not prepared to be a new parent. Behavior issues also develop when people get pets to fix inner wounds—a huge burden to place on any kid. Adopt pets to give and receive love in that order.

Many people ask me if their current pets are open to adding a new family pet, and the pets say, "Yes, I'd love a friend...just DON'T get a puppy or kitten!" But people ignore them, multiplying stress and behavior issues. I ran into an exhausted client at the vet's office who was carrying a very sad puppy in a carrier. "Oh Shannon, I wish I'd listened to you and Buttons (her senior dog). You were right. Buttons has been so unhappy since we got the new puppy, and the puppy is so sad. Buttons wants nothing to do with her."

Avoid causing heartbreaks and honor your pets' wishes. Puppies and kittens deserve families who'll match their high energy and playful curiosity. Some older pets are okay with young ones, but most prefer to date within their age group.

I spoke with a desperate woman in India who was considering euthanizing her dog, Ace, for "acting aggressive for no reason." The moment I said hello to Ace, he instantly sent me images of cactus plants. I asked his mom, Sari, if she had any of these prickly phalluses. "Yes, I just bought ten of them. Why? Does he like them?" Um, no...cactus oil is toxic to pets. While he wasn't eating them, Ace noted the plants were causing him to feel sick.

Next, my head started throbbing and I heard the toddler pop song *"Baby Shark"* blaring in my ears. The equivalent of an alarm clock that won't stop beeping until you lose your mind. I asked Sari if she ever played that song, and she laughed, "Yes, we play it all day long! My toddler loves it." Ace sighed. I warned, "You're driving your dog nuts! The song's beats are messing with his brain chemistry."

Animals of all species send me their emotional and physical feelings, and I was starting to feel aggressive too. Like animals, my senses are hypersensitive to lights, alarms, "hold" music, and anything beeping makes me batty. Animals and Shananimals love peaceful nature sounds, like birds, waterfalls, and potato chip bags opening.

Ace felt relief knowing I truly understood how he felt. Sari initially dismissed Ace's concerns until my silence screamed, "It's not funny to dismiss your dog's feelings...and he nearly lost his life." Finally, Ace said, "If you really want to know who the aggressive one is, check the nanny cam. The babysitter's hitting me!"

Aggression is often fear. Poor Ace was breathing in toxins, having his peace of mind obliterated, and getting abused physically. I'd expected Sari to burst an eyeball when she confirmed violence after reviewing the nanny cam. Instead, she commented, "Oh no...that's not good, but I'm not sure I want to fire the nanny. She's great with the baby!"

I wanted to send Sari to Aunt Lydia, the brutal dictator in *The Handmaid's Tale*, who'd shout, "Who's fault is it girls?" Animals around the world would chant, "Her fault...her fault." This situation called for compassion and common sense, two things Sari and Aunt Lydia lacked. Sari needed an empathy lesson the way Aunt Lydia needed a vibrator. Sari didn't even want to toss the plants, and wanted Ace to accommodate them whatever the cost. Finally, she agreed to move the plants outside, put headphones on the toddler, and "talk with the nanny." Animals are naturally more cooperative than most people, but are somehow the ones in cages.

Animals are often compassionate and interested in other animals' welfare, even when they've never met, don't get along, or have to live apart. Animals love more freely than people do, and happily pop into my sessions to offer wisdom or love to other creatures, whatever their species. Energetic connections activated by good intentions.

No matter how many times I tell people it's all a telepathic process, they'll often hold onto their pets like an elephant's tight trunk to make sure Sugarbutt is on camera. Human rules of time, space and structure don't apply to animal communication or mediumship. Telepathy transcends video chat. Love, intention, openness, character and communicators' skills (and no naked family in the background) are essential.

Bart is a dog whose theme song would be "Bad to the Bone," not because he's a bad dog, but because he's one of the most confident, cool, lone wolves around. Independent natured, he still wanted a family, specifically a male veteran with a tough guy exterior and teddy bear insides. Pet and people matchmaking is essential for success, and not always possible given shelter overcrowding and understaffing.

People can have insane demands: don't shed, bark, meow, scratch, poop. (Or Shannon, can you stop talking about animals for 5 minutes?) Some pets fit right into any family and successfully train their humans. Others, like Bart, need an ambassador to handle (with love) a badass recruit with paws.

Bart taught me many things about animals' inner worlds. An animal's soul is deeper than most imagine. In many ways, talking with Bart is like talking with Jesus! Both are pretty hairy, have an answer for everything that makes sense, and bring peace, love, laughter and inspiration.

Bart loved people, but was aggressive to canine comrades. He disliked the company of other dogs so much that he was given his own wing of a shelter. Bart requested his own mailbox to receive all the love letters fans sent, which were plentiful given he'd been featured on the news as a forgotten dog no one wanted. Advocates try to explain how most pets are really good when they get out of their kennel and get out to play a little, and that the same way not all people like each other, animals have preferences too that don't make them bad.

Worldwide, shelters are flooded with discarded animals, acutely aware of their often deadly situation. Being natural empaths, animals feel each other's fear and rejection when not chosen. Watching the cat or dog next to you get all the attention while being judged as too old, big, ugly, or loud is depressing. How do people judge animals by the same things they don't want to be judged by? How do people breed more suffering souls who are literally dying to be loved? The conditional love gene needs to be bred out of humans.

While it's sad to visit shelters, it's way worse living there, so please turn excuses into love stories. There are no perfect people or pets, but there are perfect love stories waiting to be let out to play and give you their hearts. People expect things from animals we'd never ask of ourselves. All things considered, shelter pets manage very well and they deserve recognition. Bart knew publicly praising and acknowledging ANY achievement would increase his adoption chances and those of his shelter mates. Despite not wanting dog friends, Bart offered ways to help the harder-to-adopts, like himself.

Bart's huge heart, combined with clever ideas and determination, were impressive. He and I would play off each other like a team of comedy writing ad execs. He knew being the only dog in a solitary wing, like a hardened criminal, would scare many adopters, but others would relate to his strong energy and independence.

Bart knew achievements don't have to be a BFD. They can be silly too, like "Stole Most Treats" or "Gave Sloppiest Kisses." He requested I ask his shelter advocate to have the staff look for what's right with Bart instead of what's wrong. Donna always put his ideas into action right away. It was refreshing seeing animal communication in action, honoring Bart's ideas to help improve his morale, educate staff and find his new daddy!

His kennel was soon adorned with many awards: "Best Smile," "Most Handsome," "Leadership Potential," "Comedy Champ," etc. Donna and I watched his spirits lighten as Bart took part in his own advocacy. Having his voice heard improved his self-worth and generated even more love for him in the community. Bart's ideas translated into awesome progress working with his trainer, and being an extra good boy on walks.

Formerly misunderstood, and the kind usually picked last for adoption (big, intimidating looking, dark colored mutt misjudged by looks or kennel behavior), he was becoming popular, although he still needed a special breed of human.

Bart sent me an image of a beautiful dog, Venus, with shiny brindle fur who I'd just met at another shelter. They'd never met in person, but Bart asked me to hang his photo in her kennel with a love (not like) letter. (Bart is no average John Tucker.) I agreed to act out the canine version of the song, "Please Mr. Postman," knowing Venus's caretakers would think I was nuts. If I'm making animals happy, the rest is small bones.

How could I prove Bart wanted to romance Venus? I couldn't. I only knew when I connected with his heart, he showed me Venus, my second grade "Show and Tell" love letter, and an opportunity to be a weirdo at another shelter—a shelter whose director judges other shelters who play relaxing music for stressed dogs as "spoiling them."

Imposing machismo on animals is an ironically non-masculine thing to do. Being a human teddy bear for a scared animal is fatherhood at its manliest by sparing, not comparing scars. So, I'll be a fool for love. The best part about being weird is people expect me to do weird stuff.

I delivered Bart's photo, with a heart shaped love note for Venus to feel special, and taped it on the bars. Energetic intentions are powerful, so even if the sign were removed, the love was not. How could a dog at a shelter who doesn't *like* other dogs not only know about a dog he's never met, but also *love* her?

Animals are not limited by arbitrary rules on love, location, or species. They don't talk themselves out of feeling good. Imagine an animal rejecting an adopter for being gay. "I'll stay in this scary shelter for life rather than go home with two dads! And turn off that girly music. It makes me happy." Animals have too much pride to be stupid. They judge character by if they're allowed on your bed, not what you do in your bed.

It's science—everything is energy—rocks, trees, oceans, planets, people, possums, and plants. Most limits to what's possible are only in our minds. Animals shape-shift, astral travel, and experience continuous life in rainbow-colored realms most humans don't believe exist. Imagine how Toto must've felt when Dorothy finally discovered Oz! She needed a tornado, a murder, and magic shoes to see the world isn't black and white. All Toto needed was to be a dog.

Animals know our past and present, and what's in our hearts and minds. Bart could've met Venus while both of their spirits were astral traveling, or through a chance encounter years ago, but in this lifetime, I was their matchmaker. Animals know who's in my energy field and extended furry family, and who they like, dislike or can help, no matter the species, distance, or issue.

Usually an animal will drop into a reading when there's a common denominator or something another animal has that they want or need, such as a specific medicine, toy, or human intervention. There will be a reason they show up in each other's sessions, sometimes to provide comfort and insights. Venus mentored me in medical cases from the first time I met her at her shelter while sitting in the play yard.

I'd recently set the intention to accelerate my gifts in medical intuition. When she happily trotted in, I was unsure why I felt a little afraid of her. Unbeknownst to me, at ten years old, she'd just been returned to the shelter she'd been adopted from as a puppy. She'd killed the other family dog in an unexplainable attack. The devastated family, frozen in fear and grief, needed relief.

When the shelter informed me of the incident, I asked Venus what caused her violence. "Degenerative brain disease," she diagnosed. The only silver lining was Venus's behavior was due to severe illness, not malicious intent. Venus wanted to comfort her family by knowing she'd never intentionally cause harm. Venus lost her family because her brain misfired, not her character. An unwitting assailant with unavoidable accountability.

I relayed Venus's medical message to the shelter director. "That makes perfect sense. Venus is a sweetheart and never did anything wrong until the tragedy. But, we'll never get funds approved for an MRI to confirm a diagnosis or get treatment." Venus and I spoke further and she humbly requested, "Please tell them not to find me another home. I'm a potential danger to animals and not quite sure when I'd snap. Please focus on the many others awaiting families. They can be helped. I know I'll be well cared for and loved here." And she was.

Venus was selfless and practical. I wish humans were more grounded this way. Animals can dream big while seeing things as they are in the present moment. They don't play mind games, pretending with themselves the way people do. Many animals had been at this shelter for years with little exposure beyond a website presence. Venus knew her circumstances weren't going to improve. She might get lucky, but time and resources beyond her medical care and love were better spent on healthy pets without murder raps.

Strategize best case scenarios, but apply common sense and priorities. Venus had remorse and self-compassion over the tragedy. She knew the disease caused the tragedy. She missed her family, but didn't self-punish like people do. Her dog sibling was safe in Spirit watching over her. Like any serious issue, second opinions are always wise. Unfortunately, the shelter director favored an animal reiki volunteer who stated she'd "not sensed any brain issue at all." While this volunteer's opinion didn't disprove what I had heard directly from Venus, it was what the shelter wanted to hear. A tricky situation as neither of us could prove our intuitive senses without medical tests, or another tragedy.

While I was open to being wrong, I wasn't guessing. I'd heard "degenerative brain disease," as if Venus had been her own physician reading her own medical chart. So I felt certain tests would confirm her message. What explanation is there for an unprovoked murder from a dog who loved her sister for ten years? There'd been no instigating circumstance or prior aggression between the two.

I'm always open to all input, a reasonable, responsible approach. But the shelter merely dismissed my communication with Venus, and chided, "Wow, this would be a real feather in your cap if you got this right, wouldn't it?" Horrified, I explained I wasn't in the business of collecting feathers. My mission is always to relay exactly what animals tell me, and exactly what I feel in my own body based on my interactions with them. People often choose what they want to hear and cast shade on unwelcome truthful spotlights.

I want to get things right. Stakes are high. But it's not about me, or the director whose ego and jealousy blocked her receptivity to a scary truth about a sweet dog. I was an easy target to discredit given I'd also told them Venus had a secret dog admirer who sent her a Valentine.

When I was initially petting Venus and "degenerative brain disease" dropped in like a paper airplane from Heaven, there was a reason. Of all the potential messages, why that one? I reached out to Glen, an animal communicator I admired who did excellent medical readings. I don't get jealous, I get inspired. My gifts are always evolving, and I set the goal to be laser-like accurate on medical cases, like Glen. The Animal Kingdom helped me achieve this.

I messaged Glen whom I didn't know well. "Hi, would you please tell me if you sense any medical issues with a dog named Venus?" At this level, we can work with as little info as that. Moments later he replied, "Venus says she has degenerative brain disease." I got chills. I could feel Venus's energy in my conversation with Glen who, unbeknownst to me, was in the hospital with brain cancer. He passed a few months later.

Had I known Glen was hospitalized, I wouldn't have intruded. Just one of many reasons we can't know everything. I know as a dedicated animal friend, he was happy to help, despite facing death. I'll be doing the same with my life until my last breath. I will always help an animal if I can. It's why I'm here. Medical cases of all species poured in after this conversation. I listened, learned and reduced or eliminated suffering.

The shelter director disregarded danger and Venus's wishes, and brought her to adoption events. No further incidents occurred, but in my opinion, it was an irresponsible decision and done in a sad attempt to prove me wrong. Venus passed a few months later from a suspected brain tumor.

Bart stayed busy suggesting fun ways to fundraise, like having staff or visitors compete with him in an ice cream eating contest (dairy free). People would pay to participate and could bet on who'd win. Bart vs. Human! Like Bart, I only wanted men who'd join him in silly, messy faced fun. Neither of us wanted a diva dude. Bart left a creative legacy other shelters could easily duplicate.

We brainstormed an "Adopt a single person & pet" campaign (which years later is finally underway) where single adults pay a donation to have their profiles featured on shelters' social media sites to match with other single pet parents and give exposure to adoptable animals. I'd use my humor and psychic skills to create profiles and people/pet matching. No more swiping or humping and dumping. Just human and furry hearts finding love. There are always creative possibilities to apply fun to challenges, like homeless animals...or women named Shannon with home repair projects needing a handy husband.

With so many people and pets looking for love, uniting paws and hands in local and nationwide campaigns would create many fairy tail endings for cats, dogs, and people, and raise lots of money otherwise wasted on dating apps and bars. Depression and loneliness would plummet, and "kill day" at the shelter could become a wedding or adoption day instead.

Bart did get adopted by a veteran, as he wished, but the man's PTSD worsened, and Bart asked me to let Donna know he needed to come back to the shelter. I'd invited the shelter to contact me on potential adopters to make sure Bart approved, but they didn't want to delay anything—fearful the man might change his mind (as adopters sadly do). Bart went home with a man who dearly loved him, but ultimately couldn't take care of him, and needed rescuing himself.

Luckily, Donna listened to Bart's plea through me to return to the shelter. Bart remained in good spirits, with compassion and forgiveness for the man. Bart was used to managing fearful emotions. Donna escorted Bart to adoption events again, placing awards and ribbons around him, so potential adopters would see all that's right with him, along with his solo dog requirement.

 Honesty is essential in any profile, whatever your species, to make sure it's a lasting match. Lying sets up heartbreak, and good rescuers work hard to set everyone up for success by being forthcoming about an animal's needs, and hoping people do the same. Bart adopted another loving, but healthy veteran and his wife, and they enjoyed many good times together.

Years later, Donna asked me how Bart was doing. I energetically connected with this party boy to see for myself. Immediately, I saw him smile and heard his confident voice answer our question. "Never better!" I saw him zooming around in a race car. Donna added, "Oh, I hope it's true that he's doing well and having fun." Animals often elaborate with images, comments, songs, sensations, etc. to confirm what I've heard them say.

Bart added, "I'm doing great!" We laughed and then Donna surprised me. "Did you know Bart passed away?" No, I didn't. I took a moment to process the bittersweet news.

Death is sad for people, but joyous for the freed Spirit. Donna wasn't trying to trick me; the news had been posted on social media since he'd been a public figure. She just assumed I knew and asked how our friend was doing. Unless someone tells me or an animal visits me, I wouldn't necessarily know they've passed. I'm not tuned into everyone's spirits all the time, nor is that possible. My head would explode with too much information and emotion.

How could a medium be unsure if someone's passed on? It's our job to talk with dead people, so wouldn't only a fraud be confused? If someone was always confused, yes. But spirits are energy and energies are ALIVE, whether or not the body is too.

I adjusted my mind to Bart being in the afterlife. I reflected on his tone of voice and how it felt slightly different when he said, "Never better!" It seemed over the top, with a hint of mischief, but I dismissed it. Only if I suspected he wasn't alive would I ask, "Bart, are you still in your body?" Asking, "Are you alive?" would likely elicit, "Yes," because the spirit is eternal. Only by asking more questions, a Spirit disclosing they've passed, or receiving other afterlife evidence (Venus) would I be certain they're no longer in bodily form.

When I saw Venus was his passenger, I understood he'd passed, and asked how he died. "Car," he whispered. Donna confirmed. "That crazy boy loved chasing cars!" (He didn't earn a ribbon for this.) Bart spared gory details, but added his people felt guilty he'd gotten hit and were heartbroken by his death. He loved them dearly and did his best to comfort them, like most pets do, regardless of whether their people recognize or acknowledge it's really their deceased pet's presence sending messages.

Bart was alive driving race cars with Venus. Good to the bone, together forever. Like Venus, disclose your fine print, forgive yourself and focus on love. Like Bart, never label yourself unwanted, celebrate your achievements, and send love letters to someone who needs a friend. See you in Heaven—extended family of all species. Thank you for teaching me so devotedly.

14
PETS KNOW BEST

Trust your pet over your vet.
Dr. Kermit the Dog Spring

When I was six years old, I contracted spinal meningitis, a life-threatening illness causing an intolerance for light and screaming headaches, the same kind that math class caused me. Two years later I was one room over with appendicitis. My parents, busy with a bridge party, took a "walk it off" approach, until I screamed, "My stomach's exploding!" Off to Paoli Hospital we went.

Prior to surgery, my inner reality show producer appeared when I asked the doctor, "Please make the scar low so when I'm older I can wear bikinis." He laughed nervously, looking at my mom to see if I was serious. She didn't blink...my vanity came from her.

I awoke to see he'd granted my wish, but my joy turned to panic when I asked to see my appendix and the doc laughed, "It's been disposed of...we threw it out." (Spitting out my Jello), "What? Go get it!" I insisted. The appendix belonged to MY body. It was MINE, hazardous waste or not, it was destined for "Show and Tell!" I was too weak to dumpster dive to retrieve it. Nurses kindly assuaged my outrage with candy and toys (effective bribes still to this day). *I wish I could say this doc met my appendix years later in Spirit and apologized to us, but nope.*

My experiences of many serious medical challenges throughout my life and healthcare professionals with kind hearts or cruel intentions offer an extensive arsenal of knowledge for animals to utilize when showing me what they're experiencing. I'll usually see, hear, feel or sense their pain level, what they need to recover, and the competence of their wellness team.

One dog sent me an image of a vet he was obviously afraid of—a dangerous dude. The image was of an actor who often plays the creepy serial killer type. I told his dad and he said, "His vet's a woman."

So I referred back to the dog who locked into the first image he showed. I repeated that the man I described is definitely involved in his dog's care and should be removed. The dad then turned pale. "OMG...that's his radiologist! I never trusted that man. He fits this description." When an image or feeling persists, it's because it's accurate. Play "detective" and act swiftly.

Since a young age, I knew to question authority of all kinds to be educated and empowered, not difficult. Blindly trusting adults and uniforms felt suspect for good reason. Respect and honoring another's dignity should be standard in medical care. Experts shouldn't forget manners, or that a body's owner might know something about it that they don't (animals certainly do). Men can let women speak for their own bodies and people can let animals speak on theirs. A cartoon where a group of dogs are ironically deciding feline healthcare holds much furry wisdom.

My experiences have made me hyper alert and aware of what animals show and tell me they're experiencing. I don't take anything for granted or make assumptions. I recall a client scoffing when I relayed that her cat disliked her food and litter. She contested, "Not possible. It's the best cat food and litter on the market. And I should know, I've been a product inspector for years!"

Ok, fair enough…but…you're not a cat, and your cat is in poor health, stating the food is causing allergies and the litter is causing kidney problems. Let's find out why Mr. Whiskers feels this way. Sometimes animals use a litter box or eat something simply because they need to poop or they're hungry, not because they like it. Although, cats are more likely to hunger and bathroom strike to make a point. "Naughty behavior" in animals is often self-preservation.

Pet, parent, and communicator are in collaboration, not competition. I have to set aside what a doctor, pet product company, or pet parent claims. They can believe something is true, but if an animal disagrees, that's what matters, because that's the truth for their body. The brand, flavor, texture or amount may be okay, but not mix well with the animal's chemistry. Defenses go down when all involved remember we're on the same team…help the animal heal. Corruption exists in both the pet and people "wellness" industries that puts profits over health. We must challenge traditional wisdom and medicine, and be open to answers coming from any source or species. Message over messenger.

In Mr. Whiskers' case, he said the smiling cats on the food and litter packages were drinking corporate Kool-aid. Don't fall for marketing ploys on what's healthy for your pets, or trust a brand just because your vet sells it. Research which companies make the pet food recall list, face facts, and make necessary changes to spare suffering, extend life, and save money. The label "human-grade meat" is alarming because the alternative fed to pets is scary stuff. Imagine "Adult grade food" labels while parents feed poor quality food to kids.

Mr. Whiskers knew his food and litter were costing him his health, and the manufacturers' facts were fiction. His mom's guilt of choosing products that harmed him caused her to be defensive. She finally accepted that guilt wasn't helping either of them and bought an all-natural litter that Mr. Whiskers asked for by name. She began making him fresh meals. Mr. Whiskers's kidney stones vanished, along with his allergies.

A client contacted me because her dog had a severe bacterial infection, and vets couldn't determine the cause or cure. The dog immediately said, "Asbestos!" I said, "You have asbestos in your house." She was certain that was impossible as she'd had her house inspected for asbestos, mold, and other toxins. The dog remained firm and then showed me an image of Johnson's Baby Powder. She said she didn't use this product. The dog was very ill and desperate to heal.

I double-dog dared myself to continue. "You are definitely using a product with asbestos. It feels like it's directly on your body. Please examine everything." And then she said… "OMG…I use a dry baby powder shampoo! Is that what's killing him?" It was, and even weirder, she had a crew cut, so shampoo would be the last thing we'd suspect! The dog smartly named the toxin, and a similar product I knew that contained it, so that I would understand. It takes detective work to identify a nearly bald woman's shampoo is poisoning her pet.

Animals will sometimes ask for name-brand products like, "I want a Bark Box subscription" (themed monthly toys and treats), or request peanut butter or sushi flavor, or reference something they've seen their people eat by describing or naming—hotdog, ice cream, steak sauce. A cat once requested a "kitty cocktail" and demanded to "try the appetizers." The woman worked at a wine club and said they didn't serve appetizers.

Again, the cat insisted they do. "OLIVES, I want the olives!" The woman laughed. She didn't consider these appetizers, and then agreed the kitty could have some occasionally, along with a seafood cocktail to join the guests in happy hour. I'm a shrewd snack broker negotiating on behalf of my clients' munchies. Snacks are serious biz!

A sick cat refused dialysis but requested whipped cream dinners on her final days. Many of my cat clients report liking sweets despite studies saying cats can't taste sweet. My sweet tooth is sharper than tiger fangs, so I do what I can to help!

I experience things through animals' and people's hearts, minds, bodies, and souls. Animals and spirits use things from my own life to communicate what's happening, no matter how personal or how long ago. They're a furry paparazzi with no regard for privacy, and since it's for a good cause, I don't mind. Messages vary based on animals' motivations and goals for their health or relationships with their people. I respect their truths. Animals don't lie.

They may play games while communicating, but they're genuinely reliable. A lost bird asked not to be found once he discovered, like the cartoon bird in the movie, *Rio*, he was born to fly! I spotted him in a tree and he said, "Shh...I'm finally free. Please don't tell them you see me." His family was looking for him and they turned the corner just after he spoke this. The bird hired me first. I didn't say a peep. Freedom prevailed.

What's written on a record by one human often isn't what's been said by another human or animal. A shelter dog named Phoebe made painful eye contact with me, and I felt how invisible she felt. When I asked to take her to the play yard, the staff said, "Ok, but Phoebe only likes to pee and then go right back in her kennel." I sensed this was off, and this was a story they told themselves based on her initial fears that now became "her story," her reality and destiny.

Remove the labels and see her soul with fresh eyes. They fed and let her out, but she was starved of affection and lost inside herself. I've been like her, and it's scary and lonely. A hug, a laugh, and an advocate can retrieve a soul from the spiritual Lost and Found.

Phoebe walked with me into the play yard, and while aloof, she was obviously relieved to not go straight back to her kennel. I asked to bathe her, and the staff said she didn't like baths. So, I pushed the issue and asked when was the last time they bathed her. They paused for a while. "Well, I guess when she first got here...so, about two years ago." WTF!

Not only hadn't they tried another bath after letting her acclimate, but their only source of bathing was a cold hose! Every pet deserves a warm, pampering bath. Phoebe came to life after her bath and they enrolled her in agility class. It all started with the way she looked at me. "See ME, know me, love me, don't overlook me. I'm shy, but I'd like to know myself and see who I can be," was what her eyes said to my heart. Trauma can mask their magic, but magic is always there.

"Girl, let your magic out!" And Phoebe did.

Imagine how often animals are misunderstood. It's why I'm so diligent in getting their exact words and emotions correct. They can feel what's being said about them, but can't speak up. Coma patients, medically disabled patients, animals, and babies are at risk of being even more misunderstood and mistreated. They're aware of what's being said, even if they're unresponsive or prelingual. What if caretakers have the best intentions, but are simply misguided on what's wrong and what can assist in recovery?

I listen to souls and deliver their messages. I'd even do charades or draw cartoons if necessary! Humor used appropriately reduces stress and gets across important information. Like when someone needs a breath or butt mint.

Handing psychic microphones to those unable to speak rectifies the records of what they really need and want. It's vital I keep my filter off of messages as much as possible. Like when I asked myself if I was projecting onto Burp the turtle that he wanted his tank decorated like my house. I need to be self-aware and understand what comes from them, me, or both of us in agreement. Burp and I have the same colorful taste and don't like lettuce!

A mother hired me to do a reading on her intellectually disabled son. He showed wanting to suck on a fire hose. "I'm dying of thirst, Shannon!" His mom was desperate to know and help her nonverbal 16-year-old son. When I described the image her son shared, Mom became angered. "That's because my ex-husband cuts off his access to water at night so he won't wet the bed! I knew he was lying when he told me he didn't do that."

Her son also had a simple request to have a cabinet with his favorite snacks at wheelchair height so he could access them himself. His mom was excited. "Of course! I want him to be as independent as possible, and I'll make certain he's never without water at his dad's house again." I am the eyes, ears, and voice peeping up to protect.

A cat once thanked me for accurately relaying her words: "It's fucking freezing in here!" not "It's a bit chilly." One means stop being a cheapskate and turn the heat on; the other is to turn down the fan, please. Many animals request blankets at vets' offices because it's fluffing freezing, or turn the TV volume down as two rabbits requested. I visited a shelter whose lobby was busy and loud, made even louder by a TV blaring.

The rabbits hailed me like a taxicab when I entered, and I knew to kindly ask the shelter to relocate them to the outdoor space for fresh air and less people peeves. The manager graciously thanked me, and the rabbits were relocated within minutes. Cheap, easy, and free solutions to make a big difference in wellness and respect.

Sadly, I'm unable to set free the many pet shop animals who suffer under fluorescent lights, loud noise, and uneducated "consumers." Rescue, rehabilitate, and release when possible, but don't support creating captivity.

I know a very happy bird who was rescued and truly did need a person when her mom saved her. Sunny found me in my dreams! I woke up recalling a dream about a sassy rainbow-colored bird, and later that day was guided to wander into a somewhat hidden *Alice in Wonderland*-themed cafe. I knew magic was afoot! Grover and I sat down for snacks. The lady next to us commented on his cuteness and I asked if she had pets. She smiled and showed me a photo of the exact pretty bird from my dream, and her last name is BYRD!

She guided me to a networking group that helped me help more pets, and I did a reading for her and Sunny that brought them closer together. Sunny's mom's heart melted with joy at how much she loved and guided her, including brilliant, playful business ideas she chirped during our reading. We were both impressed. Like many pet parents, Mom was surprised at how much her animal baby had to say, and how funny and clever. The expression "a little bird told me" made me smile mischievously at the magic my feathered friends can fly into my life at any moment!

My own goal at the time I met Sunny was to take flight in my life and business, see how high I could fly, and how sweet freedom feels when it comes from within and manifests without. Just like Sunny did from my dream into "real life." Shortly after I began hypnosis with a loving shaman, he asked, "What are your goals for your session, Shannon?" I Cheshire-Cat grinned. "Fly!" He grinned back. "Did you know I'm a former flight instructor?"

Sunnier skies were ahead for this turtle with a solid shell and a lion's courage. My rainbow-colored wings were growing stronger and cleared for takeoff. I'm all animals in one—a Shananimal.

Wally, the corgi, was obsessed with cheese, and turned everything in my house into cheese. He needed a cheese fix and asked if he could please come over to my house for some cheese, which he knew was in my fridge for my dogs. Many animals like cheese, so what's the BFD if Wally *really* wanted some? "Wally's been forbidden by the vet from eating cheese for six months, and he really misses it!" laughed his mom.

I felt for the pooch. If someone forbid me from chocolate, I'd stage a coup with the help of Fred Robbins Frog, and while he pooped on heads, I'd eat their chocolate. For Wally, cheese was life. I asked Wally if he had anything else to share with Mom. Wally said her fiancé was a "cool dude, but mom would kick him to the curb shortly after the wedding. She's already bored of him!" Then Wally rocked a blue bassinet. Mom was looking right at me, and it was hard to keep a poker face. I asked Wally to confirm if he was showing me Mom was pregnant. With a huge smile, he held up a sign: "IT'S A BOY!"

Mom was forty-two years old. (I wasn't sure this was good

news—did she want a baby?) Cautiously optimistic, I ventured, "Wally believes you're pregnant…"

"OMG…I haven't told anyone yet. Is Wally excited? Does he know if it's a boy or girl?" Yes, and a blue bassinet would say so, unless this fetus is fighting gender stereotypes. Five months later she gave birth to a baby boy named Cheese (only by Wally). Mom kicked her fiancée out soon after, and Wally became Papa Bear.

A client once asked me to assist with her cat's health issue—a rash she didn't know how to treat. "Herpes!" the cat meowed loudly. I didn't know cats could get herpes, but that's why I relay messages first and ask follow-up questions afterward. When I announced, "Butterball says he has herpes," his mom fumed. "Shannon, I can't believe you're making fun of me for having herpes!" Umm…what?

I kindly explained it was her cat talking about himself. "Your cat has herpes. Please know I'd never make fun of anyone for a health issue. Butterball might, but not me." (Because I'm a professional I didn't add, "Maybe you two can share a cream.") I hadn't tuned into her health. I only address people's health if an animal or spirit is concerned. The cat didn't rat. Mom's wounded filter projected. Butterball interrupted and asked for Neapolitan flavor catnip!

Almost every time an animal requests something I find obscure, like this or a "Cat Barbie dream house," it exists. They somehow know what exists and what's possible. Cats seem particularly aware of what's available in the marketplace. Perhaps they're the ones planting the seeds in inventors as they sleep! Cats are nocturnal and serious about getting their needs met.

People often subconsciously distort things through their filters, or willfully to suit their narratives, and project stories onto animals rather than deal with reality. "Fifi hates men." Maybe. Or, maybe just your man, or how you act around men, or she's trying to steal your man and is covering her tracks! Stay open-minded and seek answers.

Word choice matters dearly in perception and the outcome of a situation. Just ask every lawyer. Or ask me. I hate being misrepresented or misunderstood. Caution: tangent ahead! The media edit interviews and have taken serious messages I've shared and watered them down to one "woof"...that's also taken out of context. A woof can mean many things, after all.

Media once confused animal communication with animal training, despite how much I'd educated them. When they came to feature my client's success story of her multi-species family and how much "Shannon Spring totally changed our lives," they expected to see Dr. Dolittle and a zoo of talking animals. Since it's a telepathic process, not dolphin training, they'd need cameras in the animal's heads and mine if they wanted a Hollywood production.

The real story is about experiencing how the communicator translates the interspecies conversation, and the big splash is the understanding that washes over the pet parent's face. When people have preconceived notions or try to orchestrate how animals should behave, animals can "misbehave" by doing...nothing! Animal communication is letting the animals lead, the way the Mayor did when he wowed the teachers with his ability to hear and respond to the soft-spoken student. The teachers trusted me, and my furry producer, and trust creates magic. He knows what he's doing, and so do I.

When pets complain that their person is smoking, drinking, and has a lousy attitude, I don't sugarcoat it with, "Your pet hopes you'll reevaluate bad habits and be more cheerful." I'll repeat their exact message: "You're killing me with your smoking and acting like a real asshole when you drink. Grow up and be good to me. I'm sick and tired of your shit." (If they add a "talk to the paw" gesture, I'll oblige.)

Recently, at a meeting where the Mayor and I presented, a woman announced, "I don't like animals, so why are they always getting near me?" Cringe. "Let me ask Mayor Puppypants," I replied, then deferred to the insulted party. Puppypants packed a punch... "Get over yourself!" I gasped in approval and horror that I had to repeat his message aloud with a large audience watching.

I'd opened the presentation stating that my willingness to be punched in the face for my honesty is one of the things that makes me great at my job. The anti-animal lady teaches self defense and weaponry. My son had challenged her to a duel! The audience laughed and so did she. Puppypants disarmed her with his only weapons—truth and cuteness.

Pets are known for their unconditional love, but they're fluent in sarcasm too. Their time is short and people who knowingly shorten it need a wake-up call. Don't waste time. I'd rather be disliked for being honest than liked with shaky integrity. Unconditional love mixed with tough love is powerful. It'll always be your choice how to live. Animals hope you choose wellness for them which starts with your wellness.

Pets and nature are the best healthcare plan, along with chocolate, comedy, and sleep. Animals know my happy places, and what triggers murderous rage. (One of my students said she wants to hit everyone with a pool noodle when she's angry, and I had to admit it seemed more satisfying than yoga.) Kids and animals know I can laugh at myself and don't want my personality or instincts trained or schooled out of me either.

Pets are skilled at masking their pain, and people often underestimate their suffering. Many clients come to me to ask their pets if they're ready to pass, if a treatment is working, and what will help them feel better. When a tumor is malignant I'll feel nauseous. When they're anxious or depressed, my heart might beat faster, or my spirit might plummet. I'll also feel their loyalty or disconnection from their people—physically and emotionally sensing what's affecting their happiness and health.

Animal communication never takes the place of medical care. I have the vet bills to prove it. It's invaluable to also know an animal's input on their care. On medical readings, I'll triple-check what I'm hearing to make sure I gather all the details to process and relay an animal's opinions of their medications and treatments' effectiveness.

Sometimes animals mention a name brand of food or medicine they like or loathe. But usually it's, "My food's making me sick," or "YUMMY!" with an image of a common food item. Kibble is a common complaint among cats and dogs for being too dry, hard to digest, and deceptively lacking nutrients.

Fresh fruit and veggies are popular requests by dogs, and farmed animals and honey is pretty universally well-liked. Animals communicate as much as they know. "I'm allergic to sweet potatoes, chicken, essential oils, etc." If something's helping, they may give a thumbs-up gesture, and if it's not, they may shake their heads no, display a red X like a game show buzzer, or show the offending food or bottle being flushed down the toilet (it's wasting money).

For objectivity's sake, I advise clients not to disclose the names of pets' caretakers or products. There's one pain medication pets consistently boo at for being mostly ineffective, and there are certain brands or doctors that I personally know are problematic. It's the animals' experiences that should dictate readings and outcomes; my opinions are offered when asked, followed by the animals' responses to my input.

Animal communication combined with holistic and Western medicine is a comprehensive way to help animals thrive. Some of my own best care came from a vet! During COVID, Grover wasn't feeling well and, with an urgent look in his eyes, I took him to an ER vet and handed him over to a masked stranger. I wasn't sure what was wrong; sometimes it's trickier with my own pets. Sitting in my car, I became disabled with back pain.

I called a friend. "I can't believe this, but I think I'm heading to "the people ER," while Grover's at the vet ER. I really need a SHOT OF PAIN RELIEF; it hurts like hell." Then, I realized, "Aha! Grover's sending me his pain so I know what's wrong with him. He needs a shot of pain relief!" I called the vet to say I discovered Grover's issue when he beeped in.

"We know what's wrong with Grover. He's in debilitating back pain and we're going to give him a shot of pain relief." Like mother, like son—Grover and I are one. Pets often mimic their people's health issues in an empathic effort to transmute them. When the vet administered a shot to Grover, my back pain went away too!

I had been having back pain for two weeks, and lamented to this vet that pain meds weren't an option unless I was screaming. I don't want to ever fall into addiction again—something people think can't happen to them, but it's insidious. The vet recommended a specific muscle relaxer, and I joked he should be my new doctor. Grover and I played ball just an hour later.

About six months later, Grover became paralyzed overnight. It was terrifying to watch him so helpless. Our vet suggested a specialist to evaluate him, an MRI, and a costly surgery that had little chance of succeeding in cases like this. I'd have donated a kidney to pay for surgery, but when I asked Grover what he wanted me to do for him, he declined specialists. He gently said, "Mom, if I'm ever going to walk again, one day, I'll just walk."

This challenged me as a mom and Animal Communicator because I needed to honor his wishes, and yet wanted to fix him if possible. I knew I had heard him correctly. I had to TRUST Grover, even when the vet said I was making a mistake.

Grover's favorite activity is chasing tennis balls. Watching him drag his tiny body over the grass, scraping his inner thighs with a wild smile, going as fast as he could, was heartbreaking. He was Peppy Penelope Puppet in dog form, a constant cheerleader of life. I bought him wheels to attach to his hindquarters. I knew they weren't the right solution, but I tried them anyway. When the wheels failed, I pushed Grover in a baby stroller, like I did as a child with my teddy bear.

I carried him around in my arms speaking of wellness. Pets often take on our suffering, and if I could've taken on his, I would've. I stayed strong and projected strength, not pity. My mighty hero didn't need to hear, "Oh you poor thing" from anyone. Give strength. "May you heal. Peace be with you. I love you."

I'll never ask an animal to suffer for me as I've seen people do. I invite them to heal if they can, and if they choose. Don't stay a moment longer on my behalf. I love them enough to listen, nurse them through recovery, or hold their paw when passing. I let them go into the arms of angels, not nothingness.

I heard Grover's words replay about how he'd maybe walk again one day, but I also knew I had promised my pets quality of life. The wheels weren't a solution, nor was watching him drag his body. I pondered a time frame to make a hard choice, if needed. This couldn't go on indefinitely.

Never make an animal's suffering or recovery your own glory story. There are some fates worse than death (and there is no ultimate death). I wanted Grover to recover, but without pressure from me. Don't be the runner making their dog jog behind them on hot days, or inappropriately long distances, and claim they love it, or the cat parent bragging about a kitty's independence and how long you can leave her by herself. Don't exploit their willingness to please you or hold on for you. Coach Grover needed me to be the coach now and bravely lead.

Memorial Day was about two months away, and I asked the angels to please give me a sign by then if he'd recover soon. About two months after total paralysis, I was reading for a Spirit dog named Cassie whose dad previously hired me to answer very painful questions he needed closure on about her passing. Normally, I'd advise against that, but Chris desperately needed answers.

After our session, he said he felt relief knowing Cassie's suffering and the medical mistakes hadn't been in vain. The staff learned from their mistakes, and like all deceased beings, Cassie is now well in Spirit. He thanked me, stating I'd gotten answers no other medium could, and proving Cassie was alive because of the evidence she'd given. Chris had been wracked with grief believing he'd let Cassie down. Cassie was only full of love and gratitude for her dad. Her messages transformed his pain into peace, relieving his crushing guilt.

Chris now wanted to connect with Cassie for fun and hear

anything she wished to share. Immediately, I felt her joy. Chris began our video session by expressing compassion for Grover. I was looking right at Grover who was lying by the front door, when Chris gently asked, "Shannon, I'm sorry to hear about Grover. Can Cassie help Grover heal?"

An instant wave of light enveloped me as a twinkle sparked in Cassie's eyes—a fairy-dog-mother waving an invisible wand. GROVER STOOD UP on all fours, tail wagging, smiling...a divine twinkle in his eyes...and took a few steps!

I turned the iPad for Chris to see. "WOW! DID THAT JUST HAPPEN? DID CASSIE DO THAT?" Exhilarated, I cheered, "Looks like it!" Our dogs partnered together to create this WTF (Watch The Feet!) miracle. Chris wanted signs that Cassie was *still* with him because people worry pets move on and leave us. (They don't. They can be many places at once.) Cassie eagerly showed her dad that not only was she still with him, but she had impressive healing skills.

It was magical watching Grover watch himself, realizing he could walk again. We were in awe when Chris surprised me by asking, "Will Cassie send me any *other* signs she's with me?"

"You mean this Lazarus moment wasn't enough for you?" I half-joked. But I understood Chris needed more signs for himself. I smiled at Cassie. "You heard your dad. What *other* signs show you're with him?" It felt like asking a toddler to hit a *second* home run...in a row, except this was a Spirit-dog, and Cassie was already at bat. "Tell Dad to expect to meet someone named Cassie very, very soon." I thought, are you kidding me? Let's end on a miracle, but I trusted Cassie. Two hours later, Chris emailed me: "It's incredible! I took my other two dogs to the beach and within minutes, up came running A DOG NAMED CASSIE!" One of the greatest Holy Fluff moments!

Chris and Cassie reunited. Grover was running and chasing balls. I was grateful to have my furry coach/cheerleader back to his normal self. If you still don't believe animals talk and magic is real, you might be dead inside. Miracles can happen when we least expect them. Expect the unexpected.

When a pet is ready to pass on, readings help prepare both species. I'm often confirming what most people already know…it's time to say goodbye. (Really, I'll see you later…) Better to say goodbye a little too soon than too late to spare suffering and regrets. If you made a mistake, know they're now at peace. Learn from it and love on. Don't punish your heart in their honor. Expand your heart and love another animal, whether volunteering for a day or parenting for decades.

To evaluate if a product or person is helping or hurting an animal, I'll ask clients to privately write a numbered list of items including food, medications, supplements, and caretakers. Clients silently focus on one at a time while animals simultaneously express to me how each one makes them feel. Their responses range from serious to silly but are always sincere. For example, if I hear the song "I Feel Good," and see a cartoon Snoopy dancing or a giant foam #1 finger, they approve.

Conversely, Judge Judy might appear banging her gavel to render the animal's verdict or no-nonsense action plan. Game show buzzers, heckling Muppets judges, or poop emojis would indicate disapproval. I'll investigate with more questions to identify and resolve the offense.

A bird named Wingman in Argentina was adamant her medication was the correct type, but it was expired, and therefore, garbage. Mom confirmed her pharmacy often dispensed expired medication at discounts and told people it worked just as well!

Animals can share feelings on a dosage adjustment, manufacturer, flavor, pill vs. liquid or if a homeopathic solution is better and cheaper. Soliciting input from animals increases comfort and speeds recovery.

Like me, animals have strong convictions and can differentiate disliking someone based on their personality or inherent untrustworthiness. They might respect a professional's skills, but dislike their attitude, or love them but find them professionally incompetent. If the cartoon character Homer Simpson appears, someone might be lazy, unintelligent, or a beer-drinking donut addict! I dive deeper to see what the message is behind the symbol.

Sometimes images of books flying off shelves, or movie titles flashing, energetically summarizes a situation or feelings. These resources usually offer support for their person or pet. If a bird shows me *Gardening for Dummies*, it's likely because their person dreams of gardening and needs more peaceful time in nature. It could also be because flower essences will aid the pet's health. Nature speaks and heals.

Sometimes animals will ask for food my pets enjoy or that's in my fridge. They might show a product's slogan or play its jingle in my ear. Animals make credible, passionate brand ambassadors and harsh critics. They'll also tell me when something is a life-saver, defective or dishonest in its claim.

Henry Horse wasn't making any progress with an expensive new machine, championed for helping many horses, that his dad bought him. When I asked Henry to explain why he thought his body wasn't improving, he declared, "It's broken."

"Impossible!" Henry's dad fumed. "It's brand new. And it's really expensive!" Just because we don't want something to be true doesn't make it so. His dad (like many humans) made up his mind and stubbornly locked onto one way of thinking. Don't shoot the horse, or the messenger. It was an inconvenient truth to accept this brand-new, reputable, costly machine was defective. He wanted a different answer.

Henry repeated, "It's defective," then lifted his leg and smashed this particular unit to pieces at the factory. It *should* work but it doesn't. Accept facts and deal with things as they are, not as you wish. Denial is a costly habit. Dad was listing all the reasons it couldn't be true. Henry and I were in problem-solving mode. "Click, Clack, Neigh…write to the company and get a replacement machine today."

When Henry's dad finally conceded, "Ya know, I use a different XYZ machine on the other horses, maybe this particular one really is defective." Giddy-up! Dad was off his high horse, ordered a new machine, and Henry soon experienced relief from his aching muscles.

Missy booked a session, fairly certain she'd be saying goodbye to Roo, her beloved pup whom she'd scheduled a euthanasia appointment for just a few days away from our reading. I begin each reading with an open mind. Too many mistakes happen when care providers rely on other people's accounts or records. Mistakes happen in the medical version of the game, "Whisper down the lane," so stay open. Animals run the show.

Missy mentioned Roo had a tumor removed, unaware yet if it was malignant, and Roo's blood count was down. Their vet stated it would take a miracle to improve. My "Shananimal" ears perk up if I sense danger or miracle potential.

I telepathically scanned Roo's body and felt instantly nauseous. Sensing nausea can have me hurling my guts out in sympathy, attempting to relieve their symptoms. My body confirmed the removed tumor was malignant, corroborated by Missy's vet a week later.

I asked Roo if he was ready to transition to Spirit, knowing his death date (aka afterlife party date) was days away. He showed me a giant thermometer, like at fundraising events to display donations with the red line rising, predicting his blood levels would rise. He was sure of it, and then so was I.

"I have much life still to live. Mom should cancel euthanasia."

Missy perked up, and said she felt strongly this was true, that he'd recover despite appearances and statistics. In this case, I could tell a client exactly what she wanted to hear: Roo would live. Readings can help people make informed and compassionate choices, and most importantly, honor their animals' souls.

There are no certainties (other than we will all die of something). Free will determines a lot. Animal and Spirit families can provide wise counsel to help us manage or lessen stress from the extraordinary challenges we face as humans. They can guide us to avoid certain pitfalls, but can't stop unavoidable soul lessons or death.

For example, I learned and grew immensely from having alcoholism. My grandmother couldn't prevent me from taking my first drink, but could inspire me to have my last one. Roo can't control his body, but he can communicate about it and have a will to live or pass on.

Roo's blood count rose dramatically within 48 hours after our session. "I'm eager to spend quality time with Missy, and help with her book." Missy then shared she'd taken the year off to write a book, and that her birth mom (from whom she was estranged) had always wanted to be an author. Roo spotlighted Missy's birth mom who was alive, grieving, and ready to share her spirit's heartfelt messages. I needed to help Missy heal mama drama.

Missy's mom telepathically handed me a rolled-up white diploma with a red ribbon tied around it. "Tell Missy this is an apology. I'm so very sorry." Missy cried and confessed, "I've been so angry at her all these years for abandoning me and not showing up at my graduation."

Missy was eager, but struggling to forgive her mom who added, "I was too ashamed and jealous. You became everything I wanted to be, but I lacked the courage. No matter what I chose, I was going to hurt you. By abandoning you, I left you with a gaping wound, and if I'd kept you, I'd have caused you even more pain with my own wounds. Please forgive me. I love you, and am proud of you." Missy cried. Luckily, my waterproof mascara demonstrated exceptional resilience.

My mother never graduated college, one of her biggest regrets. She'd even won a scholarship, but her dad unconscionably told her to give it to someone poor. Ever since, she sabotaged good things that came her way. Missy and I both carried deep mother wounds.

It takes courage to choose joy and achieve our dreams. Our past only determines our destiny if we let it. Animals beg us to live in the present with them.

Roo, a dog near death, brought new life to himself, and healed a cavernous wound for his mom and hers. They all celebrated Christmas together that year. Miracles happen.

I joined an online women's group to make friends, but was soon kicked out for posting a picture of Mayor Puppypants posing in a *Rocky Horror Picture Show* cut-out painting, where he poked his smiling furry face through as a prostitute wearing a black leather thong and nip clips. The group founder, an ultra-conservative Christian *comedian*, banned me from the group because a dog in drag somehow either turned her on or offended her. She never clarified.

Prior to the Mayor's pawlitical scandal, I had invited three group members (all strangers to me) to see a show at McCurdy's Comedy Theatre. We met for dinner beforehand around the block.

Dana sat next to me, and it wasn't long before her dog, Lola, telepathically crashed the party with an urgent message: "Tell mom I want the surgery! I have to get the surgery...NOW!"

Lola grabbed the mic, knowing I'd be willing to replace normal chit chat for: "This is going to sound weird, but..." I began, "Dana, your dog is begging for some kind of surgery and I'd feel disloyal if I didn't woof up on her behalf." Dana was nonplussed by her dog's suffering. "Yeah, I know she's blind now. I feel bad. I waited too long, and now it's too late for surgery. Besides, the vet said it probably wouldn't work." As Dana perused the menu, I felt Lola's despair and anger at having no control over her body and her mom's dismissive decision.

I also wanted eye surgery, as I hated wearing readers and feared inheriting Nanny's macular degeneration. Lola was living one of my worst fears. She needed my help for Dana to understand surgery was the right choice. I chugged my water and strategized while Lola relaxed in my helping hands, snoozing on her sofa at home.

Dana sipped her cocktail, and one of the other two diners, Julie, said, "Shannon, you remind me of my Aunt Jackie who passed a few months ago. She was funny like you." After she said "Aunt Jackie" a total of three times, just like *Beetlejuice*, Aunt Jackie materialized.

Jackie had a lively spirit and party-animal personality, the kind that makes small talk with the living even less bearable. Julie lamented, "I don't know what to do with her ashes. I really want to do right by her." Without missing a beat, Jackie quipped comedy gold in my ear, making me her punchline puppet - emcee for a dead woman's one-woman comedy special broadcasting her wishes: "Aunt Jackie jokes you should put her ashes on eBay and auction them off to see how much she's worth!"

Julie spit out her martini. "OMG...THAT'S JUST WHAT SHE'D SAY! AUNT JACKIE WAS SUCH A COMEDIAN, AND AN EBAY ADDICT!"

I appreciated Jackie's sense of humor about her death. While sweating through my Lilly Pulitzer sundress, I announced, "I don't know how anyone wears undies in this Florida heat! Go commando or go home!" Julie screamed, "OMG...AUNT JACKIE ALWAYS WENT COMMANDO!" Naked, pink, and unafraid, I'd made a new comedy buddy who was killing it in the afterlife with nothing to sweat.

Making friends with uncensored spirits is always easier for me than trying to navigate the false personas of the living. Spirits often choose to communicate through me because of my commando-style approach to life...and the afterlife. While grief sucks, there's no reason to be uptight about death.

The collective joy of our afterlife loved ones' unfiltered spirits is a comedy club wrapped in a loving Hallmark card, served with freshly baked cookies. Laugh, cry, we're all going to die. A soulful celebration is just a breath and blink away.

Now that Dana had enjoyed a break from my peer pressuring her on Lola's behalf, it was time to slip in more surgery slobber. Lola said something so heartbreaking and desperate that I'd have donated my eyeballs to fix her. "Tell mom I'd rather die than continue to live so lonely and blind. I can't stand it. I need my eyes. Tell her it's worth risking my life, even if I can only see ten percent better afterward." I respected her passionate position. Her body, her choice. Except it was Dana's choice, and she was mostly choosing martinis.

I relayed Lola's desperate plea, and Dana sighed. "I know she's miserable. We had to put her dog brother to sleep, and I lost my father and brother this year, too. There's been so much loss...no way I can risk losing her too, especially when the vet predicts the surgery would certainly fail." Her defeatist attitude was a knife to Lola's heart and mine. Feeling Lola's helplessness and depression strengthened my determination to help and get my eye surgery too.

I invited Dana to book a private reading to connect with her dad, brother, and Lola's dog brother, Kato. I sensed this would help Dana heal, AND, they'd guide her to grant Lola's wish. Who better to guide us than those who can literally see from a higher perspective? Thankfully, she booked a private reading.

It's a delicate line I walk advocating for an animal and managing boundaries with people. I also don't want to be a salesperson. My sessions have changed many lives, but people need to trust good things can happen for them too. I can pry open closed minds and hearts, but each soul chooses to turn the light on or curse the darkness.

I don't deliver messages outside paid sessions unless, like Lola, a spirit, "dead or alive," drops in with a message I feel ethically obligated or comedically inspired to share. But details and questions must be in a formal session for my protection and theirs.

Sessions are too personal, powerful and unpredictable to risk doing them on the fly. Clients need privacy and focus, and I'd burn out without breaks or compensation. A grant or sponsor for my work would allow me to help more animals on an even broader scale.

Lola's dog brother in Spirit, Kato, excitedly dropped in on me the night before Dana's reading. Kato showed how he'd escaped every gate mom installed. Dana confirmed he was "a real Houdini!" Her brother, dad, and dogs all shared memorable evidence of their lives with Dana. Her tense, pale face turned pink and perky. Spirit joy is a contagious, energetic beauty booster.

Lola waited patiently and then began her tough love campaign to open Dana's eyes to see the truth. "Tell mom if she fearfully holds onto me, and keeps leaving me at home ten hours a day, blind and friendless, I'll completely lose my will to live, and she'll lose me, too. I love her, but I can't live like this. I'm too depressed."

Dana reiterated her fears of the vet's dismal prediction and high cost of surgery, despite having the financial means to help Lola. Dana's dad brought up the many times he'd tried to help Dana with depression, and how he would have done anything to relieve it. He guided Dana to see she had the ability and opportunity to grant Lola's wish, and if Lola passed during surgery, he was there to greet her. Kato smiled knowing what was to come.

Dana began empathizing with Lola, basking in her family's loving support, and trusting their LIGHT. "Ok, Lola. You'll get the surgery, even though it costs a fortune and probably won't work. I'll do it for you." I understood Dana's feelings, but it's exhausting working with people's pessimism. Animals are easy, honest, and realistic. A miracle was at hand...and paw. Lola couldn't guarantee success any more than I could. She stated her wishes, likely outcomes, and risk-taking comfort.

I merged with Lola's body as if the surgery was underway, and could feel her eyes getting stronger. I could feel the surgeon's skill and Lola's determination to see. Lola didn't fear death, but continuing to live blind scared her deeply. Based on what I was experiencing as Lola, I felt very confident she'd regain sight.

I could see images of Lola playing and being silly, and mom's relief she had listened. Dana had the power to create a happier story for them both. But the outcome is always in Spirit's hands.

I reminded Dana I was just the messenger, and then helped her select the surgeon based on three potential doctors, and which Lola chose—the one with golden paws.

About a month later, Dana messaged: "LOLA'S SURGERY WAS SUCCESSFUL! SHE CAN SEE!" Lola's face was exuberant, the light in her eyes brighter than the sun. I was as grateful and excited for Lola as if she were my own dog.

Two months later, I got lens replacement surgery and Lola cheered for me. Life's better when you can make choices about your own body. I help animals have some control in a world where their needs are often unmet, and bodies used for our benefit. See the light, humans!

Maria asked me to chat with Hercules and see how he was feeling. "He's saying his issues are limbs and lymph nodes," I said confidently. Maria disagreed. "No, that's not it. He's got a massive adrenal tumor." I've learned to stay steady, like a pilot experiencing turbulence. "Hmm...let me ask him why he didn't share that with me."

Hercules elaborated. "Shannon, I have throat cancer. The adrenal tumor will disappear. But if they don't treat this throat cancer, I'm going to die." (A lump formed in my throat as he spoke.)

Maria gasped. "Really? Are you sure...is he sure?" Hercules, my steady copilot, asked to be rechecked at the vet, knowing they'd confirm. Luckily, Maria listened, and they treated him in time. The adrenal tumor disappeared. Maria emailed: "Shannon, you saved Hercules's life!" Hercules, of course, saved his own, but I'm honored to be mentioned in the credits.

It's a team effort; Spirit has the ultimate say. When a person, animal and I connect, we can be the hands and paws on the ground to manifest miracles. Hercules sent me a barking bouquet. "Thank you. I woof you."

15
AFTERLIFE PARTY

Listen for the laughter.
Jack Rabbit Spring

Animals helped me to stop fearing death (all the creatures I love at an epic party with unlimited breadsticks). What's to fear? Animals don't fear death. The Grim Reaper is just a weird-looking dude carrying a giant chew toy sickle who escorts them to the most magical place in the cosmos.

Working daily with the Spirit World has made me fear life a lot less. I understand now life is a play, and when the curtain goes down it rises back up—without the chaos and heartbreaks. I merge with the playwright and become joy itself again.

"The Rainbow Bridge" is timeless and always open, just like my Open Mic for the Animal Kingdom. Animals don't lose their names, memories, voice or love for us when they die, just their pain. They don't really die; they transition into Spirit. Just like people, their lives continue and their souls grow.

Years ago, when Ducky died, Allison, a "Good Vibes" t-shirt-wearing yoga teacher snickered, "Well I mean, she was *just a dog*, right?" Ummm...no, Allison...NOT RIGHT! Alison's downward-dog pose properly exposed her as an asshole. I maintained Warrior pose and uttered something like, "Don't let the door hit you, where the good Lord split you." (Jesus first said that.)

That night I dreamed about Ducky walking through a fire (cremation) emerging ALIVE. My beloved baby Ducky was alive, and lovingly healing me in my dreams to lessen my grief. No matter what I know intellectually (there is no death), my heart always craves grief relief and comfort from my furry family.

"Ducky" was my nickname from Sister Genevieve—my beloved third-grade teacher. It means pleasing and delightful, a word that makes me happy just saying it. "How are you, Shannon?" I'm ducky, thanks for asking! Her sweet voice calling me *Ducky* made me feel special and treasured, the way I want my pets to feel.

While speaking at a pet camp to kids about animals in the afterlife, specifically about Ducky (also a lesson about black pets getting adopted last), I shared how animals love to send signs they never leave us. Right on cue, my mysterious, toy-cat-meowing-dog magically appeared on the computer screen! Her spirit lit up the kids' faces from seeing hers. And no, skeptics, her photo was not a screensaver, nor was it a tech glitch. It was, and always will be, DUCKY!

No longer confined to a body, our loved ones gain "superhero powers" and find clever ways to comfort people and animals left behind. Your cat and dog can still entertain themselves and you by leaving mice on your doorstep, or bite marks on new slippers. Don't underestimate their desire to show off and comfort you, and don't *expect* these things...*invite* them. (Maybe not *these* things, but stay open to their connection with you and their comedy skills.)

The smell of your deceased spouse's cooking may permeate the air at dinnertime to let you know they're right there! You may hear familiar paw steps, catch glimpses of spirits on their favorite chairs, or sense their presence by a special tree. Dreams are one of the most common ways spirits communicate, because human defenses are down, allowing them easier access. Ask them to visit, and to help you remember it when you wake.

A dog named Monster cleverly used sign language for his epic sign to his mom that he'd heard and understood her when she'd spoken to him shortly before he passed. Julie asked me in her reading, "What does Monster say about the moon?" Monster began playfully making shadow puppets on the moon. I was impressed and wanted to watch his puppet show. I animated my fingers into various shapes to show Julie what Monster was doing. (This is a major reason I require video readings to be able to fully express what I receive.) Monster says, "When you look at the moon, imagine him doing shadow puppets, he's having so much fun." Julie smiled, but in her raw grief, hadn't yet processed... the magnitude of Monster's moon dance.

Julie had practiced sign language in front of Monster! "Shadow puppets" was Monster's playful representation of sign laguage, the animated language of symbols which had been frustrating for his mom to learn. Monster was making it fun for her. When I explained her dog's sheer creative genius, Julie glowed from the wow factor. "I used to tell Monster to look at the moon after he passed, and we'd be looking at the same moon." Monster received her message and mooned her back with loving comedy. A week later, an image of shadow puppets in a puppet theatre on the moon appeared in my newsfeed. I passed along Monster's message to his mommy, and Julie sent me back a message radiating Spirit's love thanking me for our reading "bringing her back to happiness...a lifesaver."

While Julie (and Doug, a client you'll soon meet) received "big" signs, be grateful for the "small signs," so your spirit family know they're reaching you. Imagine someone handing you a $1 bill and you complain you can't buy anything with it. If you're grateful, you can multiply it into unlimited abundance. Loved ones work hard to reach us, so appreciate all signs, water them, and more will blossom.

Two spirit cats began laughing and made me blush as they showed whipping back the showercurtain on their proud... but nude marine dad. Like two hazing frat boys, they reveled in my sworn mission to deliver the naked truth. With my rosy cheeks, I mentally covered this soldier's sudsy cheeks, and reported for duty. "Please forgive me, Doug, but your cats are playing peek-a-boo with you in the shower..." Doug howled with feline-felicity: "OH MY GOD...I always played that game with them! I'd whip back the showercurtain and make funny faces at them...that's so awesome!" I thanked his cats for the birds-eye view and making dad laugh away some grief. While Doug tattooed his cats' faces on his body, my face is not there...yet.

Imagine all the cool things you'll do once freed from your body. That's what your pets in Spirit are feeling now! I know I'll be flying a lot. No flight attendant telling me to buckle up or deny me extra pretzels. Cats can push things off the tallest counters and leap from nowhere in acrobatic feats laughing at their previous amateur earthly forms. Dogs can dig to their hearts' content and tell every landlord everywhere to FLUFF OFF!

Spirits can do things that we consider special effects here. The higher their souls advance, the more they can do, and the more open we are to magic, the more we'll receive. However they visit, they'll show their love, support, and humor. They'll try to guide us away from trouble and steer us back into the Light when things get dark.

They'll do all in their power to make us laugh, help us love ourselves, and send special people and animals our way to act on their behalf, with assistance of all kinds. Remember, their love for you hasn't gone anywhere. Trust their loyalty. They're excited for you to notice their spirit's presence. Acknowledge them with joy.

About four years after Teddy #2 passed, he visited in a vivid dream where he sat on lush green grass under the brightest blue sky, confidently, tongue out, smiling, lit up with JOY. His chocolate brown fur was fluffed and shiny. In a semi-lucid state, I asked him, "Teddy, what did you come to tell me?" Teddy was excited by my question. "HAPPY! I'M HAPPY!" As fast as he appeared, he returned to his realm to play. I awoke energized by his magic.

Kermit, Puppypants and I walked down to the bay a couple of blocks away. As we walked, I spoke of Teddy to them, and how awesome it would be if they could all play together. Moments after arriving at the waterfront park, a dog that looked like Teddy's twin (black not brown, with the same white heart patch of fur) ran up to us. I knew something special was underway. Woohoo! Kermit and this happy, black fluffy mutt ran into the bay.

The dog's dad was shocked. "He's never done that before. He's afraid of swimming!" But, with Kermit as his swim coach, this pup was content and free. As I prepared to ask the man, "What's your dog's name?" I knew he wouldn't say Teddy, and I also knew his answer would be perfect. I fully trusted Teddy had arranged this play date.

The man smiled and answered, "My dog's name is Irie...it means HAPPY in Jamaican." Teddy cleverly made me trust him and his dream message by knowing this dog messenger came from him, with a different name and color. Despite Teddy's tragic early passing, he is... HAPPY! My baby bear wanted me to only see him this way. Forget the final sad moments; those sad moments are ashes. But the soul is IRIE! Happier than ever. Both Teddys are safe.

Teddy's big sister, Lucy, also visited in a dream (with a twist), requiring I trust what I knew...Lucy's with me...even if she doesn't completely look like herself. In the dream, Lucy came running up to me, and I pet her. I felt her warmth and love. My Lucy was a purebred Golden Retriever from Golden Rescue with strawberry blonde fur. But, in the dream, while the same smallish size, she was golden and black. I awoke feeling like Lucy had hugged me.

The next morning, Kermit, Puppypants, and I walked down to the same bay park and spotted a lady with a dog who looked just like the dog I saw in my dream, a golden and black beauty resembling part Ducky and part Lucy (these two were earth sisters for many years). This time, I knew this dog's name would be Lucy, but to humor myself, I asked the stranger, "What's your dog's name?"

She smiled and called out with pride, "Lucy! Would your dogs like to play with my Lucy?" For a brief time, my two goofy mutts got to play with "my Lucy" through this Lucy. Worlds merging, love surging. I was so jealous I wasn't a dog too!

Big Brother Rowdy added a new fun challenge to trusting it's my dogs contacting me in clever ways. I was in the water at Ft. Desoto Beach, floating, when out of nowhere, a big beautiful blonde Golden ran into the water like I was a giant toy he needed to retrieve.

Rowdy had passed about 13 years prior, and despite having seen countless Goldens since then, I'd never seen one that LOOKED JUST LIKE ROWDY in looks and energy.

I began laughing, feeling Rowdy's silliness inside me. Rowdy and I had spent hours playing ball on the beach. While this dog beside me looked and felt like my boy, I knew this wasn't actually Rowdy, but a messenger of my furry angel. Some animals reincarnate, and some visit temporarily through another being's body. Some do both.

I waved at the pup's people on shore who gleefully waved back, enjoying me enjoying their furry star. Puppypants began to sing for me to swim back in, and the golden and I obeyed. I thanked the dog's family for letting me play with her for so long, then asked, "What's your dog's name?" She continued to sit by my side as I hugged her.

"Kya," the mom answered. I couldn't wait to hear this twist; Teddy and Lucy taught me so well to trust. "What does Kya mean?" I asked, as Kya looked into my eyes. "Diamond in the sky," her mom smiled. WOW! I kissed Kya with all my love for Rowdy. I thanked Kya for being a fun divine messenger and thanked Rowdy, my diamond in the sky, for saying hello to me and his goofy siblings at my side, diamonds on earth.

A spirit cat named Arizona gave me a hairball full of nerves, delivering a potentially controversial message. After providing epic evidence of his life with his mom and grandma, he smiled slyly. "Tell them I have Archangel Michael-sized wings (Michael is the Big Kahuna of angels), and that I'm sitting on the right-hand side of Jesus!" I witnessed Arizona in all his glory sporting wings that would make even Archangel Michael question his rank.

I knew I'd heard Arizona clearly, but I worried about his people perhaps not believing in Jesus, or being atheists. I could have ended the session on a win, as they'd already expressed joy in the evidence he shared, but it's not my information to censor. I knew I needed to hit a home run now *and* be willing to eat kitty litter if I struck out.

I took a deep breath and said, "And umm, one last thing... Arizona says to tell you 'he has Archangel Michael-sized wings and is sitting on the right-hand side of Jesus.'"

His people became hysterical...with gratitude! They cheered and squealed in delight at his words. "We always told him that's where he'd be, right at Jesus's side, and he'd have those huge Archangel Michael wings in Spirit!" They were as elated as a gospel choir testifying the Lord has risen... and the Lord is a cat!

I felt giddy with relief and celebration too, as there's nothing better than making these connections for pets and their people. It's immediate intimacy when I speak with animals, and a beautiful, serious, and silly bond for life, even if we only have five minutes together. Names and details can fade, but the connection remains in our hearts, much like with my students, but even more so with animals, because they never outgrow a friend.

Arizona Cat might be sitting on the right-hand side of Jesus, but Kitty-Girl IS Jesus. My friend Rachel, a rabbit rescuer, reached out needing help with a stray kitten whom her friend Norma had been caring for until Norma had wrongly faulted Kitty–Girl for making her son sick. Norma abandoned Kitty-Girl at a nature preserve, but later regretted breaking her son's and the kitten's hearts and went in search of the stray, to no avail. Kitty-Girl was weak in body but mighty in message. "Tell Norma, I was Heaven-sent to her son and was meant to be with him. Sometimes, Jesus arrives in the face of a helpless kitten. I forgive her, but tell her she turned Jesus away today." Mic drop!

Rachel gasped. "Shannon, Norma prays daily to Jesus and is going to lose her mind when she hears He came as this kitten to be with her son! Also, she didn't want to hire you since she thinks psychics are sacreligious!" Jesus, Kitty-Girl, and I smiled. Norma misjudged me, not knowing Jesus is on my speed dial, and a feral kitten would Bible-thump her!

Spirits tell me when I arrive in Spirit, I'll feel like Norm from the TV show *Cheers*, where everyone will know my name, and I'll drop funny one-liners. Norm once said, "It's a dog eat dog world, and I'm wearing milk bone underwear!" It'll be wonderful to meet all the souls "in person" who've shared their loved ones with me, and the thousands of animals who adopted me along the way in their hearts.

An American client wanted to move to Tajikistan and hired me for psychic advice. Immediately, my "human self" thought, "Tajikistan? Hell no!" But this was her life, not mine. Her childhood cat, Tabitha, from twenty years ago, sashayed in purring, "Tell Renee she's MAGNANIMOUS!" Renee became a Powerball winner, screaming, "TABITHA SAID MAGNANIMOUS? I JUST WROTE THAT IN LIPSTICK ON MY MIRROR...TO BECOME MAGNANIMOUS!" Renee exploded with child-like wonder, feeling Tabitha's sweet soul encouraging her.

Tabitha then got down to business and grew serious when breaking open a fortune cookie about Tajikistan. It read, "Proceed with extreme caution!" Delusionally optimistic about the ominous message, Renee asked, "So Tabitha thinks I should go? She says yes?" Tabitha smacked her paw to her face, and I advised, "Tabitha's not enthusiastic about your move, but wherever you go, she's always with you." Tabitha licked her paw, knowing full well Renee had already mentally bought her plane ticket to Tajikistan.

Feeling Renee's decision, I felt short of breath, trapped. Tabitha showed me a deceptive contract Renee had to sign before moving there to teach abroad. But whatever the fallout, Renee would gain valuable life lessons. Tabitha tried to protect and warn her, but now would accompany and support her choice. However spiritual we are, challenges are part of the human condition. Animals want to help us live our dreams and heal ourselves. Renee chose to let this fortune cookie crumble, and off she went.

About eight months later, Renee messaged: "OMG, Shannon, you and Tabitha were right! My Tajikistan employers are threatening me. It's exactly as you said. Can you ask Tabitha where I should go next? I heard, "Just don't go to the Middle East," when Renee exclaimed, "Maybe SAUDI ARABIA!" Déjà vu smacked Tabitha and me on our foreheads. WHAT THE FLUFF!

Tabitha suggested Budapest, Hungary, and Renee gleefully confirmed she always wanted to go there. A tastier fortune cookie for sure. Tabitha helped Renee meet her soulmate, advising Renee, "Look for the man with the bird." And while sipping coffee at a Hungarian cafe, a friendly man with a pretty bird on his shoulder sat down next to Renee. They flirted like alley cats while Tabitha mischievously eyed the bird. Now that Renee was making good choices, Tabitha was free to be naughty!

There's too much evidence to credibly deny that animals communicate and that their lives continue after death. Animals are wise, witty life coaches because they've mastered what most humans cannot: love unconditionally, be happy in the present moment, and don't second-guess instincts.

Many concepts that once seemed impossible or laughable, to humanity (flying to the moon, dog bakeries, catios, the Internet) have since become realities. How can death be finite with *no* other worlds we can travel to, when we already physically travel to other "worlds" and planets via airplanes and rockets, and in dreams via astral travel?

Why, then, couldn't we travel post-mortem to an afterlife? Or through time portals while alive? We can and we do! Animals are natural travel guides to help us explore and expand our awareness. Be forewarned, though, that they eat all the Biscoff cookies before you board their spaceships, and all in-flight movies are reels of your most embarrassing moments.

The loss of pets is a special kind of unspeakable grief. They're not *like* family, they *are* family; they hug parts of our soul no one else can reach. My pets' love makes me feel alive, and their deaths turn me into a ravaged war zone. But the joy we share, and their souls, live on.

I peek my head through the loving afterlife portal—a world accessible through my animal visits, client readings, astral travel, meditation, and other magical moments that delight my inner Ducky. While experiencing "life after life," butterflies return, and the war of grief ends.

Grief is a powerful beast, but it cannot kill our pets or our souls. The love our souls are inherently made of is a LIGHT that transforms wounds into waterfalls, and tears of laughter replace sobs of grief.

People may or may not believe in God, but most believe in their pets. Animals don't pray to any god, and yet are loved and safe in the afterlife. Animals live on, regardless of human beliefs. In my experience, religious figures like Jesus only appear in readings and transitions to those who believe in them, but they can all act as Good Samaritans for any being, because none of this is about religion. It's about souls, our essence as Beings coming from the same Source, whatever team jersey we wear.

Some pets appear in readings with human loved ones, some with religious figures, and some are solo with a smile, booty shake, and a heartfelt message, sticky note or fortune cookie.

Jesus once popped into a pet reading to save the day for a woman whose dog, Lady, was in Spirit. Often, I'll hear many messages before a session begins. This time, I heard very little from Lady about her life as a dog with her mom, Sandy. This rarely happens, and when it does, it's because the person is most in need of the pet's guidance, as opposed to a trip down memory lane. Pets can prove their presence in many ways.

Lady shared only a few details about herself to confirm I was connected with her. She lovingly, firmly directed, "Focus on Mom, and I will guide you." When an animal says this, it's because their human is going through something major they want to assist them with. This ranges from legal, medical, emotional, and major life decisions. It's when I take a deep breath, and like an Olympic athlete, remember that I've been training for these moments my whole life, and will bring home the Gold for their people. Like Yoda says, "Do or do not, there is no try." (And no, I don't speak in his voice in these moments. Maybe I should.)

As soon as Sandy's face appeared on Zoom, Lady spoke gently, "Tell mom what she's been waiting on is soon to happen." I had no idea what this meant. "Mom has a big health challenge." After I relayed a few details, making Mom smile about Lady's personality and preferences, I gently added, "And, she's referencing a health challenge. Do you understand?"

Sandy smiled and replied, "Yes...I have lung cancer. Shannon, can you ask Lady if when she said 'what I've been waiting on is soon to happen,' is she referring to my surviving or dying from lung cancer? I've been praying this latest treatment will cure me. Does she have anything to say on this?" *Mic drop.*

Once again, I cannot tell people what they want to hear. I also don't want to cause harm. Looking into Lady's eyes, recalling her promise, "Focus on mom, and I'll guide you," I became overwhelmed with...JOY! A woman just told me she has stage 4 lung cancer, and I felt like a giddy gazelle—the excitement Lady and Sandy were soon to feel at being reunited in Spirit. Their love was overwhelming.

But I had a serious question to answer in this sacred moment and needed composure. Jesus popped in and said, "Tell Sandy to pack her bags as if she's planning two trips: Hawaii and Alaska. (In other words, be prepared to live and die.) Tell her to have fun with friends, get excited about life, get her affairs in order, and identify sentimental gifts to be given. Be prepared for both vacations." Jesus's face radiated love. His voice and energy were peaceful, understanding, and all-knowing. Lady wagged her tail.

Strangely, I never feel the need to debate Jesus with endless "what ifs." Trust envelops me. Lady beamed at this advice and woofed, "Tell mom to take me for walks again, imagining me at her side." She showed a purple leash with her name on it hanging by the door. Thankfully, the all-mighty Arizona Cat guided me to ask Sandy if she'd been praying to Jesus before relaying what I'd heard. "YES! All the time. Why? Is He here?"

Relieved, I shared He'd like her to prepare for two very different trips or outcomes. Sandy's face was peaceful as she spoke softly, "It all makes perfect sense. I've been to Hawaii many times, but never Alaska, and always wanted to go! Either place is fine with me!" Lady licked her cheek, and Jesus winked at me.

While what Jesus said made sense to me, I didn't know how the message would land. Now I see why people say, "Jesus, take the wheel." For someone else, it might have been the Spirit of Mother Nature, Allah, or Ganesh taking the wheel. Or for me, The Cheshire Cat!

No medium ever knows for sure when someone's going to die, nor should we tell them. (I'd prefer to know my death date and dress accordingly.) My bet was Sandy was going to Alaska (afterlife). Jesus will need to be more cryptic with me about my "death vacation," as I'd have deduced "H" stands for here, and "A" for afterlife. He'll likely say, "Prepare to eat cake...or possibly cupcakes," and I'll go mad trying to decode the riddle, while my dogs eat frosting off of me.

Messages and the afterlife are personal to someone's (animal or person) dreams or goals. (So, please don't panic if invited to Alaska, or believe you're immortal in Hawaii!)

Sandy's prayer to live (cancer treatment to work) wasn't

answered as her human self wished. She died a month later. But divine love and her dog's love were transforming the sadness of her prayers into her soul's freedom and light, a magic I feel with my spiritual passport.

We can feel divine love while humans. Snapshots of the big, beautiful picture we come from. Death, however, is what brings us HOME. Like Dorothy from *The Wizard of Oz* said, "There's no place like Home." The Grim Reaper and I have played many games of chess in this lifetime. He knows I'm homesick and hopes love and laughter fill my heart until death throws a pie in my face and I yell, "Good one, Jesus!"

Before Sandy and I said goodbye, she grabbed the purple leash with Lady's name, right by the door just as Lady had shown me. "I'm going to take my girl for a walk now, Shannon. I can't thank you enough." I thanked Sandy, Lady, and Jesus for trusting and guiding me to help a kind lady pack her bags. Who's walking by your side? Talk with them; they can hear you.

My life's forever easier (despite the grief I carry) with the unconditional knowledge that love lives on, and WE ARE LOVE. Whether it's resurrection, reincarnation, or the scientific reality that energy never dies, trust you'll hold paws with your pets again. Just ask Teddy and Father John, or better yet, ask your own loved ones.

You'll see your family doing whatever it was they loved doing here. You don't have to be perfect to be granted admission to the afterlife. Still, Mayor Puppypants plans to be the bouncer, so stuff treats in your pockets, and tell him you loved his mom's book.

Since time and location aren't relevant to spirits, your childhood pet, current pets, future spouse, great-great grandparents, coworkers and that hottie you slept with in the jungle can all know each other by energy. Clients are often surprised when I reference family members (of any species) that "didn't meet in real life." If your parents died before your child was born, don't worry...they've met.

The limitations of time and space don't apply to what connects us energetically. Fluffykins, born in 1950, can know Bunny Foo Foo from 2030, and be laughing together with Gramps from 1890. Your ancestors can all tune into your life's reality show and the trainwreck that is your current love life, or cheer you on in your first marathon. Once you accept there are no limits in telepathic communication, it'll start to make sense (as much as possible while human). We can be loved and heckled across the multiverse!

Spirits of all species often arrange for their people to meet or hear about me when I'm the best fit for their Earth family. Before leaving for the beach on a weirdly windy day, a spirit dog said, "Grab your pool noodle." So I grabbed my pool noodle and headed into the ocean in rare rocky water for Sarasota. A woman stood alone about 300 feet from me when I heard a Spirit woman's voice: "Go talk to her!"

I needed relaxation time, and a "No Medium on Duty" sign, as my aura tends to be a lighthouse without a dimmer switch. I replied telepathically to the Spirit woman, "If she wants to talk, she can initiate it." Spirit insisted, like a whistle-blowing lifeguard, "Shannon, you and your noodle, head her way!" I compromised. "Ok, I'll walk towards her, and if she speaks to me, it's fair game for whatever this is." It was a game. I LOVE GAMES!

Within seconds, the stranger joked, "Do you have a death wish bringing that noodle into this stormy ocean?" (No, but her daughter and dog had "death wishes" for their mom to know they were alive and well!) Caitlyn shared she's vacationing, and reading a lot. "What are you reading?" I asked. I felt similar butterflies like when I ask someone their pet's name and know it will be a sign from Spirit.

Caitlyn took a deep breath and sighed, "I'm reading a book about choosing a good medium." And somewhere, a chicken-salad-eating Spirit seagull smiled along with me at this beach bingo game. "Well, I just happen to know a great one…I AM A MEDIUM!"

"You're kidding me!" Caitlyn said in shock, and then shared she'd just lost her thirty-five-year-old daughter and dog within the same year, and sobbed daily missing them both. She asked if I thought *maybe* her daughter in Heaven had arranged our meeting. "Heaven, YES!" I thought in disbelief she could wonder how else we met like this. But again, grief clouds our ability to see miracles right in front of us. Caitlyn's soul knew, but her human self was asking me for validation.

"Absolutely! Spirits work hard to arrange these 'coincidences,' and I'm also an Animal Communicator!" Caitlyn volunteers with rescue. She began processing the "coincidence," and her face softened with love. We could both feel their presence—daughter and dog. Caitlyn confessed, "I've been to a couple of mediums who've disappointed me because they couldn't get answers to the two questions that'll prove without a doubt that my daughter lives on."

No Communicator wants someone's faith, or our reputation, to hang on "proof" we may or may not receive. It's an art form, and I can guarantee contact, but not messages. Her daughter and dog insisted I assure their mom I'm the medium that'll save the day.

As confident in my gifts as I am, I felt great pressure feeling Caitlyn's raw grief and fear. Sacred hearts are in my hands. I trusted in Spirit and announced, "I'll get you your answers!" Then I asked God to hold my ponytail while I mentally puked at any possibility of failure.

Caitlyn's proof of an afterlife hinged on my answering: "Where did we scatter my daughter's ashes?" and "Where did my daughter take her grandmother?" Readings with deceased loved ones are best focused on my bringing through the Spirit's essence and messages, not a pop quiz.

My clients enjoy experiencing the personality of their beloved pets and people—their essence— and it's best not to laser focus on one or two details. If I get most details right, but not the color of their house, hair, or favorite drink, that shouldn't invalidate the session. Especially since house and hair colors change throughout life, and people get sober! But if a medium is off the mark on the spirit's essence, and delivers *only* generic information, that's a problem.

Even if a medium doesn't get answers, never use that as proof your loved ones aren't at peace in spirit. There are too many variables in this process. Your loved ones will find a way to reach you in divine timing, method, and medium. Science dictates energy never dies, and communicating with spirits is an art. Trust they're alive—the sky still exists whatever color an artist paints it. (If Burp or I am your Medium, the sky will be Technicolor-Turtle-Rabbit-Hole-Rainbow. If you hire a puppet-hating Medium, the sky might be...beige.)

We met on Zoom, and Caitlyn was tense, having been unconvinced by prior mediums. I'd spent time with her daughter beforehand, asking her to help me assuage Mom's grief. Her daughter knew the stakes, which is why she chose me, an animal lover that Mom could relate to, and a medium with courage and humor to tame Mom's turbulent waters with nothing more than a pool noodle and prayer!

Flashes of the daughter's life crashed like waves across my mind. So many Disney references...did she take her grandma to Disney? Oh, that seems so cliché, but I'm not supposed to think, just receive. Breathe, trust, and receive. Also, she'd left behind two young kids, so Disney was a big part of her life.

I called on Caitlyn's mom, "Where did your granddaughter take you?" Faster than a flash of lightning, a giant cruise ship blipped in front of me. Like a wily game show host announcing the grand prize, I blurted out, "She took her grandma on a cruise!" Caitlyn cheered with tears in her eyes. My victory was still not complete though, as she tapped her fingers awaiting one more answer.

Caitlyn's dog, dressed as Little Red Riding Hood, began scattering white flowers from a basket all over a garden. I realized the dog was showing me that the flowers were the daughter's ashes. But why *this* fairy tale? OMG...did a big bad wolf steal the ashes and kill an old lady? NO...FOCUS!

The dog kept merrily scattering more flower ashes, excited to be our angelic messenger. AHA! Little Red Riding Hood was on her way to Grandma's house. "You scattered your daughter's ashes in her grandma's garden!"

Little Red Riding Dog took a bow, and Caitlyn's face lightened from anguish to peace—feeling her daughter's and dog's spirits. "I can't believe it; my daughter really is alive. Thank you, Shannon!" I thanked them all for creating this fairy-tale ending.

What color is the sky in your story? Lilac Lucy? Grover Green? Turquoise Teddy? Blue Sky Belle? Belle is my spirit Golden who loves all the animals terrified of thunder as she was in her time here. Tom and I tried EVERYTHING, but the storms in her mind were a Category 5 hurricane. For the love of Belle- Jesus, drop a note in the suggestion box to retire thunder (and mosquitos). Humans, forget fireworks and love your animals more than explosions. (Tom was the man I almost married. I would've been deeply loved, but never have become me. I am now ready to be loved like that because I learned to love me.)

Tulip's parents were fighting for months about whether to euthanize her. They called me in for a house call to settle the dispute. Tulip hadn't been eating or drinking, and hanging on by a thread when I met her. She was in pain, ready to pass weeks ago.

Grief and resentment permeated the air. Dad wasn't ready to let go.

None of us are ready to let go, but we must honor their lives through the moment of death. No animal would ask us to suffer on their behalf, and we must be as kind. Choose mercy.

Both parents stared intently while I silently spoke with Tulip, listening about her wishes for euthanasia. After being motionless before my arrival, Tulip stood up and drank water! Dad snapped at Mom, "See, she's not ready!" It can be very tricky when we see an animal perk up right before euthanasia. Miracles do happen, but unless Tulip started singing show tunes while doing zoomies, I knew she was ready. She'd been suffering too long.

Tulip, like many pets, was already sensing imminent relief. Animals are very skillful at traveling between worlds, and can experience a preview of coming attractions they'll soon enjoy: peace, relief, joy, freedom, food buffets, and reunions with loved ones. They aren't headed to a pity party. They're a Guest of Honor at their baby shower/graduation/birthday party combo. The same soul we know and love begins a new life, as present life worries slip away.

Her parents continued to fight as I asked Tulip why she finally arose to drink water. She threw me a funny bone. "I knew I'd get thirsty doing so much talking with you!" So I repeated aloud her carefully chosen, playful, sincere words, and her parents laughed. It was the first of Tulip's two parting gifts. I was honored to be her advocate, communicating messages to her beloved parents whose relationship was suffering as badly as Tulip's body.

Tulip said, "I'M READY TO GO NOW. I'VE BEEN READY. PLEASE, I BEG YOU CALL SOMEONE NOW." Dad agreed now that he felt Tulip's soul speaking. Mom called a home vet that came within a couple of hours.

I thanked Tulip and her parents, and before leaving, Tulip performed a miracle of love. She said, "Tell them, Surf's up! I'll surf my way into Heaven." I shared the image Tulip sent me of herself in a pink bikini singing, Surf's up! Tulip was more than ready, and the image brought her parents comfort. They had met each other while surfing, mom wearing a pink bikini.

Don't mistake signs of life for wanting to extend a painful life. People and animals in transition often show life and joy so that we don't remember them as the frail suffering body, but rather the happy soul who deserves to fly free with our love sending them. We want them to go have fun, not worry about us.

Parents fight back tears on their kids' first day of school so kids can feel secure in their new adventure. They retrieve their kids at the end of the school day, and your loved ones will retrieve you when your life's bell rings. Until then, you'll visit each other in dreams, through mediums, and amazing connections that will perfectly unfold as you invite and allow them. Don't freak out if you feel you're not receiving signs. Maybe they've come and you don't remember, or you discounted miracles as coincidences. Stay open, ask, receive.

Animals don't *wait* at The Rainbow Bridge. Their lives immediately continue, even if they rest before exploring their new forms. The "Bridge" is a symbol, like gates, tunnels, and lights. I've seen people and animals arrive in Spirit in as many ways as there are personalities. It's a personal, beautiful process. There's not a separate afterlife for people and animals. God doesn't discriminate. If you want to bounce over the rainbow, walk, run, swim or dance through a light tunnel or a cupcake paved paradise, God speed!

The afterlife seems to resemble what's in our hearts, which for animals is pure love. People should choose wisely how they live, because spending eternity re-living pain they caused others would be hell. As Kermit wisely taught me, we don't take our designer tote bags with us. We bring love, regrets and memories. Lessons. It seems Spirit finds a place for everyone, with varying amenities depending on our earthly resumes.

Dads who lose their titles won't be in a daughter's afterlife, unless she welcomes the reunion. He will be in his own afterlife (same hotel, different floors). There is nothing to fear about anyone or anything.

One client's granny insisted she bring her purse to Heaven. I spoke with her spirit (she had dementia) when she was soon to pass. She kicked off her shoes and said, "I won't need these, but please ask Jesus if I can bring my purse." I respected and relayed her message. (I wouldn't mind bringing my teddy bear!)

Jesus, of course, smiled. "Well, Shannon, you can tell her she doesn't need her purse. We don't check ID (sorry, Puppypants), and she won't need Earthly possessions. But, if she really wants it, sure she can bring it!" My client (the granddaughter) affirmed, "Granny never goes ANYWHERE without her purse, and kicks off her shoes immediately, wherever she is!"

I knew her purse wasn't actually flying to Heaven (maybe in the future), but that Jesus meant her purse, like a boat or car for people who cherish those, or Puppypants' dirty tennis ball collection—these "amenities" will be there for them.

Granny began our session highly agitated, screaming for her purse, and then rested peacefully after our session, bringing my client to happy tears. Thank God Jesus didn't mention a TSA purse check! With Spirit having an open-door policy with everyone crossing their border, it would be silly to have a bag check after all. (I suppose if someone wants that job though, they'll have at least one customer.)

Randy, my Spirit Shih Tzu, reminds everyone to have a Pet Guardian assigned in case of illness or death. Who will care for your animals? Include them in a trust and your will. Randy came to me full of life at fourteen years old when his mom died, and he landed in a shelter. We locked eyes when I was volunteering, and I adopted him at first glance.

He looked enough like the Mayor to fool my landlord that they were the same dog. A fluffy *Parent Trap* type caper. So which mom will Randy be with in the afterlife? His first mom or me? Both! Spirits are multidimensional beings capable of simultaneously being with loved ones here, in Heaven, and beyond. Superheroes with unlimited sky miles.

Randy guided Grover (Shih Tzu brother from another mother) through a near-death medical challenge while writing this chapter. I don't hear from Randy often, but silence doesn't mean absence. Randy gave Grover new life. I know this because whenever I looked at Grover's fragile little body, I felt Randy's spirit, and kept calling Grover, Randy.

I had accepted Grover might fly home, but Jesus packed his bags to stay in Sarasota. A wake-up call for me to play more and worry less. Our pets' short lives matter above all the rest. Grover will play ball until his last breath, and then retrieve it on the other side. (His high-pitched bark might get him bounced back to me! Depends who's working the door that day.)

Death is an angelic friend who restores our youth. A client's mom in Spirit—a beautician in life—laughed, "There's not a plastic surgeon on Earth who can make people look as beautiful as we do here in the afterlife!" In the meantime, thank God for cruelty-free cosmetics, and the beautiful smiles our pets put on our faces every day. May we see ourselves through their eyes, and never say unkind things to our faces in the mirrors. (Grover's listening.)

Pit Bulls and Parolees star Tia Torres gets it right by not labeling dogs or people by their looks or painful pasts. In one episode, I was thrilled to see their beautiful rescue dogs drinking water from a cooler labeled, "The Fountain of Youth"! There are so many fun ways to reinforce wellness. I've labeled my dogs' water bowl and my fridge dispenser this, too. Cheers to all of us—young, healthy spring chickens. May we keep our animals and ourselves young at heart.

Among many creatures, from human spirits to horses, animals have shown me greeting every nameless homeless animal, the ones who weren't chosen, the ones who were forgotten, harmed in exploitation, or only lived in fear. Without exception, every single one is escorted, loved, and welcomed HOME to Spirit.

For everyone who's cried that an animal went unloved, they didn't. They were unlucky, but not unloved. Never doubt the power of the love you send to lonely souls. Keep sending it, it's reciprocated.

Go beyond thoughts and prayers, and use your voice and hands to help paws in need.

Animals can recall a painful life, but they FEEL only love as a Spirit. They wish for humans to be more like animals. Darwin can kiss my mutt because humans are the students; animals are our teachers. Evolve to be furrier, sillier, and freer while here on Earth. Don't spoil precious memories with guilt. Learn and do better when you know better.

Trust they're divinely happy and can always see you, so amuse them! Death proposes toasts to eternal life and laughter together. Death is a temporary thief who redeems itself on reunion day and pours divine magic—signs of life all over us and our animals. Death takes the body, not the soul. Cheers, you heart-breaking frenemy. In the end, we shall laugh together.

16

EXTRA FUR AND SLOBBER

If everyone likes you, you're doing something wrong.
Shannon Spring

Kermit offered me advice on finding "Mr. Spring." "He'll find you, Mom. Don't ruin your surprise party trying to figure it out. Trust." In Animals I Do Trust. Thanks, Dr. Kermit. I can't wait to woof him. Spirit has already told me his first name many times through clever games. He'll jump off the pages of my mind and write himself into our life's play. Will he ride up on a Harley, a boat, or a unicorn? And will he have cake or a Cheshire Cat grin? Spirit plays a fierce game of poker, but my money is on Cupid for the win.

Humans presume to know me. Animals do. Animals have wisdom and secrets deep within the same way my backyard has my dogs' beheaded stuffed animals buried beneath. They feel their way through life and are fearlessly, divinely connected.

Smiley is Carol's therapy dog who brought love to kids at a domestic violence shelter and kept his Pops (Carol's dad) laughing while she was at work. Smiley insisted, "Tell mom I NEED a sock monkey doll!" Carol dutifully bought the monkey, which Smiley then ignored, making Pops laugh hysterically. Carol joked, "Why'd you make me waste $20 on that damn monkey?" Smiley flashed his proud smile. "Just wait, Shannon."

A few months passed and Carol messaged: "He has still not played with that damn monkey. I'll put it away." The day Pops passed, Carol arrived home to find "that damn, adorable sock monkey" in the middle of her living room floor. The two men in her life, dog and dad—heroes and partners in crime—pulled one last prank to make their girl laugh. Everyone laughed.

Two years later, Smiley went into a medical crisis and Carol called asking if Smiley was ready to pass. Smiley was in bad shape, but said he wanted to fight for his life. An emergency vet triaged him and they went home with hopeful determination, but a grim prognosis. While laying on Carol, Smiley confided to me, "Tell mom to watch Farley for signs when it's time for me to pass. He'll know, he'll guide you."

Carol has a large pack of rescues. Farley is a big, loud bloodhound who Smiley appointed as First Responder, foretelling, "Farley will lay by me and hold my paw when it's time." Exactly one week later while Smiley lay on the floor, Farley jumped off the couch, curled up next to him, and laid his giant paw on top of Smiley's. Carol sent me a photo of the brotherly love. It was time to say goodbye. Pops was waiting with open arms, and a spot on his "barker-lounger."

Animal communication is unique to each animal's personality, and connection with their people. No pet replaces another. They work together to keep our hearts open so we may continue the hard work of being human. Adopting again is a tribute, not a betrayal. More rescues joined Carol's pack.

While snacking on my favorite contraband...pretzels, Carol's Spirit dog, Sarge, dropped in, chomping popcorn. Sarge directed, "Message Carol NOW. Tell her I'm eating popcorn like this (loud cow chewing sounds). She'll love it!"

I obeyed and Carol exclaimed, "Shannon, I'M EATING POPCORN RIGHT NOW! SARGE WAS THE ONLY DOG IN THE PACK I FED

POPCORN. SHE CHEWED SUPER LOUDLY, SO OTHER DOGS WOULD BE JEALOUS!" Pets always know what their people are doing (and eating). Before accusing someone of eating your snacks, make sure it wasn't an afterlife animal first!

MJ hired me to talk with her boyfriend's cat and hers about why the two cats began viciously fighting since moving in together. "Hi, cats, I'm Shannon, and I'm curious why..." Telepathic fur flew; they interrupted to meow disapproval of the couple. "DO NOT PROCREATE!" They repeated it for emphasis: "Do NOT procreate!"

They were adamant MJ and Doug not make babies. MJ's cat warned, "Tell MJ to CHECK HER BIRTH CONTROL!" MJ rolled her eyes at me. "Sorry, Shannon, you're way off." I waited a moment... then MJ freaked out. "OMG! I know what my cat means...my birth control implant expired three months ago...I totally forgot...how did she know?"

They know. These cats knew she'd forgotten her birth control and this couple shouldn't procreate. It wouldn't last. They abhorred the couple's "mating rituals" which, according to the cats, "sounds like feral cats scratching each other's eyes out!" #DoDoggyStyle. #CatStyleIsScary.

Chester the Dalmatian's parents wanted to experience animal communication for fun to know what he's thinking and feeling, and consult on a minor health issue. I asked, "What would make you happier and healthier?" I felt Chester's giddiness being in the spotlight, woofing his wishes to me. Chester said his family was fun, requested bananas, and said he's lonely when they're away.

Animals speak in a stream of consciousness like I do. I asked, "Do you need to see the vet?" Chester shook his head no, and confidently announced, "I need to see Dr. Ruth!" Enter Dr. Ruth Westheimer's face, the ninety-year-old famous sex expert and radio host. Mic drop!

I felt like an awkward guidance counselor with my student's parents. "This is going to sound weird, but...Chester says he needs to see Dr. Ruth!" They burst out laughing. "We just talked about Dr. Ruth last night! He's right! We need more sex!" Chester felt Dr. Ruth sounded way more fun than the vet, and that if she could fix his parents, she could help his minor limp (and love life, too).

Jellybean, an emotional support pig, and I spoke so his adoring mom could learn what he desired to feel happier and healthier. Jellybean said, "I love listening to Lady Gaga and Michael Jackson, and I'd like to learn to spell my name. I'm also very concerned about Mom walking. I have to watch her carefully." I was fascinated, but confused. Sally wasn't blind, so why did he protect her while walking?

Sally squealed in joy. "We always listen to Gaga and Jackson during playtime, and I just began teaching him alphabet letters using those big kindergarten ones!" Sally kissed him with pride. "How exciting, now Jellybean wants to learn his name too! I'll teach him how. He's such a smart piggy!" I felt elated for Jellybean to learn to arrange the block letters to spell his name and impress his fan club.

I could only see Sally's face via video chat, so I asked, "I know you're not blind, so why is he concerned about you walking?" Sally pointed down to a big cast—foot surgery. "Jellybean's making sure I don't fall! He's so sweet." Jellybean, like Benny Pig, loves deeply. Two pigs in blankets safe at home loving their families.

A sanctuary asked for my emergency help on a goat who couldn't walk. Sweet Gertie said, "I have Lemonade Legs." I knew I'd heard her correctly, but hadn't a clue what it meant. Gertie wisely knew to use a term I could easily research, given my limited scientific knowledge. Animals, and human spirits alike, know I need to be able to say it, spell it, mime it, relate to it, or Google it. Lemonade Legs is a magnesemia disorder, and the sanctuary was grateful they could help Gertie, now that they had an answer.

Then I met Spice, a beautiful red dun horse, who said, "I have spaghetti legs" (weakness), and showed me in my high school field hockey uniform and shin guards to convey that she had shin splints. Her mom confirmed these injuries. As pet parents know, it can be challenging to know exactly what's hurting them, to what degree, and if an issue is medical, emotional, behavioral, or a mirror of us. And, what can help reduce or alleviate suffering?

Spice previously carted her heavyset mom around in a wagon in a brutal temperatures. Her mom asked me if Spice enjoyed her job. Animals will do almost anything to make their people happy, and Spice loved making her mom happy. We can always ask ourselves if we'd like to trade places with our animals, and let that guide our choices. Spice needed to be a horse whose only job now was to love and be loved, and heal. Thankfully, unlike too many horses I meet, Spice's mom agreed. "Spice Girls" must be in harmony after all...and being Mom's workhorse was out of sync with kindness.

Spice requested pies galore and then surprised me with, "I'd like Sam Adams Pumpkin Spice Ale...yummy," and licked her lips. I mused, "Can you have beer? OMG, your mom's going to think I'm a bad influence...and I'm sober! Ok, I'll tell her that you're old enough, and maybe horses can have beer." (Animals mostly only ask for things that'll help them or that won't hurt them.) Mom laughed, "I used to buy Spice *Sam Adams Pumpkin Spice Ale* for years. Sure, I'll buy more. I didn't know she missed it!"

Spice loved her name monogrammed on things, and mentioned wanting to leave a legacy. A few months later, while working on my agent query letter (my book's dating profile), I knew it needed more flavor. My writer's group leader joked (unknowingly being hightailed by a horse), "Do you have like...an alcoholic animal you could mention?" Spice grinned, galloping in to lend a hoof! "Yes, I have an alcoholic horse who mentioned wanting to leave a legacy. I guess she wants to be honored in my book!"

Horseplay rescued my query and made the whole class smile—a spontaneous moment even seasoned writers couldn't have scripted. But a horse on a mission could! Well neighed, Spice! As I emailed Spice's mom about her cameo, I felt a wave of sadness. I hoped my feeling was wrong, but her mom replied with both enthusiasm for Spice's literary debut, and that her euthanasia was scheduled within two days. I felt Spice was eager to be free of her body, and recovery wasn't possible. Spice created magic through a fun, timely way to get my attention to help them say goodbye. We had a reading to help them process the transition.

Spice was proud of her stunning beauty. "I'm just so Divine (spoken as De-vine)." Mom smiled. Spice's paperwork stated: "Devine"—a nickname. Spice sassily pointed at the stacked cases of spice ale beer. "Take it to holiday parties, Mom, and tell people there's plenty of Spice to go around!" She then showed cherries jubilee, a reference Mom couldn't place. Whenever that happens, I tuck it away—it might unfold for my client, or be a message for me.

As I felt Spice's body preparing to transition, I wanted to CHARGE LIKE A RACEHORSE, feeling like a "force of nature" —power that was imminent the moment she released her body. Freedom! Inside me, I felt the laughing trees in Scotland, Charlene Tiger's majesty, Sniffer Bear's hormones, and Spice's fire. The excitement coursing through my veins was intoxicating and liberating. Giddy up!

Spice flashed to her Spirit self, solo in a lush green meadow, soaking in the sunshine, taking a few minutes before other horses would summon her to join them. Cheers...Spice is Free!

Release guilt knowing animal friends are free of suffering, thriving in a higher realm. We're only sampling the sweetness of our souls here. The afterlife is like an overflowing jubilant dessert fountain of youth vs. this hangry human sample. About a year later, I received a surprise—cherries jubilee from a client whose horse's life I helped save. (She didn't know about Spice.)

"Thank you, Shannon. We wish you *spicy* good fortune!" (A "typo" meant to say, "sweet." But I knew it was divine horseplay—a hello from a sweet and spicy friend.) Spice taught me that people will stop saddling me with their heavy carts when I stop handing them the reins. I'm a mustang, not a maiden, simply alter my gait and the gates of prosperity break open. Sweet freedom!

Jazzy the Cat earned extra catnip cookies when she clawed at her elderly mother, making the woman bruise and bleed. Agnes and Jazzy had been Mom and cat for 16 years when Jazzy began "attacking Agnes," according to Agnes' three grown daughters. Two daughters were angry and frightened enough to euthanize Jazzy. But the third daughter, Leigh, reached out, stating Jazzy told her to contact a pet psychic. Leigh took a chance, paws in prayer, that I could help explain what the fluff was happening.

Jazzy, Leigh, Agnes, and I gathered for an "interpawvention." I knew the second I read Leigh's email that Jazzy was on a sacred mission to help her mom. Jazzy immediately apologized for her maniacal methods stating, "I had to do something drastic, out of character to draw attention. Something is seriously wrong...but with Agnes, not me."

Jazzy hadn't turned into a demon cat out for blood. Animals are limited in their ways to communicate in ways people can understand. Jazzy was a devoted daughter like her human sisters. She knew Agnes was being overmedicated, and was fearful Agnes was in danger and could die, leaving Jazzy helpless.

The women wrote down a list of the meds, and Jazzy then described the effects of each one, without my knowing the medication names or purpose. Agnes confirmed the debilitating or unpleasant side effects Jazzy relayed. "Double Trouble," Jazzy insisted. The daughters were accidentally double-dosing Agnes, who was on fourteen meds—a recipe for death more than life.

Jackson Galaxy, from the series *My Cat From Hell*, would have to change the show's name to *My Cat From Heaven* because Earth Angels like Jazzy are working miracles to save their people.

I once taught my very successful animal communication kids' camp through an online school that later banned my class when a religious zealot freaked out over my being a "psychic." Despite dozens of five-star reviews, they needed a villain—a teacher who dared teach kids they have magic inside, and that animals are emotionally intelligent beings. Number-two-pencil-minded-minions don't have bubbles for empathy on their robotic achievement tests.

I attempted a productive conversation about animal communication being intuition and empathy (something non-psychopaths are born with). Our sixth sense inner wisdom is for survival and compassion. *Sesame Street* teaches empathy and kindness for all creatures, and that the world is a rainbow of feelings and lifestyles. Argue with a Muppet, and you'll be the puppet! And that's what Faye and her joyless legal goon did—spouted pitiful platitudes with smirks.

Teachers should nurture, inspire, and protect childhood innocence while also preparing kids for life. Respect for animals is essential for character development. I was out-loving and out-funning a narrow-minded platform that boasts a nonsecular agenda, but presupposes zealots know better than parents do when choosing courses for their kids.

The curriculum hunter, Social Studies teacher Faye, labeled my class pseudoscience and drooled over re-enacting 1692, featuring me in their wannabe Salem witch trial. They held the matches, and I held the truth, so, "Light the fire, basic bitches. Cackle on, my ancestor witches!" Magic is our birthright; I RSVP'd to their fight. Kids and animals know wrong from right, and they are my people.

Not only is yesterday's metaphysics today's science, but labeling the "supernatural" as inappropriate for kids is comically ignorant. Kids are already tuned into things adults shut down out of fear or self-judgment. Empowering kids to understand their sixth sense can reduce anxiety and poor decisions (like adults make, too). Teach them to listen for answers their hearts already possess, and maybe they can learn to be something schools don't teach—happy.

The supernatural is simply nature which doesn't require approval or applause to create butterflies or The Butterfly Effect. Cracking caterpillar people out of their cuckoo cocoons is one of my specialties, although I do prefer flying with fellow butterflies. Label me a rebel with a cause for paws. I'm teaching kids camps on my playground now.

As Faye furrowed her brow at my invitational play-bow, her cat made a "Psst" gesture with his paw in front of his mouth. Kitty whispered, "Psst…Shannon…Mom needs a BUTT MINT…she's being a real stinker!" I laughed through my anger because Faye was being an asshole (my word) who needed a butt mint to freshen her attitude. Her cat supported my cause— his cause—allowing a class that gives voice to his "people."

The moment he'd whispered *Butt Mint*, like a secret game show password, Faye began squirming in her seat. I realized while I'd lost, I'd really won. Because while I'm having fun talking with her cat, she's stuck in her puritanical hell, forgetting about one famous talking snake, who, if you ask him, is also innocent. No one forced apples into anyone's mouth, or parents to enroll their kids in my talking animals class, and write glowing reviews. Faye was served a telepathic booty mint for a fresher perspective on her crappy attitude.

Mint isn't just a treatment for emotional buttheads, but also helps reduce gas, upset stomachs, and seasonal allergies, along with a host of other healing qualities. I know this because a dog once demanded, "Empty grandma's purse! The cure is in her purse!" Grandma eagerly emptied her giant black bag and a tin of mints spilled out, along with a *Golden Girls* keychain and hairspray.

Poochie exclaimed, "Bingo! Get me some mint herbs please," which soon thereafter remedied his gastrointestinal distress and made Grandma a hero. It's vital to differentiate between herbs, oils, roots, etc. Going hog wild for everything mint can be toxic. Type, flavor, dosage, possible interactions, and many other considerations have to be made on all treatments, along with a vet consultation. Poochie knew we'd honor his request responsibly, and sang, *"Thank you for being a friend."* (Got that song stuck in your head now?)

A group of cats once demanded grapes, and I recalled grapes were toxic, which they knew I'd research. And in so doing, I discovered grape seed oil is what they needed. While they could've just said that, it was important for me to learn how animals use what I know to teach me how to help them. Never discount what they say, find the truth in it. I hear you say grapes, but those are toxic, and you aren't letting this go…what is it you need me to know?

Remember when mosquitoes showed me a giant chocolate bar? I had to follow the cacao crumbs those psychos taunted me with.

The more informed and confident I've become, the more specific animals' requests become. Instead of just "bones," they'll say, "I want big, beefy, broth, bonafide good boy bones from Barking Bistro!" Animals and spirits make it clear how urgent a message is by locking on it, repeating it, and the feelings and words they send me. (Including a person's need for a super-size butt mint!)

I enjoyed working with the animals at a farm sanctuary in New York, where their caretakers love and individually respect them. Molly the duck had recently lost her duck boyfriend, Mike. Many animals grieve their people and animal companions with overt suffering; others miss their physical presence, but focus on their beloved's spiritual presence.

And then there's Molly, who if she were human, could be considered a suspect for Mike's death, given her rapid rebound. Did she have a secret life insurance policy on him? "How's she doing? Does she miss him?" the director asked. Mike's death hit the people hard. So it was comic relief when Molly nonchalantly replied, "I've moved on. I have a new love interest!" I shared Molly's confession as sensitively as I could. Immediately, the director confirmed, "She does! OMG, she does have a new boyfriend! His name's Boysen."

Whew! I know animals are practical, but Molly easily waddled back to fluffing her feathers for romance. I admire her. Molly still loves Mike, but Boysen can bring her a good (non-auto-corrected) "duck." Mike's spirit was equally unflappable. No duck would replace him, just provide companionship for his lady. Unselfish true love.

Boysen enjoys his study role and told me he's popular with the ladies. The director informed me Boysen has a second girlfriend, "Shannon," a needy duck much like a Shannon McDevitt I once knew. A quackerific love triangle that I needed to get to the bottom of! Who would Boysen give the final rose to? How did the lady ducks feel about each other? Was I secretly rooting for my duck namesake? My beak was all up in their business!

Boysen chose Shannon (even though he didn't have to choose because…he's a duck) because she needs him more. Previously an unlucky duck, she follows him everywhere now. "Besides," he said, "Molly's heart belongs to Mike," and he's more than a one-night cluck. Molly expressed compassion for Shannon (not me, I'm on my own in the dating world). There'll be no feathers flying in this love triangle. A sister-wife situation where everyone gets what they need, especially Boysen.

Animals grieve, get jealous and insecure, and fall in love. They can also cut themselves and each other a break. Since I was unaware of this plucky situation until the director confirmed, I preempted anthropomorphism. I support their free bird lifestyle—every duck deserves to honk the one they're with without judgment. Despite my open mind, it's safe to assume I won't receive the final rose. Speciesism works both ways.

Shelters are tasked with many tough assignments, but naming animals is fun. It's not fun seeing animals named after trauma, disability, or perceived flaws: one-eyed animals named Pirate, three-legged ones called Tripod, big-eared "Dumbos," a flea-infested one named FLEAS, and an abused dog whose head was stuck in a bucket and animal control named...Bucket. Lack of creativity is also one of my biggest "people peeves."

It's people having buckets on their heads who post laughing emojis on compassionate comments expressing disapproval. Names are powerful. Cheap laughs aren't worth sabotaging a desperate animal's chances. Humans excuse cruelty as traditions or jokes, with chilling disregard. Substituting ego for compassion is irresponsible and dangerous.

Animals respect authenticity, and people who can laugh at themselves and learn from their mistakes. Accountability is more important than infallibility. Put ourselves in their paws and ask how we'd feel about the decisions we make that affect animals' fates. I know a few government officials who need to be renamed and deserve 23 hours without a potty or play break because of understaffing and underfunding.

In 2023, Manatee County, FL commissioners (one being a marine) starred in an anti-animal cruelty marketing video with shelter pets after they'd just voted AGAINST anti-puppy mill legislation. Manipulative self-promotion after empowering PETLAND and other corrupt (follow the money) pet businesses that prioritize profits over animal welfare, and denying punishment for repeat animal cruelty offenders. #BeAPuppyMarineNotAGreedMachine.

Closed minds dismiss animals' voices and the validity of animal communication, and label animal activists crazy, while normalizing cruelty. Animal Communication is similar to employing the services of a talented trainer or nutritionist. Well-behaved and healthier pets are overall easier to adopt and cost less time and resources to care for. Greedy government officials cost animals everything. Spay and neuter corrupt officials.

Even rescues can mistake animal communication for creating work for them, rather than solving problems. One shelter wanted to name a big, dark mutt (already the hardest to adopt) Zodiac. I said, "You mean like the serial killer?" I offered to ask "Zodiac" what he'd like to be called, and the director agreed, mostly to shut me up.

Zodiac was thrilled to be seen, and now heard, through me. While chatting, he shared, "My last mom was a bag of Cheetos, and I really want some peaches please." I sympathized—my family are gas station hotdogs. "What would you like your name to be?" I asked excitedly. "I want to be called (movie star) PATRICK SWAYZE! He's so handsome...and I'm handsome, but I don't know if people see that!" Mic drop. (Nobody puts Zodiac in a corner!)

My heart melted in adoration of his cuteness. I knew this was a perfect example of something that could look like bullshit to the shelter. How the fluff could I prove this is truly what Zodiac, the non-serial killer dog, wanted to be named? I crunched on some pretzels and rewarded my psychic detective brain with a mindless Netflix binge to solve the mystery.

Zodiac was secretly influencing my program selection. I began watching the comedy series, *Insatiable,* and in one episode, the two main male characters get into a silly fight about an upcoming production of...*Dirty Dancing* (it gets weirder). "I'm Patrick Swayze! You're Jennifer Gray!" argued the first man. "No, I'm definitely Patrick Swayze in this duo, you're the girl!" Character bitch slapping ensued, and I was happily spooked.

While Zodiac's body was curled up on a shelter's cement floor behind bars, his spirit and I were spooning, enjoying an actual "Netflix and Chill" having the time of our lives. The series was so funny I kept watching, and nearly twirled my dogs in the air at what happened next.

A few episodes later, "Patrick Swayze" (the character who fought to play him in the production), announced something like, "I could go for some Cheetos..and peaches!" In no universe has anyone ever said the words "Cheetos and peaches" in the same sentence. This abandoned mutt's new movie star name would shine the spotlight to guarantee adoption. Zodiac vs. Patrick Swayze….it's obvious which dog's fan club is going to explode. Patrick was adopted before ever hitting the red carpet. With a mutt muse, magic multiples.

The moment I met Goofy, a macho Pitt-Bull mix, he begged to be called Harley. The shelter agreed he was definitely a Harley, and bestowed him a dignity that might've helped his love life pre-neuter. Goofy is a cute name, but not for a large, clever athletic player who could inspire rap music history.

Harley told me they could help him find just the right person to adopt him if he was marketed at local Harley-Davidson shops with flyers and cutouts of himself. "I want a cool motorcycle Dad with a sidecar I can ride in." An image straight out of a biker dude mag.

When I arrived at the shelter later that day, I saw two nondescript men arriving. I instantly liked them, but didn't know why. I relayed Harley's wish to the director to have his face featured at a Harley-Davidson fundraiser. "Huh, that's funny, those two men just in here are from Harley-Davidson, wanting to help with a fundraiser!" He knew I had no way of knowing that, so maybe I was the real deal. Anyone could agree he looked more like a Harley. But this twist of fate piqued the hardened director's curiosity.

Our shelter meeting had gotten delayed, which caused me to arrive at the same time as these men I didn't know existed. No coincidence! This was the first shelter animal I'd delivered a message for. He was ready for game day.

The director had tried to trick me earlier by having me ask Goofy how Goofy felt about "Dave," one of the shelter volunteers. He scrunched his face the way I had when trying to discourage Puppy-pants' potential adopters years ago. So either he was psyching me out, or playing double jeopardy, making me think he was psyching me out!

No matter the circumstances, I don't make assumptions based on human behavior. I always go straight to the biker dog for answers on what's really blowing in the wind. Harley shared, "Dave's a FUN guy who takes me on field trips and buys me burgers. He's awesome!" I was grateful to Harley for giving me the last laugh on the psychic trap. I didn't blame the director for testing me. As long as someone isn't endangering an animal or wasting my time.

Harley desperately wanted a lure course to sharpen his prey drive. He once stole my favorite Cheshire Cat thermos and raced around the play yard playing keep-away. No way could I catch him, so I silently asked him to please bring it back to me because it was *my* toy. He did, and I thanked him for being a silly good boy. He drove staff crazy, not coming when they called. He threw me a bone that day. I didn't demand or get angry. I surrendered as the older, slower dog.

He's easy to love—a challenging and brilliant showman. Not every animal we love is meant to be ours or will fit in with our pack. Harley waited years, but a cool bachelor with a motorcycle adopted him and made his dreams come true. I keep a cut out of him in my window. Even in cardboard, he's full of life.

Privacy in the shower or sex isn't one of the perks of being an Animal Communicator who runs a 24/7 Open Mic. A horny black bear named Sniffer knew I'd often claimed, "Nothing's weird to me." Sniffer accepted and won that challenge. A talented animal friend and wildlife photographer with a Mr. Rogers-like soul was concerned he hadn't seen Sniffer in a while. I decided to reach out to the bear and report back to "Mr. Rogers" any info, excluding that I was now Sniffer's human honey.

Sniffer, like all animals, is aware when his species or any is under attack. He was brokenhearted about the upcoming state-sanctioned bear hunt. He loved his life and lamented that humans can't find better ways to entertain themselves or feel powerful, and then defend their barbaric torture of bears by labeling them nuisances and dangers.

"Mr. Rogers" works tirelessly to show bears peacefully living and loving in hopes people will see them as souls, not trophies or commendable kills. Sniffer showed me what depression felt like through a bear's spirit. It was no different than the cellular sadness I've known.

Finally Sniffer, like I often do after pouring our hearts out, added comic relief to his grief. He lifted his giant paw and slapped me on the back (telepathically, but it physically sent me flying forward) and exclaimed, "Life's hard, but there's always sex, Shannon. Am I right? SEX IS FANTASTIC!" His flirtatious side was hilarious and freakishly foreshadowing.

Later that night, Sniffer merged faces with my boyfriend, mid-thrust during sex. Sniffer had called my bluff. A BOYFRIEND WITH A BEAR FACE WAS WEIRD! A bear was co-opting this man's body and making me roar with laughter. Well-played, Sniffer. Sniffer's sex bomb was an interesting twist to his sensitive side, an alpha male with a teddy bear heart. But this interspecies threesome was weird, even for me.

I cannot haphazardly send out challenges to the animal kingdom anymore. They're always listening! Sex with a bear would be intense… perhaps unlike Goldilocks's one-star review, for me, it would be just right. (Reincarnated bear-me is already living that fairy tale.)

About a year later, I met Sniffer in the furry flesh. He snuck up behind me out in the wild where I knew he foraged. I turned around and WOW…what a magnificent beast with a wildly curious look in his eyes as to what my Little Red Riding Hood hiney was doing in his forest. Was I finally going to shed my human suit and switch teams? My heart already had.

His face fascinated me as I inhaled his powerful presence—600 pounds of love. But it's one thing to speak or mate with a wild animal from the safety of my tempurpedic, and quite another to encounter them in-person on their turf. Yelling, "WASSUP!" to Sniffer seemed foolhardy. I tiptoed away with my heart screaming, "HOT HONEY, that's the bear from my bedroom!" (Later, I texted him an eggplant emoji.)

People can coexist with wildlife, but we must play by their rules and not endanger them. Hugging a wild bear is something that remains a fantasy, since finding myself in a precarious hibernation situation isn't this fairy tale's ending. While I have to respect interspecies boundaries, Sniffer has VIP access to me, my cottage, and my future unsuspecting husband, anytime. A 600 pound wildly inappropriate teddy bear doesn't have to knock. Perhaps I should forewarn "Mr. Spring." Nah, this Goldilocks will let future husband-bear prove he's "just right."

17
TUSKS FOR TRUTH

The highest form of knowledge is empathy, for it requires us to suspend our egos and live in another's world.
Plato

One of the reasons kids and animals take so much abuse is their eyes speak love and truth. They see through people, which terrifies dark hearts and dishonest characters. Inhumane circuses and SeaWorld staff dress to look like the animals they exploit. They project happiness onto animals who perform tricks out of hunger and fear of punishment, making animal abuse "family entertainment." Kidnapping kids of any species is creepy.

Many kids even think animals come from zoos. Some zoos do good work caring for animals who can't care for themselves, and some successfully rehabilitate and release them. But capturing healthy animals for "educational purposes" only educates us on human greed. Locking up beautiful beasts to study and enjoy them is narcissistic delusion. You are now studying a prisoner. This book helps you learn about my world without staring at me in a cage, and hopefully inspires more respect for animals.

Cows consider the "Happy Cow" campaigns…udder bullshit. Gentle souls experiencing extraordinary violence doesn't make for a great "Got Milk?" campaign. #GoMilkYourself. A bull named Larry showed the children's book, *Click, Clack, Moo*, by Doreen Cronin, which told me he needed his voice to be heard. The book is about cows making demands of the farmer by typing letters negotiating their needs and the farmer's demands of them. The farmer learns a valuable lesson: "Moo" means something.

Larry requested a gentler caretaker, a massage for his migraines, and to join "Big Bessy," his best friend who'd been sold. All of Larry's wishes were granted. Bessy's mom had just become vegan, loved her new connection with her animal family, and welcomed Larry with love.

There are two types of people when it comes to animal welfare: those who understand why it was a BFD when animal crackers boxes stopped picturing animals in cages, and those who whine about woke-ness. Cruelty is insidiously normalized. It takes courage to question tradition. It's not about the cookie boxes, and if you don't understand that, no cookies for you!

Naming the elephant in the room is hard not to do when I can talk to the elephant. While most won't acknowledge the elephant, I'm willing to talk about it. Animals are dying to name the "elephant in the room" so they can heal the obvious wounds people pretend not to see. Speaking their truths and being heard helps them feel loved, respected, and truly seen as individual souls.

One of the first elephants I spoke with was Renny, who lives in Nepal. He's a flirty, fun, proud, and playful soul. Animals and people share the same desire to be free spirits and free of persecution. When people feel captive in their lives and hearts, they'll often find ways to impose their suffering on free spirits by capturing or controlling animals for amusement and profit—a threat wild animals live with every day.

Renny, like all elephants, wants to peacefully live his life in nature. Humans feel entitled to steal this natural-born right. Some Nepalese men accused Renny of "murdering" a villager. Immediately this reeked of manure to me. Some other Animal Communicators and I discussed the incident in question, and talked with Renny to hear his side of the story.

Some colleagues, along with local villagers, thought Renny was guilty of purposely trampling a man. The Nepalese press did a stellar job painting a picture he was hungry for humans. The accusers wanted a villain, and Renny made a fine one for insecure men wishing to be as mighty as an elephant.

Power, jealousy, and money motivate cruelty around the world. Fearful men wanting to feel powerful taunted Renny. I felt Renny's sensitive soul and good-natured heart, as I asked him to describe how he felt being accused of the murder.

He expressed great despondency at the human capacity for cruelty and injustice. He felt ganged up on and misunderstood, something I'd felt my whole life—weak people wanting to steal my sunshine and thunder by targeting me with gossip, lies or misdirected anger. While I've never been accused of murder, I've been in virtual lineups for crimes the accusers themselves committed.

Renny's spirit radiated strength, confidence, and majesty. When I connected with his abusers and accusers, I felt chained up inside and understood why they craved an elephant's authentic power...TRUNK ENVY!

Renny did what was needed to survive and escape their abuse. The men were calling for his execution—payback for an elephant killing a man. I trusted Renny, and he gave me additional telepathic backup to use when advocating for his innocence. His reputation mattered to him. He was not a killer elephant, but a self-respecting one protecting himself. Some beings start fights, others end them out of self-preservation.

This brilliant, resourceful elephant on the other side of the world scrolled through my memory banks to locate an episode in my life's reality show where I'd also been framed. He referenced my painful memory to validate my conversation with him and express mutual angst. I also have the memory of an elephant, and never forget how someone betrayed me or helped me.

Back in 7th grade, a couple of mean girls pretended to be me and prank-called (long before cell phones and caller ID) another student's parents. They cursed, lied, laughed, and hung up. I'd been at the mall at the time with my best friend eating pizza and playing arcade games. I was new to their school and they were jealous of the attention I was getting. "Haters" who framed me to destroy my reputation. Haters fear happiness because they lack the courage to heal their wounds.

I tried to clear my name, but the parents insisted I sounded just like the girl who'd harassed them. A girl named Annie later admitted to a mutual friend what she'd done, but never apologized or cleared my name. Renny showed himself tossing Annie around with his trunk forcing her to apologize. I laughed in hysterical gratitude wondering if wherever she was she felt seasick.

A fellow communicator relayed my messages to Nepalese elephant caretakers and advocates. Renny was spared execution and while loved by many, remained hated, feared, and in danger. In a future conversation, he shared he'd fathered a calf, and was spending time deep in the wild, but visited town when he needed a social fix.

Together, Renny and I felt loved, understood, and validated by each other—someone who knew the truth about our characters. Renny and all animals use their wisdom and wits to survive circumstances and people the same as me. Developing comedy skills early on helped me build confidence and resilience to ward off people poachers.

Renny taught me to remember that the weak will always hunt the strong—a painful compliment and destiny that requires insane bravery. I can be a human on the outside, but remain an animal within until I fly HOME and shed this skin. We united our hearts in justice: *Law & Order Elephant Unit: Tusks for Truth!*

My abilities continue to accelerate as I become more animal and less human. Being with animals is being with authenticity itself. Instead of wearing a "People Suck" shirt (just be a person who doesn't suck), lead by example. I hope you're inspired to call out injustice and imagine what it's like to be in someone else's shoes, paws, hooves, fins, wings, or invisible magical pants.

Once you experience soul connections with animals or mystical realms beyond the matrix, it's like stepping out of a black-and-white world into full technicolor. Imagine someone on a beautiful sunny beach trying to convince someone in a blizzard that it's a perfect day for a swim. Until the skeptic makes it to the beach, they'll never *feel* the ocean, and may not even believe it exists. Reality is relative, but if you believe yours is the only one, then reality bites.

I hope wherever you're at in your spiritual awareness and awakening, this book helps you dip your toes in the ocean. Or run into it buck naked yelling, "OMG, this is the ocean? I've heard of it, but didn't quite believe something this vast and magnificent could be real! Look at these waves, they roll out... then roll back in! How far does the ocean go...how deep...are we all a drop of the ocean, and the whole ocean at once? Yippee!"

That's just a taste of what it feels like to develop your intuitive abilities and discover there's this whole magical ocean to dive into at your own pace and comfort level. Remain in shallow waters, or go off the deep end and party with mermaids.

No one ever has to believe you when you tell them how rough or calm the waters were that you swam in or how crystal clear the color was, because you won't care. You'll know it's real—you were there and will forever "sea" life differently now that you know the ocean exists. There are creatures we'll never see deep in the ocean, but they're there and we can talk with them. They don't question their existence based on humans' awareness of them.

Think of the things we can only see under microscopes. Without the necessary equipment, we might not know bacteria existed. People with extraordinary intuition can see, hear, and feel things others can't because we've fine-tuned our senses. Many, like me, were born to do this playful, sacred work. Perhaps there's a sea creature forum right now discussing if humans are real or merely a myth. Maybe it was me who was the imaginary friend all along.

I'm having too much fun swimming in the healing waters of the animals' love and truth to ever go back to life as I knew it. Happy hour is any time I spend *present* with animals. No doubt, I've gone off the deep end. Shallow waters have no appeal to me, having made me restless for so long. Unplug from the noise of the news, listen to the wisdom in the wind, and go with the flow.

Animals can show you uncharted territories within yourself. Are you open to worlds that have always been, and always will be, whether or not you dare to leave the shore of your comfort zone? Come on in, the water is beautiful.

May you be so lucky to never be down on your luck, and be so wise to see life through empathic eyes. May you be so kind as to help those left behind, whatever their species, color, or creed. Always use your voice, and do good deeds. May you share your sandwich at traffic lights. Respect our bodies, our choices, and who we love, is a human right.

May you free animals from slaughter trucks and show them all you give a fuck. May Heaven's light shine on your life and give you the heart to end animals' strife. Talk with animals, fairies, and trees. Listen to birds, and plant flowers for bees. Show love to humankind, speak kindly and proudly what's on your mind. Know yourself and your truth. Live your own magic, be your own proof.

To all those I've lost to death and said goodbye as you took your last breath, my grief becomes joy, untouchable by pain. Our hearts and souls will meet again. To all my pets in Heaven and those laying by my feet, and the many still I've yet to meet, thanks for all you do for me. You set my spirit, my heart, and mind free.

Together forever, there is no end, my furry family, my best friends. I love you more than words can say...walk with me, it's time to play. You are loved, speak your words, wherever you are, your voices are heard. Love is real and never dies...whatever your species or insides. Until The Big Paw in the Sky woofs us HOME, no animal friend is ever alone.

EPILOGUE

Keep some room in your heart for the unimaginable.

Mary Oliver

I'd envisioned my whole pack being at my book signing one day, not writing an epilogue on the passing of one of my children. Saint Jack passed shortly after I'd finished this manuscript. His body was shutting down, his spirit ready to soar.

Goodbyes are bittersweet when we know relief is imminent. Jack amped up the sweet part by soaring in to lift me every time I dipped into despair in the weeks after he passed—a multitude of signs from which I've chosen a few to share. But first, let's say goodbye before we say hello again.

Knowing my past, present, and future pets and animal clients are always with me, whatever form they're in allows me to serve as their playground on which they can constantly say, "Mom/Shannon, look what I can do!" and my heart beams with pride, excitement, and awe of their new tricks and devoted love for me.

Jack's a patient teacher who guided me through his passing. I'd planned on a home vet, but Monday couldn't wait, so we chose a vet open on Saturday referred by a friend. Before we said goodbye, we laid as a family next to Jack on a big comforter on the floor at home. Kermit lovingly sent healing energy to Jack as I spoke softly while he solemnly rested in the middle of our family sandwich. It was calm and surreal.

Grover, however, squeaked his toys, trying to invite us to play, while the Mayor laid above my head to keep me grounded. Each member did as we knew best to process the gravity of what was underway. One moment our bodies are here, and the next, gone. The physical absence of a beloved's body is a lonely, blinking VACANCY sign, and it was flickering.

Feeling Jack's beautiful, warm, wolf-like body...
   breathe up and down right next to me;
     knowing one moment soon, he'd be a force of LIGHT-
   the very definition of FREE.
I love his body and all its bumps...
   looking into his eyes gives my throat a loving lump.
Ok, Jack's body, you can power down...
   there's a puppy inside who needs to play...
   and I won't stand in a puppy's way.
Free of the body, unlimited by rules...
   waving goodbye to pain, and this Earth school.
My inner puppy also hungers to play,
    and part of me went with Jack that day.
But, I had bellies to rub and feed;
   the remaining puppies needed a mom who'd lead.
And in their eyes, I saw the same knowing...
   that one day too, it'll be their homecoming.
These bodies are costumes, this world is a stage.
   Some days a comedy, and some days a cage.
Jack helped me stay grounded as he took to the sky.
   He'd prove to Mommy again, that death is a lie.
While each play, each show comes to an end...
   our souls are more than plot twists and stories,
   we are forever friends.
When the curtain goes down in an hour today,
   it also rises on Jack's spirit, a rainbow away.
I trust that my pain is not in vain.
    It's a warmup for my heart to explode in joy again.

. . .

We can astral travel the world, and we can send love anywhere, anytime with our thoughts, but holding my baby's body was something I had to let go of. Jack's eyes carried the wisdom of the multiverse—of HOME—a home I've been aching for my whole life. His eyes hugged me. "Mom, I'm not leaving you. Where I'm going is beyond words. It is so BIG and MAGICAL and full of LOVE...and I am sending its energy through my eyes to you now. Do you understand? I will be with you in a new way. You will feel me, I will see you and you will join me in this place one day. Do you trust this? I believe in you, Mom. Feel my love, it's EXPANDING. I will protect and love you forever." I held his gaze and he knew I understood. He was free to go be and do what his soul now needed. Jack's Graduation day was here, and I wanted to stay steady for my son on his big day.

Kermit, Jack, and I drove to the vet. I brought Kermit as moral support for Jack and me, knowing Kermit was strong enough to be present during the process. He and Jack walked side by side on so many walks, and now Kermit would walk him to retrieve his diploma. Kermit was a saint, too, that day, with a brotherly loyalty no trainer can teach.

On the drive, my Heavenly pack popped into the car. They said, "Tell Jack...LISTEN FOR THE LAUGHTER." I smiled. I believe this is the greatest death coaching advice ever given.

Jack always loved trying to push his way into the front seat and leave his claw marks on the armrest he drooled over. "Big dogs in the back, little dogs in front," I'd always smile and say, as I pet under his chin and stole a kiss at red lights.

This car ride was different. Jack was lying down, solemn, with Kermit glued to his side. I told my boys, "Mom needs to drive Jack to the airport to Heaven, which today is through the vet's office." I stayed strong and alert, driving us safely, and remaining fully present for him. I'd promised to tell my kids the truth, the way my parents never did. And when I told him everyone is safe, angels are here, it was the definition of "God's honest truth."

My tears were on standby for now; they weren't going to steal the show. Jack didn't need my pity or the burden of my grief. He was teaching me I practice what I preach: TRUST. This isn't to say we can't cry and feel all of our emotions. I've sobbed over many parting pets. I wanted to do this differently. I'd release my patient tears afterward. For now, I wanted to be his mommy—strong enough to do this without losing my mind to the heartache building inside me.

The vet was gentle and respectful, but the two techs kept saying, "Jack looks so sad!" (Perhaps because he's dying, ladies.) Their inappropriateness annoyed my inner puppy. I've been a compassionate presence for so many people in their moment of need, and the techs made this about them. Jack couldn't comfort his mom...this was going to hurt us both, and he definitely didn't need the burden of comforting the staff. Again, I learned patience from Jack. I could use my energy to be annoyed at their immaturity, or to show love and focused devotion to Jack in our final physical moments.

Graduation days are sad and happy, but at this moment Jack was sad. He was leaving Kermit and Mommy and heading off on an adventure we'd be a part of, but not able to smooch again for a while. (Or, so I thought.) And so when Jack took his last breath, I whispered, "LISTEN FOR THE LAUGHTER," and the kind vet looked at me quizzically, like a dog does when uncertain of the words spoken. I knew no one had said the "L" word before in "the euth room." Laughter angels were standing by, but the euth room is where people cry.

Jack's many spirit siblings—Teddy #1, Hellion, Rowdy, Stormy, Lucy, Ducky, Belle, Teddy #2, Randy, and Rainbow, who'd passed just months before—huddled in for the MVP crossing over. A family clubhouse where I can visit just by thinking of them.

A special dog I helped pass once said that the euthanasia room should be renamed "The Reverence Room." It's a sacred space; grief and laughter are sacred emotions. Laughter was just a breath away for Jack. As someone who used to get in trouble for giggling at church, I know there's no better way to celebrate life than with laughter. Grief was always on standby.

Jack knew the wails of grief were just a moment away for his mom. Kermit and I would be one dog down on the drive home. In reality, we were one dog UP! Jack peacefully left his body and Kermit and I walked out emotionally…not here…not there…breathing in strange air.

Once home, Grover and Puppypants greeted us, and I watched the two little dogs sniff and grab toys. Kermit lay on the grass soaking in the sun. I was smiling at him, proud of his strength, when I felt a massive warm hug around and inside me gently whisper, "I'M HERE SHANNON, I'M RIGHT HERE!" Kermit circled his head in awe, seeing what I could only feel. Jack was HOME right here with us… and with the angels. Limitless across worlds. Like two paws on the beach and two in the ocean, except all of him was everywhere. I was so lit up with LOVE, I nearly birthed a rainbow out my puppy portal.

That night, Jack visited me in a little spaceship, like the ones in the cartoon, *The Jetsons*. Jack is a lookalike for "Astro," the cartoon dog. Jack was JOYFUL and told me he was "flying through time and space!" He beamed me up into his passenger seat, with his Earth brother-pups in the back. We all went flying with Jack as our pilot. Fearless, ALIVE, and laughing at the sheer grandness of Jack's new adventure. It wasn't a dream, but more of a lucid experience—a reality much like this world.

Jack is a skilled pilot and we didn't have any baggage with us. We were all FREE—the natural state of all of our souls. I am not one for cliches, and one of the ones to avoid telling grieving souls is, "They're in a better place." And yet, it's true. This better place is so much better…that it defies anything people can perceive. So Jack transported me there to experience it. I breathe easier knowing Jack is SAFE and having the time of his afterlife!

A year later I did a reading for a spirit dog named Stella, a beautiful chocolate colored mutt who wanted to show off, in her own stellar way, to comfort her grieving mom. Stella began our reading by having me demonstrate how her parents used to call out, "STELL-LA!" like Stanley did in *A Streetcar Named Desire*. Stella showed me that after she passed, she hovered in a little spaceship over her body and beamed a ray of light upon her sobbing parents. I was concerned that after relaying concrete evidence that brought tears of relief to Stella's mom, this spaceship sighting may alienate her trust in my messages. I took a deep breath. "Stella shows her spirit watched over her final moments from a little spaceship. She sent a loving white light to heal you."

Then, as if Stella yelled, "Aliens have landed!" her mom exclaimed, "Shannon! I swear I felt a spaceship hovering over us, just as you describe!" I was relieved, ecstatic, and curious. Had Jack and Stella met? Do all dogs acquire a spaceship? Stella's mom smiled. "I can't believe I didn't tell you this when you said spaceship. Our last family trip with Stella was to Roswell, New Mexico (renowned for UFO sightings)!" Our pets' love really is "outta this world," and whether your pet is napping, farting, or flying around in a spaceship, please know, like Jack and Stella, they are flying safely and joyfully through time and space and will beam us up with their light—sometimes when making breakfast.

One morning, my heart ached lamenting Jack's empty bowl. My inner Charlie Brown was missing my fourth little Snoopy. My pain broadcast like a lighthouse to Jack's heart. I began scrolling through Facebook and came across an antique note paper image instructing: "Go find the nearest book, go to page 18, line 4." A hopeful wave rolled over me, and I eagerly obeyed this mysterious command.

I had recently rearranged a stack of books I'd had for years, but never read. I danced with joy when I saw THE MAGIC OF DOGS was on top! Like tearing open a present, I flipped to page 18, which was Chapter 6 (my birthday 9/6) titled, "ALWAYS WITH ME STILL," and line 4 (four dogs) mentions, A DOG NAMED JACK AND THE CLEVER SIGNS HE SENDS HIS MOM FROM SPIRIT! My son is a magician!

As always, there were signs within signs to uncover. I floated through most of my day on Jack's wings, carrying me into his world. He was everywhere, from cardinals flying up to my face and butterflies chasing me and his brothers, to something a stranger said when we took our first pack walk "without" Jack that let me know he was right there.

I was always annoyed when people hollered, "Ya got your hands full," upon seeing me walk my pack, mostly because everyone said it as if it were funny, when it was just an ordinary comment void of truth or fun. Once in a blue moon, someone would holler out, "Beautiful family!" and we'd all wag our tails!

In our first threesome dog walk, a stranger looked at my pack, locked eyes with me, and I thought, "Oh great...here it comes again... got my hands full." But instead, this construction worker we'd never seen looked at Kermit's side and said, "You're missing a big dog. You have a tiny, little, medium, and now you need a big one. You're missing a big dog right next to that one." I replied, "We just said goodbye to the big one this week."

The man looked embarrassed for what he'd said, but I smiled and reassured him. "Please don't feel bad. You just made our day. We are indeed missing a big one and your eyes went right to where he's walking with us now. You've magically picked up on his spirit, not ripped open a wound." The man relaxed. He wasn't expecting praise, and was as surprised by my words as I was by his. We walked on, a beat happier from Jack reminding me to expect good things. Lose a body, gain an angel.

Later, a friend texted me that he had prayed to Jack to ask him how to help me, and he gave him one word: "Pinocchio." I knelt in gratitude, understanding what it meant, something this messenger could not have known. About a month before Jack passed, the pack snuggled in bed and watched the remake of *Pinocchio,* a beautiful tale of a man who loses his nonhuman son who had brought him so much magic, and then inconsolable grief in his passing.

I cried along with the death scene, and spoke aloud to my boys. "Boys, I know one day each of you will leave your bodies. And it will break my heart. Know that I know you'd never do anything to hurt me. All of us die. Know that when you go to Heaven, I know you'll still be here, too, that you'd never leave me, just as I'd never leave you. I trust you completely and know you'll send many signs you're with me. You'll watch me grow old, and one day, you'll greet me when I die. I will say goodbye to you 'here,' and you'll say hello to me 'there.'

And the boys listened. More than I knew. *Pinocchio* was much more than a movie title in our family. In the final scene, Pinocchio is gifted with eternal life and watches his dad grow old and die, free of his body now too, together forever.

My friend was delighted to be a sacred messenger, and then added a ribbon around Jack's gift. "Jack spoke of a tapestry of many colors that represents Shannon's boys—green and yellow, blue, purple. He says you'll know." No one but my dogs knew of the paw painting they made. A tapestry of blended puppy toes. Priceless art.

Another friend knew nothing of how I'd mused aloud to all the boys that I wondered what they'd be getting me for Valentine's Day. When the holiday arrived, so did a package from Jack! I opened a gift of the softest blankets and pillows with hearts and spiritual messages. The card read: "Thinking of you. Love, Jack and Bridget."

I'd helped Bridget's dogs, Monkey and Pickles, cross over months before—silly pups who always appear side by side, giggling, eating sundaes, or jumping with joy. "Forever Toddlers," they'd joke. Bridget said she had wanted to send me flowers, but Jack told her to send heart-shaped gifts. She didn't know that every night I wrapped my dogs in blankets, tucking them in. Jack knew. And he had one more Valentine's gift to give.

The final glance and kiss Jack gave me from his body while lying in our family sandwich had sent an otherworldly surge through me.

A kiss straight out of a furry fairy tale, like he was transitioning into a prince. It stopped my heart with its unmistakable, "THIS IS MAGIC," energy.

Jack knew just the prince to deliver his laughing, kissing message—a beautiful, barking, boomerang brother mutt, assuring me he'd be my Valentine for life. He'd seen the message I had written in a journal about missing my "fourth little Snoopy." One day, while rearranging things, I felt compelled to place my tiny Snoopy doll with the red "Be My Valentine" ribbon around its neck right above Jack's bed. When squeezed, Snoopy makes laughing and kissing sounds that always made me laugh.

After I positioned it as a Guardian above the bed, I sat a few feet away in a rocker. About 30 minutes later, the Snoopy doll began kissing and laughing all on its own! It was Jack telling me, "LISTEN FOR THE LAUGHTER!" Moments later, a rescue dog's pic popped up on my screen, bringing Jack's energy all around me.

"Ethan" had a "Be My Valentine" heart caption above his head, and wore a heart bow tie that read, LOVE. His lopsided ears and innocent, sweet smile won me over. Jack knew that this stray pup without a mommy and a mommy who'd lost her Jack were destined to be together. Ethan means "strong," "enduring," "long-lived."

Of course, I needed the approval of Jack's siblings. Before the meet and greet, Jack led me to an Akashic records class (past lives and soul records). I asked the instructor, out of playful curiosity, "Do you see anything on a dog named Ethan's soul records?" She laughed and said, "This is weird... he's afraid you won't recognize his soul." But his halo was too bright to miss.

Mayor Puppypants nearly wagged his tail off his little body when they met. He definitely recognized Jack's soul. The first song Siri played on the way home was "Motherless Child." I renamed him Charlie after my first childhood stuffed dog toy I loved.

Charlie is a kissing Cupid whose all encompassing smooches make me giggle like the laughing Snoopy. I see him as Jack's long-lost twin brother, like on a soap opera when the first brother passes, and it's discovered he has a handsome twin! Charlie, like Jack, is a peaceful, humble soul who brings out my best. Grateful for the smallest things, he brings me the biggest message: "I LOVE YOU, MOM!" I love you too, Charlie-Jack Spring.

I, Shannon, take you Jack, and all your brothers and sisters, to have and to hold, until death do us reunite in magic. May my tears of grief and tears of joy dance together and form a triple rainbow that leads me laughing all the way back to you in Eternal Spring.

Paws in gratitude to anyone who's made my life lighter, and who shows kindness to animals. Please use your voices to speak their truths. May you have the courage to find and live your own. May peace, paws, love, laughter, and joyful surprises follow you throughout your lives.

WOOFMEOWT!

Follow the Spring family's channels and podcasts at:

ShannonSpring.com   JustHumorMe.com
@MayorPuppypants   @JustHumorMeFriends
ShannonSpring.substack.com

Please share how my book impacted your life with animals. Buy a copy for the animal lovers in your life, those who believe in magic, and those who need it. Magic Awaits...

ABOUT THE AUTHOR

Shannon Spring, M.Ed, PhD-og is an Animal Communicator, Psychic Medium, Comedic Keynote Speaker, and Author. She's been in tune with animals and the spirit world since she was a child, and finds being a human inconvenient when she'd much rather be an animal.

The founder of Mayor Puppypants Unleashed, she offers: psychic readings, classes, events, and Just Humor Me™ comedic keynotes and HAHA (Humor and Healing Adventure) Retreats, including programs for people in recovery. Shannon's helped thousands of animals and their people live happier, healthier lives by getting answers to behavioral, emotional, and medical challenges; and connecting grieving people with their beloved family of all species in Spirit.

Shannon graduated with an M.Ed. from The Citadel Military College and a B.A. in Human Development and Communications from Boston College. She graduated from The National Speakers Academy and is a Certified Creativity Coach. Shannon enjoys performing stand-up comedy, doing psychic detective work, and volunteering with animal rescues. She lives in her colorful cottage with her rescued paw-spring in Sarasota, Florida, and will spend half her time in the mountains with her future human husband and their many animals.

Shannon long ago gave up caring about who thinks she's crazy because laughing with the animal kingdom and attending the afterlife parties brings her too much joy to worry about people who haven't yet awakened. Look for the signs, and listen for the laughter, Shannon will lead the way!

www.ingramcontent.com/pod-product-compliance
Lightning Source LLC
Chambersburg PA
CBHW070049080526
44586CB00013B/984